정보화와 복지국가

최영진 지음

Informatisation and the Welfare State

양성원

머리말

송파 세 모녀 사건이 일어난지 햇수로 4년이 지나고 있다. 그러나 아직도 한국에서는 이와 비슷한 사건들이 뉴스에 오르고 이에 대한 해결책들에 대해 의견이 분분하다. 그렇다면 그간 우리는 이런 복지사각지대에서 발생하고 있는 일들을 방관하고 좌시하고만 있었을까?

그렇지 않다. 지난 4년간 우리는 송파 세 모녀 사건 이후 여러 방법(예: 단전・단수 가구 정보나 건강보험료 체납 가구 정보활용)을 통해 복지사각지대에 있는 위급한 사례들을 발굴하고, 다양한 복지 대상자들의 복지욕구(needs)를 충족시키며, 유사한 사례들의 재발을 막기 위해 다각도로 노력해 왔다.

위급한 경우 바로 전화를 할 수 있는 상담소가 생겼고, 복지 기관들은 더욱 세분화되고 전문화되었으며, 현장에서는 복지공무원의 방문과 상담을 통한 사례관리가 이루어져 왔다. 이러한 변화들 중에 가장 눈에 띄는 것은 사회보장정보시스템(행복e음)을 통하여 대부분의 복지 사례들이 전산화되어 기록되고 저장됨으로써 현장에서 보다 효율적이고 효과적인 복지 대상자의 관리와 자원의 연계가 이루어질 수 있었다는 것이다. 또한 복지 사례의 축적을 통한 통계적인 평가들은 관리와 감독에 투명성을 확보하게 해주었으며 새로운 복지정책을 만드는데 길라잡이가 되고 있다. 지금까지의 요람에서부터 무덤까지 이르는 생애주기에 따른 삶의 질의 향상을 위한 거대한 프로젝트 실현은 복지현장과 복지기관의 전산화와 자동화가 없이는 불가능한 것이었다.

이 책은 송파 세 모녀 사건을 시발점으로 복지 전 분야에 걸쳐 새롭게 떠오른 화두인 '정보화와 복지국가 발달'의 관계에 대한 고민들로 채워졌다. 지난 20세기 중반 이후부터 급속하게 이루어진 컴퓨터, 인터넷, 전화, 휴대폰 그리고 영상매체의 발달이 과연 복지국가의 역할인 복지서비스의 제공 및 관리에 어떠한 영향을 미쳤을까? 이 책에서는 OECD국가를 대상으로 '정보화는 사회복지지출을 증가시켰는가?' '정보화는 소득불평등을 심화시켰는가?'라는 두 가지 질문에 대해 일련의 통계분석을 통해 그 해답을 찾고자 하였다.

이 책은 총 8장으로 구성되어 있다.

제1장에서는 현대 사회에서 복지국가 및 정보화의 의미가 어떤 것인지 그리고 이 둘은 어떠한 관계에 놓여 있는지를 간단하게 살펴보았다.

제2장에서는 복지국가 발달에 대한 기존 이론들의 소개를 시작으로 복지국가와 정보화의 개념화를 통해 새로운 이론적 관점으로서의 '복지국가 발달에서의 정보화'에 대한 이론적 논의 가능성에 대해 고민해 보았다.

제3장에서는 역사적 맥락에서 정보화의 의미와 정보화에 의해 야기된 사회변화를 다루고 있다. 또한 정보화에 따른 사회불평등 현상과 이에 대한 복지국가의 대응들을 검토했다.

제4장에서는 연구가설을 설정하고 연구 수행을 위한 조작적 개념화가 이루어졌다. 계량적 통계분석방법 및 변수들을 설정하고 이에 대한 설명이 추가되었다.

제5장에서는 정보커뮤니케이션 산업의 발달과 복지국가의 역할 변화의 관계에 대한 분석을 확대 34개 OECD국가를 대상으로 1985년부터 2010년에 걸쳐 시계열 분석이 수행되었다.

제6장에서는 인터넷 사용과 복지국가 발달의 관계에 대한 분석이 이루어졌다. 마찬가지로 전체 34개 OECD국가를 대상으로 1985년부터 2010년에 걸쳐 시계열 분석이 수행되었다.

제7장에서는 전자정부의 발달과 복지국가의 발달간의 관계를 분석하였다. 전체 34개 OECD국가를 대상으로 분석기간은 2003년부터 2010년이다.

제8장에서는 일련의 분석의 결과들을 토대로 과연 연구가설이 증명되었는지에 대해 논하고 있다. 이 장에서는 더 나아가 복지국가 발달에 대한 이론적 관점으로서의 '정보화 이론'의 가능성에 대해 고민하였고, 향후 연구를 위한 제안들을 담고 있다.

정보화는 이미 우리의 삶에 깊숙이 자리잡아 그 의미가 특별하게 다가오지 않을 수 있다. 아침에 일어나 스마트폰으로 날씨와 메일을 체크하고, 인터넷 뉴스를 읽으며 출근하는 우리의 모습들은 더 이상 낯설게 보이지 않는다.

이러한 정보화는 복지현장에도 깊숙이 침투해 있다. 복지현장에서의 복지공무원은 출근하면 사회보장정보시스템을 열고, 전산망에 올라온 복지 대상자들을 확인하고, 방문과 상담을 계획하며, 기록을 작성하여 저장한다. 이렇게 저장된 기록들은 통계적으로 처리되어 그 결과가 보고되고 새로운 정책을 만들 때 중요한 데이터로 활용된다. 이렇게 정보화란 화두는 복지국가의 역할을 논하는 데 있어 중요한 부분을 차지하고 있다.

따라서 역사적으로 그리고 거시적으로 정보화란 큰 물결이 과연 복지현장과 복지행정 그리고 더 나아가 복지정책을 형성하는데 어떠한 영향을 미쳐 현재의 복지국가가 형성되었고, 앞으로 어떻게 변화시킬 것인지 이론적 관점에서 살펴볼 필요가 있다. 앞으로 이에 대한 꾸준한 관심과 지속적인 후속연구가 진행되길 바란다.

마지막으로 이 책이 나오기까지 함께 해주신 출판사 양성원에 고마움을 전한다.

저자

2018년 5월

Contents

Chapter III Informatisation, Inequality, and Public Social Welfare: • 29

Chapter IV Hypotheses and Method of Analysis • 65

Chapter I

Introduction

Chapter I Introduction

1. The Purpose of this Study and a Statement on the Current Socio-economic Climate

On February 27, 2014, a mother and her two daughters took their own lives in the Songpa district of Seoul, South Korea. This event caused Korean society to reel in shock and begin asking serious questions about the public welfare system. The following excerpts are from related articles:

> A mother and her two daughters, surnamed "Park", committed suicide after leaving their last 700,000 won to their landlord for rent and bills. They also left a message that read, "We are really sorry". Rent and bill money aside, the family had spent the last of their cash on two coal briquettes (600 won), one piece of charcoal (1500 won), and a letter (20 won) before they took their lives. Park's husband died of bladder cancer 12 years ago, and the long battle for his life had left them in debt. Additionally, their eldest daughter suffered from diabetes and high blood pressure. The mother allegedly earned 1.5-1.8 million won per month working at a nearby restaurant, but she injured her arm in late January, rendering her unable to continue work. After enduring these numerous hardships, the 61-year-old woman and her two daughters, both in their 30s, were driven to suicide. President Park Geunhye announced her deep

> regrets that Korea's social security net and emergency welfare support system was not well enough organised to avert this tragedy ("Could the Sonpagu", 2014).
>
> After the 'One Mother Two Daughters in Songpa District' case, President Park Geun-hye spoke in response to the rising issue of the so-called 'welfare dead zone', saying that we need to "find and help people in need". As a result, the Ministry of Health and Welfare promptly advertised the 'Emergency Welfare Support System' on the first page of the major daily newspaper, touting the slogan "When in danger, call 119; when experiencing difficulty, call 129". They also promised to add thousands of employees to their work force ("Killing Each", 2014).

South Korea is beginning to recognise social adversity of serious scope. The above incident reflects the inadequacies of the current state of the welfare system, raising many fundamental questions. It is not known exactly why these people were moved to take their own lives, or whether public services were even available to them. The Emergency Welfare Support System is designed to support low-income families during a crisis, but it seems highly likely that this family was unaware of the existence of such a system.[1]

As mentioned in the article, this group suicide incident prompted the government to publicise the Emergency Welfare Support System via all available media in an effort to "find and help people in need." This study concentrates on examining the development of the public welfare

---

1 Tragic thought it is, it can hardly be said that the 'One Mother Two Daughters in Songpa District' case is special among accounts of suicide due to personal shame. It is clear that similar suicide cases caused by poverty have been increasing rapidly during the last several years. In 2010, the poverty rate for South Korean senior citizens was among the world's highest at 48.5 percent; far in excess of the OECD average of 13.3 percent ("Older Generation's Suicide", 2011). According to the results of a 2012 Household Finances and Welfare Survey released by Statistics Korea, the poverty ratio based on the 2011 disposable income was 16.5 percent. This ratio measures the portion of the population who earns half of the median disposable income. These people make less than 9.98 million won (9,300 U.S. dollars) per year. The poverty ratio of households with people aged 65 or older was 67.3 percent, accounting for the largest portion, while that of single-member households was 50.1 percent ("Nearly 20 pct.", 2012). 1238 people committed suicide among recipients of the National Basic Livelihood Assistance during 2010-2014 ("Not Qualified", 2015).

system; pinpointing social problems that affect disadvantaged people such as those involved in the unfortunate tragedy above. From a macro-level perspective, this study explores how well the public welfare system is developed, and whether the measures taken are sufficient to protect the public. Also taken into account is the available information on socioeconomic issues, and whether said information is reaching its target audience in the public welfare sector. It is imperative that these issues are looked at because, while a state may provide a social welfare service with the aim of guaranteeing a reasonable minimal living standard for all citizens, this system is insufficient if welfare service providers and recipients do not have access to the relevant information. The overall problem becomes even more profound with the introduction of income inequality in polarised societies.

Since the mid-20th century, in western industrialised countries, comparative studies on the welfare state have been conducted on an ongoing basis. Currently, similar studies based in Latin American and East Asian countries are also being expanded. It is not surprising, then, that numerous theories have emerged surrounding the establishment and development of the welfare state. Many of these theories are supported by the results that have surfaced from the extensive body of comparative studies. Evidence reveals that the historical development of the welfare state depends on political, economic and social changes. Therefore, the three key elements affecting the construct of theories based on the welfare state are capitalism, democracy, and the state's involvement in public welfare (Marshall, 1963, pp. 306-307).

The history of the welfare state can be summarised thus: From the nineteenth century, acceleration of industrialisation spawned the introduction of many social policies in western countries. Consequently, numerous social issues were addressed and a higher level of egalitarianism achieved. After the 1970s, however, the dissemination of the welfare state slowed due to endogenous and exogenous factors such as economic, political and financial crises (Pierson, 1988, pp. 28-37). The term 'globalisation' was popularised in the latter half of the 1980s, foreshadowing a number of changes in the macro-environment during the 1990s. These changes prompted the welfare state to introduce a new phase, or 'era', in which there were attempts to repair previously existing systems and create new programs (Giddens, 1998, pp. 28-37; Lewis & Surrender, 2004, pp. 3-4, 16).

The welfare state was confronted with a myriad of new developments during the second half of the 20th century. One of these developments was given the label 'informatisation'.[2] During this period, due to the remarkably rapid advancements in information & communication technology, society experienced changes at an unprecedented rate. Today, it no longer seems odd to shop online with Smart Phones, work on Tablet Computers, give and receive UCC (User Created Contents) through LTE (Long Term Evolution) services, and watch the latest movies on HD Wide Screen Televisions at home. These environmental changes have caused a tectonic shift in the roles of governments, businesses, and individuals, giving birth to even more changes in society in an almost cyclic fashion. Referring to these fundamental changes spurred by technology, Alana Northrop and Kenneth L. Kraemer coined the phrase 'the information revolution'. He believes the information revolution to be the biggest change in human history since the industrial revolution (Northrop & Kraemer, 2000, pp. 265-280). As a result, the 'information society', which describes the fundamentally important role information plays at all levels of society, became one of the characteristic trends of modern times.

The ultimate goal of this study is to uncover how the development of the information society impacts the development of the welfare state, with a special emphasis on the links between informatisation, the state's ability (or lack thereof) to provide at least the minimum standard of human living, and the level of inequality in a society. These are the two major questions presented in this study:

I. Does informatisation hinder increasing public social spending?
II. Does informatisation deepen income inequality in the society?

---

2 The discussion on informatisation is continued in more detail in the next chapter.

2. Outline of the Study

Chapter 2 provides a theoretical background, introducing established welfare state theories and the content of this study. As informatisation and the welfare state are the key concepts, a brief historical overview is provided. Previous studies on the relationship between informatisation and the development of the welfare state are investigated, giving rise to the implications and contributions this study may add to the overall picture.

Chapter 3 presents the meaning of informatisation in a historical context, including the economic, political, social and cultural changes caused by informatisation. In addition, several inequality phenomena caused by informatisation are observed and the response of the welfare state to such social problems is examined.

Chapter 4 outlines hypotheses, operational definitions, and the method of analysis in this study. In order to perform the analyses, independent variables, dependent variables, and control variables are introduced and explained briefly.

In chapter 5, the relationship between the development of the Information & Communication Technology industry and the welfare state is analysed. This analysis is performed by utilising all 34 OECD countries as analysis objects and creating a time-series cross-section data spanning from 1985 to 2010; a total of 26 years. Descriptive statistics, correlation analyses and causality analyses are performed.

In chapter 6, the relationship between the increase of ICT usage and the welfare state is analysed. The analysis is performed utilising all 34 OECD countries as analysis objects and creating a time-series cross- section data spanning from 1985 to 2010; a total of 26 years. Descriptive statistics, correlation analyses and causality analyses are performed.

Chapter 7 analyses the relationship between the development of the e-government and the welfare state, once again using all OECD countries as analysis objects. Descriptive statistics, a correlation analysis and causality analyses are performed in order to investigate changes over the period 2003-2010.

Chapter 8 presents the conclusion, wherein analysis results are summarised; demonstrating whether proposed hypotheses are ultimately proved or disproved. Drawing from these results, the current condition of welfare states and informatisation in OECD countries can be deduced. Finally, the results of this study are explored theoretically, including what manner of study might be performed by scholars and citizens in the future to further the understanding of the relationship between informatisation and the development of the welfare state.

Chapter II

Theoretical Overview

Chapter II Theoretical Overview

This chapter provides study trends, analytical framework, and theories of the welfare state's development, thereby validating informatisation and the welfare state as the appropriate key concepts to explore in this study. In addition, the extent to which current studies have advanced regarding the relationship between informatisation and the development of the welfare state is explored.

1. Background and Scope of Studies on the Welfare State

1.1 Analyses over Time

In order to definitively identify changes expected to occur within welfare states over time, the data looked at in this study falls between year 1985 and 2010.[3]

The development of information & communication technology (hereafter ICT) accelerated alongside the development of computers and

[3] This is partly due to the limitations of data collection. Indices published by international organisations were less developed and/or incomplete before 1985, so to ensure accuracy in this study, the limited timeframe in which the analysis falls cannot be avoided.

proliferation of mobile devices throughout the 1980s and the 1990s. Since the 2000s, the field of ICT has changed rapidly, transforming humankind's lifestyle in a variety of ways. Computers, the most important aspect of ICT, have been in a state of perpetual development since the 1950s. However, they existed only as individual systems until the early 1980s. The Internet was introduced in 1983 and, while it was initially adopted for mainly academic uses, it quickly escalated to become one of the most commercial and popular forms of media. By the mid-1990s, millions of computers were connected around the world (Baek, 2013, pp. 30-50).

Historically, studies show that the welfare state's development since World War II can be divided into three phases: from post-World War II until 1970, from 1970 to 1990, and from 1990 to the present. These phases reveal that, over time, the welfare state has undergone a 'building-reduction-rebuilding' process (Nullmeier & Kaufmann, 2010, pp. 81-82). This overall timeframe is therefore a felicitous period in which to observe the relationship between the transformation of the welfare state and changes of informatisation in political and economic environments. Based on existing literature on the welfare state and informatisation, a visual representation of their concurrent growth can be presented as in Figure 2.1.

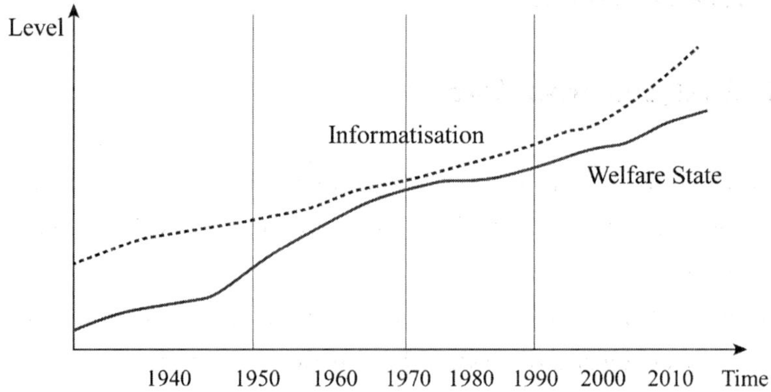

Source: The figure is drawn by the author of this study.

<Figure 2.1> **Informatisation and Welfare State**

1.2 Objects of Analysis

In reality, it would be a folly to argue that all 34 welfare states are of the same type and have reached the same degree of development in the public sector. Scholars have discovered a range of differences as well as similarities while conducting comparative studies on the development of welfare states (Esping-Andersen, 1990, pp. 20-23). For the last half-century or more, there have been many attempts to classify the welfare state in advanced western countries. During the last few decades, as studies have emerged from Latin America, East Asia, Eastern Europe and Russia, achieving classification has become increasingly important (Arts & Gelissen, 2010, p. 569). Since the 1990s in particular, there has been an increase of studies on welfare state typology that focus heavily on the 'convergence phenomenon'.[4]

This study deals with all OECD countries, regardless of whether they are at the frontier of developmental changes. For the purposes of this study, it is irrelevant where the country falls on the spectrum of welfare type and advancement. The fact remains that these countries do indeed share the status of 'welfare state', and rather than focusing on their differences, the focus remains on the developmental features they have in common.

1.3 Contents of Analysis and Analytical Framework

It is important to keep in mind that this study is about the relationship between the development of the welfare state and the development of the information society.

Discussions about whether modern society should be referred to as a 'post-industrial society,' a 'post-modern society,' or an 'electronic community' are left to other scholars.[5] Since the birth of the post-industrial

4 Iversen summarised that theories about the development of the welfare state have arrived in three big waves, starting with structuralism (focusing on the convergence phenomenon), moving to institutionalism (focusing on the divergence phenomenon) and then to new-structuralism (focusing on the convergence phenomenon) (Iversen, 2010, p. 194).

5 It is also sometimes referred to as a 'network society' or 'smart society' (Webster,

society, the type of information has changed, the complexity of information has deepened, and the importance of information has increased. These developments are all addressed in this study, alongside an attempt to determine how these phenomena influence the changes in our society; particularly where public welfare and inequality is concerned.

To achieve this, it does not matter whether the information society is cast in a positive or negative light. It does not matter whether the idea of 'continuity' or 'discontinuity' is emphasised. Despite the various viewpoints on social change through information, it is indisputable that social change does indeed occur through information (Kim, 2013, p. 20). To allow for a wider scope, this study is therefore conducted drawing from the fundamental reality that information does affect social welfare; especially public policy, with an emphasis on social policy.

Due to the considerable period of time studies have been conducted on the welfare state, scholars have accumulated a diverse range of results across various fields, including political science, economics, sociology, history, and so on (Leibfried, 2010, p. xxiii). This study is not a summation of studies that came previously, but rather an examination of the determinants of the development of the welfare state, and an exploration of potential areas of study left untouched. Its scope is limited by environmental and technical constraints that come with the territory of rigorous analysis; a necessary sacrifice in order to allow for an optimal level of accuracy. This era is one of rapid change in all areas of information. This study aims to address the growing expectation that these changes are unequivocally linked to the development of the welfare state.

There exist several welfare sectors: Public welfare, mandatory private welfare and voluntary private welfare. In most of the 34 welfare states, the public welfare sector has been developed continually alongside the private sector (Amenda & Whiteford, 2010, pp. 121-122). Furthermore, how public social spending is conducted can reveal both political priorities and the original extent of welfare needs. This is exemplified in this

2006, pp. 35~37).

excerpt from an article written by Herbert Obinger and Uwe Wagschal:

> The budget is a sort of fingerprint of government. The innumerable figures listed therein not only tell us about a government's political priorities, but also reflect the preferences and demands of the population (Obinger and Wagschal, 2010, p. 333).

Moreover, the size of the public welfare sector best represents the state's efforts towards the development of the welfare state, which is why the public welfare sector has been chosen as a focus for this study.

This study seeks not only to identify factors that impact the development of the welfare state as explained in previous studies, but also identify influential factors that remain unexplored. In addition, if informatisation has an impact on the development of the welfare state, positive or otherwise, this means that informatisation affects inequality; the very condition that the welfare state seeks to amend. Indeed, it is the condition of inequality that gave birth to the welfare state in the first place (Saunders, 2010, p. 526, 532, 538). It naturally follows, then, that this study deals with inequality issues in addition to public social spending.

Therefore, this study is conducted within the following analytical framework:

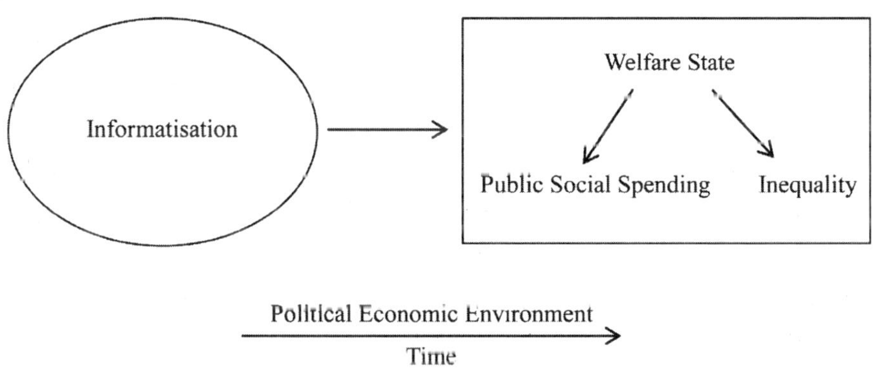

Source: The figure is drawn by the author of this study.

<Figure 2.2> **Analytical Framework**

In order to understand the relationship between informatisation and the development of the welfare state, the association between informatisation and public social spending must be dealt with first, taking time-dependent variables in the political and economic environment into consideration. The question of whether informatisation leads to the exacerbation of public social spending is therefore posed. Next, by examining time-dependent variables in the political and economic environment, it is determined whether informatisation deepens income inequality. The question is also posed as to whether informatisation has an impact on income inequality.

2. Conceptualisation: Informatisation and the Welfare State

2.1 Informatisation

To fully grasp how times have changed, the definition of 'information' prior to the conceptualisation of informatisation must be discussed. Frank Webster, a sociologist whose writing on the information society is widely and critically discussed, defines information as being the guidelines or instructions for an object or person as a meaningful thing (Webster, op. cit., p. 28). Annie Brooking, the author of 'Intellectual Capital' and 'Corporate Memory,' argues that information is composed of organised facts or data used to describe a particular condition and/or problem (Brooking, 1996, p. 23). Gordon Davis, a scholar of political science and business administration, and Margrethe H. Olson, an influential economist, are the authors of the acclaimed 'Management Information Systems.' They posit that the value of information is determined by its effect on behavioural changes in regards to decision making (Davis & Olson, 1985, p. 226).

Taking all schools of thought into consideration, information could be recapitulated as a meaningful description with potential impact on human behaviour and therefore outcomes and/or results. How, then, can 'informatisation' be defined? Most scholars have not defined the term precisely; instead mentioning it in passing within explanations relating to the information society. Daniel Bell, a sociologist and futurist, refers to the role of information in a post-industrial society as follows:

> A post-industrial society is based on service. Hence, it is game between persons. What counts is not raw muscle power, or energy, but information (Bell, 1973, p. 127).

Alvin Toffler, a renowned writer highly intuitive in regards to technology, society, and digital revolution, anticipated in 1980 that the information society would possess characteristics of diversification, decentralisation and individualisation; whereas the industrial society was standardised, uniformed, and centralised (Toffler, 1980, Chapter 13, Chapter 14). He argued that an information bomb was exploding in our midst, showering us with oftentimes jarring shrapnel in the form of images, resulting in a dramatic shift in the way each person acts and perceives their private world.

Manuel Castells, a sociologist whose interests centres on globalisation and the information society, posits that the concept of informational capitalism is the combination of informationalism and capitalism (Castells, 1996, pp. 18-19, 338). The term 'informationalism' indicates that information technology itself is a major source of productivity, and the term 'capitalism' is indicative of the basic economic relationships between 'profit-seeking individuals and organisations, private ownership, and market principles.' In other words, countries in which informational capitalism flourishes, information is a factor in determining the basic economic relationships within the capitalistic economy.

Herbert Schiller, a sociologist, scholar, and media critic, stressed that, in the midst of this explosive increase of computer use (such as computer processing, storage, retrieval, and data conversion), information itself is becoming one of the most significant products of the day (Schiller, 1986, p.72).

According to the above assertions, informatisation implies a relative increase in the significance of information in society, especially affecting the value of information and the criteria by which a society functions and judges itself. Informatisation means that information is moving into the category of 'goods.' It is a key factor in the increase of productivity through information technology, and remains so for nearly every field within society. This increased productivity eventually leads to the development of the 'computerised' society, as well as the development of information technology useful for networking.

For the purposes of this study, informatisation is recognised as a process that causes the proliferation of information. According to Schiller's observations, the concept of information includes the 'commercialised' product, which may be produced, consumed, transported, as well as a source of investment. Certainly, information is traded in the market via the principle of supply and demand, including the intervention of the government, who routinely regulates information according to their policies and motives (Schiller, Ibid., p. 34).

This study, however, does not necessarily conform to Schiller's argument that the government must actively interfere with the commercialisation of information. For the sake of neutrality, this study contains no bias that information itself, or the commercialisation thereof, is beneficial, harmful or profitable for society. Informatisation is viewed from a purely objective standpoint, paving the road for an accurate assessment of its impact on public welfare and inequality.

2.2 The Welfare State

The scope of this study is necessarily determined by humankind's perceptions of the welfare state. It is, of course, a concept which has been defined by many scholars (Esping-Andersen, op. cit., p. 1). For this reason, several of the more prominent viewpoints on the welfare state must be touched upon before delving deeper into its complexities. Here are three definitions as described by different scholars:

> The basis of the welfare state is a government-protected minimum standard of income, nutrition, health, housing, and education. These things must be provided for every citizen not as charity, but as a political right (Wilensky & Lebeaux, 1975, p. 1).

> The term 'welfare state' can be characterised as a descriptive concept; a specific type of government activity. It identifies countries in which the state adopts an active role in the management of economic and social progress. A considerable portion of this type of the state's resources is dedicated to social purposes, thus meeting the need for greater equality and a higher chance of adequacy or success when it comes to income security, health, housing, and education (Nohlen, 2001, p. 580).

> In modern political science and sociology, the welfare state serves mainly as a neutral descriptive term for a government's activity, especially in wealthy democracies with a predilection for liberalism. The status quo in these countries has historically been realised via industrialisation and democratisation in response to social problems. Through government intervention in income distribution, the aim is to ensure safety for each individual, as well as adequate health care, housing, education and employment (Schmidt, 2004, p. 806).

As outlined in the above definitions, the welfare state can be characterised as a state that implements social policy with the purpose of equality and safety in specific areas. This concept is explored and substantiated by Gosta Esping-Andersen, a sociologist whose specific focus is the welfare state, especially in capitalist economies:

> A common textbook definition is that it involves state responsibility for securing some basic modicum of welfare for its citizens. Such as a definition skirts the issue of whether social policies are emancipatory or not; whether the help system legitimation or not; whether they contradict or aid the market process; and what, indeed, is meant by 'basic'? Would it not be more appropriate to require of a welfare state that it satisfies more than our basic or minimal welfare needs? (Esping-Andersen, op. cit., p. 18)

Some aspects of the common definition of the welfare state remain unclear. However, in line with Esping-Andersen's perspective, this study defines the welfare state as a state that takes responsibility for ensuring a minimum standard of life quality, protecting its citizens from social risks, and (on one level or another) striving to obtain equality, thus providing increased opportunities for all.

3. Theories of Welfare State Development

Continued attempts by scholars to elucidate the origins and development of the welfare state have resulted in various hypotheses and theoretical perspectives. After World War II, studies continued to scrutinise the effects of social, political, and economic factors on the welfare state. As aforementioned, this study is conducted to uncover unexplored factors that affect the development of the welfare state, while simultaneously re-evaluating those factors that have been established by other scholars. The following looks at the main elements of the origin and development of the welfare state as presented by some of the major theoretical perspectives.

3.1 Structural-functionalism Theory

The earliest school of thought on the origin and development of the welfare state is the structural-functionalism theory, developed in the 1960s and 1970s.

Émile Durkheim was a prominent structural-functionalist, and recognised that modern society was becoming increasingly complicated due to the process of industrialisation. The new world meant that the pre-existing rules and values people relied upon to maintain social order were no longer applicable, resulting in a variety of dilemmas. He believed that, in such circumstances, society is able to maintain equilibrium through an adaptation process, ultimately overcoming associated dilemmas and allowing continued development within society. However, he also recognised that industrialisation increased labour specialisation and division, triggering a degradation of the pre-existing order and yielding some maladaptive results among workers in the labour market. In order to expedite the resolution of these issues, he suggested strengthening solidarity by creating professional corporations composed of the employer and employee, avoiding direct intervention of the state (Coser, 1984, pp. ix, x, xxi-xxii).

Talcott Parsons, another structural-functionalist, deviated somewhat from Durkheim's stance, positing that society is a system that consists of interrelated elements which interact with the external environment, resulting in the development and maintenance of the entire societal system. He postulated that there was no real need to expedite the process of resolution, and that change in the political and economic environment naturally leads to functional adaptation within the social system. Moreover, he believed that this is exactly what led to the development of the welfare state in the nineteenth century. In other words, he deemed the industrial revolution and democratic revolution to be the very reasons for the origin and development of the welfare state (Parsons, 1977, pp. 298-300).

Structural-functionalism has been supported by the results of a number of comparative studies using quantitative data. The results of such studies show that the increase in urbanisation, economic influence and a rising elderly population are among the main factors that cause the emergence and continued development of the welfare state (Wilensky, 1975, p. xiii; Huber & Stephens, 2012, p. 117).

3.2 Power Resource Theory

The power resource theory was popular from the 1970s through the 1980s. This theory focuses on the development of the capital society, democratisation, and the resulting conflict caused by the division between social classes (Lessenich, 2000, pp. 45-46). The divide of social classes can be traced back to uneven distribution, with a particular emphasis on political and class conflicts between capital owners and wage earners. The power resource theory highlights the importance of a collective, organised approach among the working class. This approach involves a higher level of involvement in left-wing political parties and trade unions in order to increase equality and encourage a more generous welfare state.

The power resource theory also acknowledges that political parties view the relatively disadvantaged in terms of economic resources. Political parties rely primarily on labour power to bring about the development of the welfare state, the effect of which is the modification of conditions and outcomes related to market distributive processes (Korpi, 1985, p. 39; Korpi, 2006, p. 168).

Scholars adhering to this perspective have used quantitative comparative studies to try and demonstrate the relationship between the political mobilisation of the working class and the development of the welfare state. The main factors discussed are the density of trade unions, the number of people who belong to trade unions, and the power of left-wing parties (Ebbinghaus, 2010, pp. 200-204).

3.3 Neo-institutionalism

There was considerable criticism surrounding the power resource perspective, providing impetus for the beginnings of the neo-institutionalism perspective. The neo-institutionalism perspective focuses on the state playing a central role in the introduction and spread of welfare programs. It is this perspective that prompted a proliferation of institutional theories from the mid-1980s onwards.

Students of this view highlight the effect of a state's level of autonomy on the development of the welfare state. The development of institutions and competition (both internal and external to a country) is explored from a sociological standpoint (Lessenich, op. cit., p. 49). A typical example is that of Germany introducing social insurance. This was not the result of political struggles among wage workers ('von unten'), but the result of the integration strategy of the state ('von oben') (Alber, 1982, p. 150).

The essence of this perspective, expressed with brevity, could be 'institutions matter.' The idea is that pre-existing institutions can become a catalyst for the establishment of more institutions. Furthermore, they can affect the speed and direction of the development of other institutions; whether or not the affected institutions are newly established. Consequently, creating a new institution or abolishing an old one is not a trivial decision because of the impact it will have on existing institutions. This phenomenon is called 'path dependence,' and is the reason the basic characteristics of an individual welfare state should not change significantly from this perspective.[6]

To discover the relationship between the development of the welfare state and the various facets of institutions, neo-institutionalists have performed a number of quantitative studies, the main focus of which is the development of political institutions; including federalism, multi-party systems, and direct democracy. Other quantitative studies typically performed by neo-institutionalists focus on the development of the structure and function of state administrations; including modernisation, centralisation, bureaucratisation, and specialisation (Skocpol & Amenta, 1986, pp. 131-157; Wagschal & Obinger, 2000, pp. 466-497; 2002, pp. 235-271; Castles et al, 2005, pp. 215-237; Immergut, 2010, pp. 228-240).

3.4 Globalisation Theory

This theory involves globalisation's impact on the welfare state. By the 1990s it was a well-recognised concept, the spread of which many students considered overdue, and has been met with increased enthusiasm and fervour as it developed into a theory (Rieger & Leibfried, 2001, pp. 29-45). There are both positive and negative results exemplifying the link between globalisation and the development of the welfare state.

Many globalisation theorists approach the associated issues from the 'compensation perspective,' which asserts that globalisation leads to a welfare state which is continually amended and enhanced. It recognises that, while open economies tend to be exposed to riskier and more unstable conditions, this is the reason that individual states must strive to strengthen social security programs. The result is that the extra measures taken help assure some protection for the domestic economy, as well as security for workers and stability for labour relations. Second, globalisation incites public political demands for public social spending in order to compensate for and mitigate the risks involved with an open

6 This explanation is an apt argument for the maintenance of the basic elements of individual welfare states during the retrenchment phase.

economy. In this situation, pre-welfare political measures are often formed as a result of 'policy feedback' (Iversen & Cusack, 2000, pp. 317-318; Swank, 2010, pp. 320-321).

Here is where complications arise. Others adhering to the globalisation theory focus more on the 'efficiency perspective.' This describes the recognition that globalisation, from an economic viewpoint, increases the international capital mobility limit, putting pressure on states to roll back social spending and reduce taxes, thus securing mobile assets from the beginning. In response, states hesitate to do what is necessary to properly fulfil the goal of 'safety and security,' because trade openness also raises pressure to reduce public debts, labour costs, interest rates, and decreases incentives to work and/or invest. From this viewpoint, the welfare state has a negative influence on investment, profits, job creation and so on. The comparative advantages of foreign investment environments mean that business interest groups and business economists put pressure on policy-makers to impose reforms (Mishra, 1999, pp. 115-116; Swank, 2010, op. cit., pp. 318-320).

The above 'efficiency' thesis was challenged by authors who argue that the impact of globalisation is mediated by domestic politics. From this perspective, the pressure caused by globalisation is seen to influence domestic political and/or economic institutions (such as labour market institutions, electoral and representative systems, and formal institutional veto points). The institutional mediation process, caused by the impact of globalisation as aforementioned, necessitates decisions on the part of welfare states regarding their internal operations, prompting them to find paths towards heightened security for their citizens (Garrett & Lange, 1995, pp. 627-655).

Students of this perspective commonly rely on various political and economic variables to draw conclusions. They mainly draw from variables in statistics and/or other information relating to direct foreign investment rates, foreign exchange reserves, interest rates, inflation rates, the density of trade unions, etc. (Jahn, 2009, pp. 87-105).

3.5 Post-industrialisation Theory

With the globalisation theory, concerns over the causal relationship between the welfare state and de-industrialisation began to become apparent. The post-industrialisation perspective concentrates on the social risks of the modern world caused by changes in family structure and the labour market; changes that inevitably occur during the process of economic structural change. A notable concern is de-industrialisation.

Paul Pierson, a highly acclaimed professor of political science, was one of the first scholars interested in the implications of post-industrial changes. He was concerned with the slower productivity growth, service-based employment, the welfare state's maturation, the aging population, the structure of households, and the transformation within advanced industrial democracies. He argued that the changes mentioned above act as contributing factors regarding the pressure to reform and restructure the welfare state. Specifically, some reform initiatives can transform 'winners' and 'losers' into wildly competing coalitions; a process that tends to contribute to the transformation of the welfare state in individual countries. This is one of the many consequences of conflicting interests that arise during the process of distributing benefits and burdens (Pierson, 1996, p. 176; 2001, pp. 82-98, 102-104).

Anthony Giddens, an influential sociologist who can boast the publication of at least thirty-four books, also argued that the welfare state must be reformed to solve the series of new social problems in the post-industrial society. He suggested mapping out and adopting a 'social investment strategy' for sustainable growth. This social investment strategy includes the expansion of investment for human capital with an emphasis on technology development and infrastructure, the environment, the support of growth-promoting industrial policies and active labour market policies. Venturing a little deeper into the issue, he emphasised the importance of the welfare state's active intervention of social welfare issues and the diversification of welfare supplies through combining universalism and selectivism, thus improving efficiency and effectiveness (Giddens, op. cit., pp. 118-128).

This perspective mainly utilises various quantitative comparative studies regarding employment rates in the service sector, as well as unemployment rates, birth rates, divorce rates, the size of the aged population, etc. (Iversen, & Wren, 1998, pp. 507-546; Esping-Andersen 1999, pp. 148-166; Iversen, & Cusack, 2000, pp. 313-349).

Having touched on several theories on the origin and growth of the welfare state, along with the implications of those theories, this study henceforth attempts to substantiate some of the existing theories via the key variables thereof, also thoroughly examining the causality between informatisation and the development of the welfare state by utilising informatisation-related variables.

4. Informatisation and the Welfare State: Theoretical Potential of this Study

In recent years, many studies have drawn the attention of scholars to the welfare state's relationship with globalisation and de-industrialisation. Another area of focus is the growth and transformation occurring within the welfare state; the main continual focus being on the responses of the welfare state to newly-emerging social issues related to socioeconomic change, globalisation and democracy (Esping-Andersen, 2002; Taylor-Gooby, 2004; Alber & Gilbert, 2009; Obinger et al, 2010).

In the beginning, studies on the welfare state concentrated on industrialised western societies. However, as aforementioned, more recent years saw a rapidly building list of studies on emerging welfare states, including countries such as East Asia, Latin America, and Eastern Europe (Peng & Wong, 2010, pp. 656-670; Cook, 2010, pp. 671-686; Huber & Stephens, op. cit.). These studies have contained familiar goals; namely, to substantiate previously discussed welfare state theories related to changes in political and economic environments and the impact of these changes on the ongoing restructuring of the welfare state. Also emerging from these studies, however, are attempts to determine the impact of the countless new factors associated with the welfare state, such as the aging population, corruption, low fertility rates, and an insufficient state administrative capacity to meet welfare needs in the modern world. Consequently, some of these newer studies contain points previously irrelevant or unexplored that now require attention.

The purpose of this study is to discover whether the development of the information society impacts the growth and transformation of the welfare state, carefully taking into account the evidence presented in previous studies. Therefore, this study belongs to the category of the de-industrialisation theory, from the theoretical perspective. As mentioned earlier, since year 2000 there have been an abundance of studies conducted in relation to the rapid development of the Internet and the information society, information inequality, and the digital divide (Lee & Park, 2009; Min, 2011). However, there has been a conspicuous lack of action towards proving a causal relationship between informatisation and the development of the welfare state, with studies failing to closely examine the potential theoretical relevance of such a relationship.

Here, it should be noted that there have been some articles and books about the relationship of informatisation and the welfare state. Manuel Castells & Pekka Himanen wrote about the characteristics of information and the welfare state in Finland in 2002 (Castells & Himanen, 2002, pp. 77-102). In addition, Yeongbin Han published an article about informatisation and national strategy in Sweden in 2005 (Han, 2005, pp. 59-80). However, rather than concentrating on how the relationship between informatisation and the development of the welfare state can be explained from a theoretical standpoint, these scholars primarily focused on how informatisation makes progress alongside welfare in individual countries. In other words, they incite discussions focusing more on the 'information society,' or simply 'information,' giving the concept of the 'welfare state' a more subsidiary role within case studies.

The ITU also published a number of reports and statistics related to informatisation in conjunction with relevant international organisations, such as the UN, EUROstat, the OECD and other national institutions belonging to individual countries with an interest in the development of the information society.[7] However, these documents do not deal with issues surrounding the impact of informatisation on the development of the welfare state.

Articles and books searched under the terms 'informatisation' and 'welfare state' yield discussions and arguments on information inequality, the information gap, reproduction of income inequality and social stratification. As a result, because of the eagerness of scholars, administrators, politicians, etc., to achieve information equality, new terms such as 'information welfare' and 'information welfare state' have been proposed (Son et al, 2000, pp. 5-35; OECD, 2001; Yang et al, 2002, pp. 79-112; Kim & Kim, 2002, pp. 123-155; Go, 2012, pp. 5-35). However, these publications begin with a different outlook on the impact of informatisation on the development of the welfare state. They contain studies which suggest the key to producing successful information welfare or an information welfare state is through resolving income inequality. The weakness of this approach is that most of these studies are at least partly subjective and value-implied. This study, however, begins with the view that informatisation is a phenomenon born of the modern society. The driving purpose is to discover the impact of informatisation on the development of the welfare state; also ensuring that the information herein maintains an objective and value-neutral perspective. Moreover, in contrast to the aforementioned studies, the influences of informatisation (as one feature of the de-industrialised society) on the development of the welfare state are explored and explained from the theoretical perspective. In conclusion, this study does not oppose but builds upon the post-industrialisation theory by explaining the growth and transformation of the welfare state.

---

[7] The ITU, the UN specialised agency for ICT, publishes the official source for global ICT statistics every year. In the case of the OECD, the OECD Communication Outlook is released every two years, providing indicators for the development of different communications networks and comparing performance indicators such as revenue, investment, employment and prices for services throughout the OECD area.

Chapter III

Informatisation, Inequality, and Public Social Welfare:

The Mechanisms of Informatisation and the Development of the Welfare State

Chapter III

Informatisation, Inequality, and Public Social Welfare:

The Mechanisms of Informatisation and the Development of the Welfare State

Chapter three briefly describes the historical meaning of informatisation in the second-half of the twentieth century, as well as numerous changes in politics, economy and social culture caused by informatisation. In addition, there is an investigation into the problem of inequalities that arise due to informatisation. The welfare state's response to these hitherto uncharted types of inequalities is also explored.

1. Informatisation in the Historical Context

1.1 Informatisation and Social Paradigm

First of all, it is necessary that the meaning and characteristics of informatisation is dealt with in a historical context.

Daniel Bell was concerned with changes that occurred in occupational structure alongside economy restructuring, which in turn caused changes in social structure. Making his mark as one of the leading intellectuals of the post-war era in American society, he identified five characteristics that differed from those in the industrial society. First, in the economic sector, changes appear from a goods-producing economy to a service economy. Second, where there is occupational distribution, the professional and technical classes grow. Third, theoretical knowledge plays a significant role as the source of innovation and policy formulation for society. Fourth, the future is oriented through the control of technology and technological assessment. Fifth, new 'intellectual technology' affects decision-making processes. In summation, Bell asserts that technological knowledge ultimately changes the social paradigm thorough the transformation of production processes and forms of communication in society (Bell, op. cit., p.14).

Alvin Toffler posits that, historically, society experienced three waves through technical transformation.[8] The first wave of change is prompted by the invention of agriculture. The second wave is propelled by the industrial revolution. The third wave is unleashed by an information revolution, which can only come about via the proliferation of information technology. He understood that management of knowledge, information and possession became increasingly important as digital technology developed throughout the second-half of the twentieth century. For these reasons, during this period, people who dominated in dealing with information and knowledge were the leaders of social change. He also saw that the system controlled through the bureaucratic centralism of the industrial age was replaced by Adhocracy; with a temporary, flexible, adaptive, and innovative structure (Toffler, 1980, op. cit., pp. 25-34).

Manuel Castells emphasises the difference between the information revolution and previous technological revolutions (Castells, op. cit., pp. 46-47, pp. 60-65). He calls attention to the unique features of the new information technology paradigm in the 1970s as follows: The first feature is that technology as raw material can act as information itself. The second refers to the pervasiveness of the effects of new technologies. New technologies influence most activities undertaken by humankind in society. The third is the dramatic effect of these technologies on the logic of networking within any system or set of relationships. The fourth feature is that the new paradigm is based on flexibility, the outcome of which is construction, demolition, and reconstruction of organisations – especially those related to networks. The fifth and last characteristic refers to the increasing convergence of specific technologies into a much

8 The information revolution created a divide in history, and owed its uprising to wide changes in specific technology production methods, social structure, social values, etc.

more highly integrated system. For example, computer technology is integrated into medical technology, which naturally results in the creation of new computerised medical technology, affecting human health on a societal level. With all five features combined, Castells asserts that the essence of the new information technology paradigm is as follows:

> The information technology paradigm does not evolve towards its closure as a system, but towards its openness as a multi-edged network. It is powerful and imposing in its materiality, but adaptive and open-ended in its historical development. Comprehensiveness, complexity, and networking are its decisive qualities (Castells, 1996, p. 65).

As aforementioned, Bell, Toffler, and Castells argue that informatisation can be understood as a 'transformation into a post-industrial society,' an 'information revolution,' or an 'information technology paradigm.' They all agreed the focus must be on increasing the significance and the effect of information and technology on society during the second-half of the century, emphasising the transformation of social structure.

In reality, the phenomenon of informatisation originally emerged from several areas. Above all, informatisation would have been utterly impossible without the invention of the computer and the enhancement of its functions, resulting in ICT. As computer processing costs decreased, its popularity and usage increased. New networks for telecommunications were established and became widespread. In addition, there were demands for energy-saving, demands for heightened speed and accuracy in every field of society, demands for intercommunication to improve the sharing and acquisition of various kinds of information, and requests for the use of resources without space and time limitations. Most of all, each country developed the need for change and reform of policy decision-making processes. These processes had to be more rapid and transparent in order to quickly and appropriately respond to the many demands of the citizens. All this aside, urbanisation, the development of faster transport systems, soaring capital and workforce exchanges between countries, and rising education levels were also catalysts for informatisation.

2. Politics, Economy, Social Culture, and Informatisation

Here, several of the changes generated by informatisation in economy, politics, and social culture are briefly examined.

2.1 Informatisation and Economic Change

1) Development and Spatial Spreading of the ICT Industry

First and foremost are the more obvious characteristics of the ICT industry. OECD countries agreed to characterise the ICT sector as a combination of manufacturing and service industries that capture, transmit, and display data and information electronically (OECD, 2002, p. 81). In the manufacturing industry, growth spurred the production of information processing devices, such as computers, mobile phones, TVs, and tablet computers. Mass production of devices, of course, also spurred the production of the components that make up these devices, such as TV and computer monitors, semiconductors, and communication equipment. In the service industry, development revolved around the circulation of information through technologies such as wired and wireless networks, mobiles, and mVoIP (Mobile Voice over Internet Protocol).

Second, UNESCO's definition of ICT is the combination of informatics technology with other related technologies; especially communication technology (UNESCO, 2002, p. 13). As can be seen from the above descriptions of ICT, the ICT industry is not only field-independent, as in the semiconductor industry and the electronics industry, but also closely associated with the broadcast and communication industries. Therefore, industries dealing with content delivery services such as broadcasting and communications can also be viewed as ICT-related industries. It is not surprising, then, that these industries have also grown at an unprecedented rate.

Third, ICT includes characteristics such as base technology, which involves networking, computing, sensing, and actuating. This introduces the possibility that ICT affects or is linked with all industries. Indeed, it is observable that new industries were and continue to be created by converging sciences and technologies that involve culture, the humanities and content. (Cho, 2010, pp. 3-4). Furthermore, as software continues to emerge with full force and increased complexity, platforms are also built at a high rate. This means the core of the ICT industry is increasingly transferred from the manufacturing of ICT devices to the building of platforms.[9]

Put simply, the development of ICT led to changes in industrial structures as well as the development of new industries. It is a notable point that the development of ICT also contributed to the spatial spread of the industry (Castells, 1989, pp. 156-168). For some time now, spatial movement for making high quality products at low production costs has occurred not only within individual countries, but also at an international level. Domestically, technology centres continue to be created in order to maximize the efficiency of development and production, while experts are called upon to skilfully handle information technology in the process. The industrial complex called 'Technopolis' concentrated on research centres for universities, the government, manufacturing companies, venture capital, the information market, and skilled workers. Over time, countries began to move their business to better production sites, so that upgrading ICT and producing higher quality products at lower production costs was possible (examples include labour, land, tax, and regulation). In the meantime, countries were beginning to actively move towards wider markets where ICT products could be consumed. Additionally, the development of networks over the Internet accelerated aforesaid spatial spreading. As a result, countries steadily increased investments in ICT industries, developing progressively higher levels of information technology, making the competition fierce in the interna-

---

[9] A platform can be defined as an environment built by many of participants, such as providers and consumers, in order to transact for value acquisition. The platform of computers and the Internet can be classified by the computers' operating systems (Windows, Linux, Mac OS, etc.), smart phones' operating systems (Android, iOS, Windows Mobile, etc.), the smart phones' application market (Apple's App Store, Google's Play Store, Daum Kakao, etc.), and web browsers (Internet Explorer, Firefox, chrome, etc.) (Yun, 2012, p. 45, 49).

tional market.

2) Informatisation, Changes in Employment and the Relations between Labour and Capital

With the ICT industry and the development of related industries, an increase in employment can be seen as a natural consequence. Above all, the development of the ICT industry led to an increase in the employment ratio of technicians handling ICT to total employment. At the same time, industries closely related to ICT developed in a widespread and rapid manner, i.e., the service industry; including circulation, finance, health care, education, and welfare. Needless to say, this created a high demand in the labour market (as shown in Figure 3.1). These types of service industries require a large range of workers with high or sufficient levels of education and ICT skills (for example, computer proficiency, Internet proficiency, etc.) (OECD, 2013, pp. 48-49)[10]

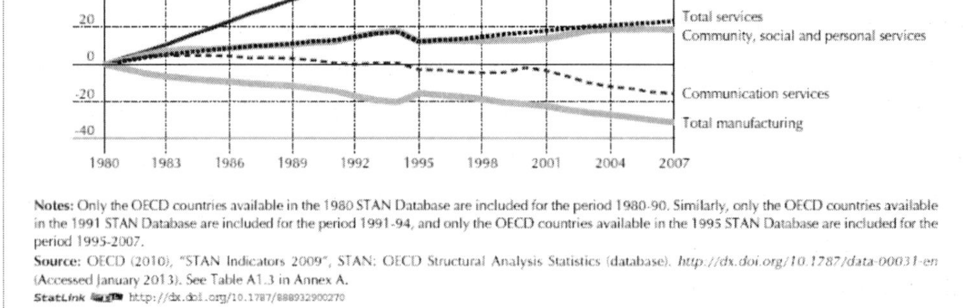

Source: OECD. (2013). OECD Skills Outlook 2013: First Results from the Survey of Adult Skills, Paris: Author. p. 48.

<Figure 3.1> **Change in the Share of Employment by Industrial Sectors**

---

10 According to the results of this analysis, in over half of all OECD countries, at least one-third of economic activity is concentrated in high-tech manufacturing, communications, finance, real estate and insurance.

Businesses computerised and automated production methods and production processes through skilled ICT workers. Middle-management positions for the management and control of production processes disappeared slowly because of the application of the standardisation program, which contributed to the decrease of unnecessary labour hire and production costs (Castells, op. cit., pp. 321-335).

These changes in labour and employment have led to changes in relations between labour and capital. Since it has been possible for employers to increase productivity by employing specialised workers and manufacturing quality products through innovative technologies, more flexible employment contracts became popular. Compared to the more traditional contract, these contracts often include varying timeframes and employee numbers (depending on a company or employer's needs at any given time). In short, this enabled the establishment of flexible and open relations between labour and capital.

3) Economic Growth and Informatisation

First, looking at economic improvement, ICT has made prompt economic growth possible through accumulating and providing information as a new production factor. In addition, the development of ICT such as computers and software increased the efficiency of the production process, while the development of the Internet improved the efficiency of the distribution process by overcoming time and space constraints. Products and services produced in the ICT industry and ICT-related industries became value-added products, and contributed to economic growth by expanding new consumer markets (Jung, 2011, p. 26, pp. 48-49). Moreover, active investment in ICT resulted in more diverse and flexible work conditions, such as flex-time working and telecommuting. Therefore, women, the disabled, and the elderly are able to participate in economic activities, thus improving economic growth by expanding the nation's work force (Lee, 2013, pp. 23-27; OECD, 2012, p. 16).

Secondly, interest in the role of human capital and social capital increased as society became increasingly information and knowledge-based. 'Knowledge Power,' obtained through education and training, was able to contribute to economic growth through the accumulation of human capital (Lee, 2008, pp. 26-29). Unlike physical capital and its externalities, human capital relates to public goods, so it can have an impact on society as a whole. In fact, the development of ICT continually expands educational opportunities and plays a role as a mediator, facilitating the accumulation of human capital by the seamless sharing of knowledge and information.[11]

Thirdly, the development of ICT affected the formation of social capital, such as social ties between members in the community (for example, trust, networks, etc.) and governance (for example, social norms, social rules, etc.). Janine Nahapiet and Sumantra Ghoshal, the authors of 'Social Capital, Intellectual Capital, and the Organizational Advantage,' define social capital as the sum of the actual and potential resources embedded within, available through, and derived from the network of relationships possessed by an individual or social unit. They emphasise the presence or absence of network ties between actors; network configuration or morphology, describing the pattern of linkages in terms of such measures as density, connectivity, and hierarchy; and appropriable organisation (Nahapiet & Ghoshal, 1998, pp. 243-244). The OECD defines social capital as networks with shared norms, values and a shared understanding that facilitates cooperation within or among groups (OECD, 2001, p. 41). In this sense, social capital is physical and human capital combined, and plays an increasingly effective role as economic capital (Rupasingha, Goetz, & Freshwater, 2000, p. 565; Woolcock, 1998, pp. 180-182; Bousrih, 2013, p. 41, 51). Informatisation brought economic benefits by inciting communication through online access and by increasing transparency and fairness within personal relationships and organisations. Governance was formed via active exchanges through social ties, which would not have been possible without the Internet and smart phones (essentially, cyberspace). These ties increased confidence and stability within societies, resulting in the reduction of social costs due to crime and social disorder (Seo & Park, 2003, pp. 43-45; Jang,

11 For example, various types of Internet-based distance learning courses improved educational opportunities and prompted the sharing and distribution of information, consequentially contributing to economic growth.

2006, pp. 15-22).

2.2 Informatisation and Political Change

1) Electronic Media as Political Instruments and Political Strategies

Informatisation affects the methods by which political power is accomplished and political debates are carried out. Politicians increasingly and actively utilise more advanced mass media as an instrument to ensure political power and public appeal. Recently, for example, newspapers, television, radio, and the Internet have been used not only actively, but also widely in the political process. In particular, the influence of the electronic mass media in the political process has been escalating. In fact, many researchers have analysed the political influence of these media through the assessment of political awareness and participation (Hwang & Kim, 2005, p. 118, pp. 148-149; Lee and Kim, 2012, pp. 105-106). The results of these studies identified that political influence of mass media increased when people encountered it directly and often. Even more importantly, it demonstrated that the development of interactive communication through mobile phones, the Internet and smart phones has been increasing the influence politicians wield. Manuel Castells says the following about the role of the electronic media:

> Not that all politics can be reduced to images, sounds, or symbolic manipulation. But, without it, there is no chance of winning or exercising power. Thus, everybody ends up playing the same game, although not in the same way or with the same purpose (Castells, 1997, p. 311).

> I shall argue, on the basis of evidence, and with the help of a number of cross-cultural examples, that this framing of politics by their capture in the space of the media (a trend characteristic of the information age) impacts not only elections, but political organization, decision-making, and governance, ultimately modifying the nature of the relationship between state and society (Castells, Ibid., p. 312).

Here, Manuel Castells is asserting that the role and function of electronic media in the political arena enables political discussions on television, computerised political marketing, and public opinion polls with a rapid rate of release. All of the above are political instruments that in turn allow personal attacks, political shows, and the planting or incitement of scandals through cyberspace. Such political strategies alter political methodologies and political results in the information society (Castells, Ibid., p. 485, pp. 486-527).[12]

2) Network Social Movements and Network Politics

The development of the Internet and mobile communications enabled people to actively follow political issues without the constraints of time and space, thus making it possible to respond individually or collectively. Now, the Internet plays a key role as a channel of interaction in the information society. Debates on political issues among people in cyberspace are possible, allowing for citizens from many socio-economic backgrounds to have some influence over political decisions without the direct intervention of politicians (Castells, 2004, pp. 46- 47). With cyber network politics becoming livelier, electoral strategies and marketing campaigns used by previous political parties became outdated. The nature of social networking on the Internet is based on openness and individuality, with the possibility of perpetual expansion. A higher level of transparency allows various limitations to be overcome, and consequently, people's voting tendencies and the manner by

---

12 For example, in South Korea, the National Intelligence Agency's chief, named 'Won Sei-hoon,' was convicted due to a political scandal operation on the Internet. After taking office in March 2009, Won Sei-hoon ordered several staff members to post articles slandering the opposition and specific politicians on Internet websites that progressive netizens actively participated in. The articles also beseeched people to support the activities of the current government. Articles were posted repeatedly, displaying accusatory content such as 'North Korea-following leftists cause confusion over the Ms. Park's bid for reconciliation,' 'Ahn is going to lie, I saw him in a room salon,' and 'Moon Jae-in is the weakest body of all time.' Since January 2011, his staff had also been actively participating on 'Twitter' where, again, progressive netizens were active. During 2012, the year that the last Presidential elections took place in Korea, this activity was expanded into an organisation which consisted of four cyber teams with seventy to eighty people in order to effectively and rapidly post such comments on the Internet ("National Intelligence", 2015).

which politicians deliver messages are significantly altered in current political landscapes.

In fact, cyberspace may be the most common place in which citizens can express public opinions on social issues. If these opinions are demonstrated by a sufficient number of people, they may also be incorporated into the political agenda (Castells, 2001, pp. 188-227). The online meeting of like-minded people and social movement groups accelerate the political process, spurring more emphatic opposition or support, as well as funding for desired leaders.[13] Hence, the new system of political participation among politicians and citizens alike.

3) E-government, E-governance, and E-democracy

Informatisation brought greater efficiency in the area of administration, which allowed the development of the 'e-government.' Because the e-government is multidimensional and complicated, various different views on the concept have emerged, all depending on the specific interests and/or characteristics of governments, organisations and researchers (Alshomrani, 2012, p. 412). The OECD states that the e-government utilises new information and communication technologies (ICTs) for a diverse range of government roles and responsibilities. In particular, networking opportunities offered by the Internet and related technologies have the potential to transform the structure and methods by which a government operates (OECD, 2009b). The UNDESA states that the e-government is the application of ICT by the government to help provide information and public services for the people. More specifically, the aim of the e-government is to ensure efficient management of in-

13 One well-known demonstration of this in Korea is when the former Korean President, Roh Moo-hyun, was elected on December 19, 2002. At that time, online supporters called 'Rohsamo,' short for 'people who love Roh,' played an important role towards the election victory. The election campaign continued over a few years, during which time these supporters provided a vital political force through Internet based networks. On the Election Day, the main method of attack was to mobilise young voters to support Roh through mobile devises. Consequently, the voting results were overturned at the last minute. The election victory of Roh Moo-hyun and Nosamo are prime examples of the power of information technology, which can be systematically utilised via a combination of communication methods via the Internet on devices such as mobile phones (Castells et al, 2009, pp. 271-277).

formation for citizens, better service delivery to citizens, and to allow citizen empowerment via easy access to information and by encouraging participation in public policy decision-making (UNDESA, 2005, p. 14). Virpi Timonen, Orla O'Donnell, Peter C. Humphreys posit that the e-government is the use of public bodies of information and communication technologies to deliver information and services to internal and external customers and organisations, elected representatives, and other stakeholders. This is done in such a way as to complement, replace or improve traditional delivery systems (Timonen et al, 2003, p. 11). As demonstrated by the above definitions, an e-government includes three elements: The introduction of ICT to the public sector, the active use of ICT by individuals, businesses, and governments, and the appropriate supply of various administrative services connected to the network.

Historically, the e-government started with administrative agencies offering general information or official documentation through websites. Over the years, e-government services gradually improved, providing search capabilities through integrated links and making civil affairs administration (such as certificate insurance and tax payments) available online. Now, the range and utilisation of services online are increasingly fast, extensive, accurate.[14]

The aforementioned developments of the e-government increased transparency and efficiency of administration and enabled citizen participation in political decision-making processes by intercommunication. Alvin Toffler asserts that informatisation lowers overall administrative costs by facilitating citizen access to government information and lowers political costs by enabling citizens more active participation in political decision-making processes; bringing about an era of semi-direct democracy in which countries can undergo the merging of direct democracy and representative democracy (Toffler, op. cit., pp. 443-447). In fact, where there is a distribution of public information, debates over political agenda, and discussions about social issues, the electronic public sphere

[14] The proportion of citizens and businesses using the Internet to interact with public authorities grew rapidly in many OECD countries between 2005 and 2010. During year 2010, an average of 40% of the citizens and 80% of all businesses in OECD countries interacted with public authorities via the Internet. (OECD, op cit., p. 46)

is most able to contribute to the development of its democracy (Park, 1995, pp. 157-161). This results in citizens actively expressing their interests and/or concerns and directly participating in decision-making through a variety of online forms of communication; all of which promote the development of e-governance (UNDESA, 2008, pp. 3-5).

2.3 Informatisation and Social Culture

1) Work-Family Relationships and Informatisation

Information has begun to change society's understanding of the traditional male-breadwinner's role in the labour market. New forms of employment, which put an emphasis on information and knowledge rather than physical labour, is creating a new paradigm of male and female roles in the workplace. In other words, biological differences are no longer necessarily the deciding factor in employment (Castells, 1997, pp. 286-304).

In addition, the development of the ICT industry, which is related to online sales, distribution and management, contribute to the increase of flexible working hours (such as temporary or short-term employment and telecommuting). These flexible work hours are another factor to have changed work and family life environments. This is particularly evident where women are concerned. Traditional female roles in the home, such as childbirth, childcare and housework, brings with it heavy time restrictions. However, flexible work hours and opportunities (such as telecommuting), enabled through ICT, allow women to move between house and work environments much more freely; improving their economic independence, as well as giving them the chance to meet their needs for self-realisation through economic activity (Kim, 1998, pp. 47-49).

Informatisation reduces time and space constraints in economic arenas, increases the demand for knowledge and technology labour, and facilitates change in the balance between work and family life through more progressive ideals regarding the gender roles.

2) Social Relationships and Informatisation

Informatisation also spawned a new form of intercommunication. Drastically unlike communication via face-to-face networking of the past, computers and the Internet enabled anonymity, speed and openness. In cyberspace, it is now common that social relationships be formed and dismantled depending on needs and interests. Above all, with the development of the Internet and mobile communications, people meet each other on a global scale on a regular basis, often forming ongoing and close relationships through a rapid exchange of information and cooperation without temporal and spatial limits.

In addition, the development of online intercommunication secured the freedom to express the thoughts and opinions of the 'I' through various passages.[15] Freedom of speech and self-expression are denied people in many countries, counties and states due to stigma surrounding politics, economic status, religion, gender, race, age, etc. However, many of these people can now express themselves freely on the Internet, where they are not limited to one cross-section of society.

These changes in communication and therefore building of social relationships enable participation in community meetings and discussions on social issues; even international issues (such as war, famine, the environment, human rights, etc.). The widespread natures of these online discussions give hitherto unseen strength to national and international communities (Castells, op. cit., pp. 33-35).

3) Life Style and Informatisation

Informatisation has brought extensive changes in our daily lives. People were once accustomed to slow, one-sided communication mediums with text and possibly pictures or photographs. Now, people prefer quick and cutting-edge interactive communication, with sounds and displays to accentuate messages. People increasingly want to chat online and use mobile phones for real-time, long distance forms of

---

[15] Various communication pathways such as Internet cafes, blogs, websites, Twitter, Facebook, Youtube, etc., are utilised by millions; a fact which can be easily confirmed by studying uploaded data and views.

communication.[16] Internet newspapers have come close to making physical newspapers obsolete, due to their ability to update articles in real time. Rapid information acquisition has never been so possible or important to people.

Today's information-sharing process also appears to put an emphasis on individuality and diversity. People create their own online presence through websites or blogs based on their knowledge or opinions, and allow others to visit their sites and evaluate their ideas. An ever-growing number of people are using SNS (Social Networking Services) like Facebook and Twitter, actively exchanging opinions or giving suggestions in real time.

Whether it be workers attending meetings, married couples recording household accounts, or students writing papers, the use of the Internet, smart phones and tablet computers are common and usually essential elements for everything from finding information to using word processors (Castells et al, op. cit., pp. 109-178). Companies hold video conferences, and send and receive documents via e-mail. They announce job postings, obtain applicants' resumes, and employ staff through job interviews online.[17] Homemakers perform banking tasks via home banking or mobile banking and buy household items through online shopping. Parents book family outings or dental visits for their children online from the living room. Students study through teaching syllabus and assignments posted on school websites, exchanging questions and answers with teachers in real time.[18]

Highlighting some slightly less-known examples, the Internet is also often utilised for remote video training, remote medical treatments, and remote video trials, showing that ICT is irrefutably useful in multitudinous areas associated with people's every day and professional lives

---

16 From 1999 to 2009, the number of Internet subscriptions has mostly tripled and the number of mobile phone subscriptions more than tripled (OECD, op. cit., p. 46).

17 In the year 2010 (or the latest available year the given OECD country provided data), more than 70% of households in OECD countries had access to computers and the Internet at home (OECD, Ibid., p. 46).

18 In the year 2010 (or the latest available year the given OECD country provided data), workers in over 95% of large businesses and those in over 85% of medium-sized businesses required the Internet as a part of their jobs. Workers in at least 65% of small businesses utilised the Internet for some aspect/s of their work (OECD, Ibid., p. 46).

("The First Televised", 2015; "The Evolution of Video", 2014).

3. Inequality and Informatisation

So far, the political, economic, social and cultural changes caused by informatisation have been discussed. Now, some of the social inequalities that arise due to the information process are examined.

3.1 Digital Divide and Social Exclusion

During the development of ICT, the importance of information has been rapidly increasing. However, there have also been shifts in the possession of information technology, and increases in the number of people taking advantage of their level of access to information. This is, of course, due to the profits to be gained from informatisation (Kim, 1998, pp. 51). These differences in access to and usage of informatisation are referred to as the 'digital divide.' Scholars have defined the digital divide as follows:

Eszter Hargittai, an influential sociologist whose research focuses on information technology and its effect on social inequality, asserts that the digital divide is the gap between those who have access to digital technologies and those who do not; or the gap between those who use digital technologies and those who do not understand in binary terms the 'haves' from the 'havenots' (Hargittai, 2003, p. 2). The OECD posits that the digital divide is the gap between individuals, households, businesses and geographic areas at different socioeconomic levels. This relates to both to their opportunities to access information and communication technologies (ICTs), and their level of Internet usage for a wide variety of activities (OECD, 2001, p.5). If the above definitions are considered in conjunction, the digital divide can be understood as the divide between people who can access and use information, and people who cannot access information, or who have difficulty using it. Furthermore, this divide can cause inconveniences and/or disadvantages in politics, the economy, and society.

In reality, the digital divide (otherwise known as the information gap), has generated various inequalities through discrimination and exclusion in different areas of society, quickly turning it into a social issue (Jin, 2013, p. 162; Kim, 2014, p. 82). Many scholars have identified the fact that women, the elderly, the disabled, low-income earners, the less educated, and rural populations often experience social disadvantages due to the digital divide (NIA, 2014, pp. 15-16, 27-35). Moreover, it has been discovered that the digital divide can be the main factor in a negative cycle which affects income, employment, as well as political and social participation (Foley, 2004, p.140; Chigona et al, 2009, pp. 3-4; Hargittai, op. cit., pp. 4-5).

Therefore, the information gap can be seen to come under the purview of social exclusion. Ronald Labonté, Abdullahel Hadi and Xaxier E. Kauffmann, who collaborated on the publication 'Indicators of Social Exclusion and Inclusion: A Critical and Comparative Analysis of the Literature,' posit that social exclusion indicates one or several of the following situations: The lack of essential material resources for social activities, the lack of income required for living, access restrictions to formal labour markets, a lack of adequate housing, a lack of access to education and health care, the inability to avoid discrimination, a lack of social-participation rights in social networks, etc. Furthermore, social exclusion indicates the lack of opportunity to access or find information that may affect all the above necessities, which is one reason these issues can be cyclic (Labonté et al, 2011, pp. 25-26). A number of studies on the relationship between social exclusion and the digital divide clearly show that the information gap is the leading factor in social exclusion. These study results reveal that, in order to better use ICT, knowledge and skills are required. Furthermore, people who possess ICT-related knowledge and skills have an advantage in gaining economic status, while those who lack these skills have no such advantage (Kennard, 2001, pp. 553-554). Another feature of social exclusion is political isolation. People with little access to ICT show low political participation and civic engagement, leading to frustration that their situation or opinions have no effect on decision-making process (Van Winden, 2001, p.866-867).

However, the Internet can also remove obstacles for the

disadvantaged. For example, people unable to travel significant distances, disabled people lacking an extensive social environment, and those who are financially disadvantaged, can all benefit from reaching out via the Internet from their own homes. In particular, Internet usage can improve the quality of social interaction among the blind, thus increasing the numbers of this minority group who utilise it. Conversely, when interpreting the results of aforementioned related studies, it can be seen that disadvantaged people who are restricted in their access and utilisation of ICT can easily experience difficulties in social participation and social relationships.

In regards to the informatisation process, it seems evident that the information gap must be considered as one of the essential social problems to be solved, as it is a primary factor causing social exclusion in the majority of the disadvantaged society.

3.2 Segmentation of the Labour Market, Job Insecurity, and Unemployment

The development of ICT industries and related industries have changed the structure of the labour market; especially occupational structure. Rules and regulations in the labour market born of the industrial revolution were heavily affected by informatisation. Such rules continue to be modified and in some cases completely transformed through the informatisation process. It is undeniable that the informatisation process has paralleled serious social problems, such as job insecurity and unemployment. Here, the four major social issues that occurred in the labour market in the second-half of the twentieth century are briefly discussed.

First, phenomena such as emerging ICT industries, rapid technological developments, and globalisation incited a sudden change in employment structure. The 'skill and function mismatch' phenomenon became apparent in the labour market, leading to the increase of structural unemployment (Park, 1999, pp. 75-80). With changes in industrial and employment structure, a number of companies began recruiting highly educated and skilled professional technicians (OECD, op. cit., pp. 49-50). However, the demands of the industrial world were high, and the education system was not yet prepared to cultivate that level of manpower with the technical skills that were needed. Hence, the ICT sector and ICT-related sectors suffered a shortage of employees with relevant skill-sets, while large numbers of people without the necessary education were at risk of unemployment (Lee, 1993, pp. 242-244).

Second, the development of ICT gave rise to segmentation in the labour market. Automatisation decreased the demand for certain members of the replaceable labour force, such as production workers and office personnel (back-office workers). On the other hand, it also sharply increased irreplaceable workers, such as managers, service personnel, designers and other employees whose job description is based on creativity (front-office workers). Core expertise workers were supported by employers through investment in continuous education and training, often resulting in opportunities for higher income and promotion. In the meantime, the periphery technical workforce tended not to be invested in financially. This sector of the workforce's fungibility resulted in a lack of opportunities for education and training, causing job insecurity and tangible income inequality (Park, 2007, pp. 100-101).

Third, the speed of technological development was increasing the volatility of the business environment, which companies promptly countered by becoming flexible to changes in product demand and the economic environment (Song, 2010, pp. 19-62). Creating a more flexible labour market was accomplished through numerical flexibility, functional flexibility, and wage flexibility. Numerical flexibility was carried out in the form of lay-offs, hiring more temporary workers, and increasing flexible work hours. Rather than regular personnel, more companies came to prefer non-regular forms of employment, such as the aforementioned temporary workers, daily workers, part-time workers, and people working from home. In addition, in order to increase the adaptability of jobs when production conditions changed, (i.e., functional flexibility), measures were introduced such as multiskilling, labour turnover, new personnel systems, etc. Besides this, devices for wage flexibility were introduced. Many companies shifted the focus of wage structure towards efficiency and capability in order to achieve more profits. The labour market might have been adapting, but at the expense of job security for the unlucky ones. Peripheral workers are still considered as buffers for the economic cycle, or reduction targets of personnel and administrative costs. There is an ongoing pursuit for organisations to become more highly efficient by supplying higher wages, career development and vocational training for the selected essential workers. This leaves many others behind, at risk of unemployment and even povert y.[19] Fourth, in a digital and knowledge-based economy, workers with the ability to create and use knowledge and information, (in human resources, for example) are highly important for efficient production within companies. It follows, then, that the continuous investment in education and training for workers is an important strategy to improve competitiveness. Due to the rapid acceleration of informatisation though time, the softness of ICT and motility of business have also continued and strengthened. Thus, the long-term relationship between labour and management ran into difficulties due to the weakening of the internal labour market, extinction of lifetime employment, and the decrease in costs spent on finding employees and filling positions. Ultimately, 'flexible' labour relations have led to company apathy in certain areas, especially in regards to protecting employees. Likewise, it has led to the

[19] Recently 'Wemakeprice,' one of three major social commerce companies in Korea, is showing negative changes in labour relations due to the informatisation process. Wemakeprice fired all probationary employees, who were employed for Internet sales last December, 2014. The reason for their dismissal was the lack of sales performance during the probationary period (two weeks). In fact, since 2011, Wemakeprice have repeatedly employed young people as probationary employees, only to fire them after the short-term probationary period. Thus, the performance of all staff was made known in real time through a sales performance check program called 'admin,' applying immense pressure for sales performance improvement. When sales performances were poor, Wemakeprice exported staff to irrelevant departments or lowered their rank within the company. They often put staff under enormous pressure, and easily terminated their employment due to low sales performances. Wenmakeprice continues to recruit new employees for the same type of work. The behaviour described above can be seen as typical black company behaviour, in which the stability of youth employment is abused under the pretext that the company is experiencing financial difficulties and needs to proceed with cut-backs ("Wemakeprice Creates", 2015). During the 2000s, the emergence and expansion of black companies became a social issue under changes in corporate environments in Japan. It can be assumed that the increase of these black companies became a serious social problem to be solved during the acceleration of informatisation (Konno, 2012, p. 12; pp. 28-32).

weakening of confidence and loyalty among workers, not to mention a decreased level of cooperation with the companies for whom they work (Song, Ibid., pp. 63-68).

3.3 The Income gap and Polarisation of Wealth

Social problems such as the information gap, social exclusion, segmentation of the labour market, job insecurity, and unemployment, ultimately led to the income gap, and finally polarisation of wealth.

Changes in industrial and occupational structure due to informatisation brought about the income gap. First, combining ICT with traditional agriculture and manufacturing changed the form of labour in these fields. As a result, while employment increased for those in professional, managerial, and technical areas that require advanced ICT, employment in manufacturing fields decreased conspicuously. This is, again, due to automatisation. Where non-skilled white collar workers (such as secretaries and office assistants) and assemblers, production controllers, etc., were once essential, they have now been largely replaced by technology.

In fact, low-level manufacturing and white collar positions still occupied by people tend to be occupied by the women, minorities, low-skilled and under-educated persons. Statistics show that such demographics suffer low wages, low career prospects, and underrepresentation in labour unions. On the contrary, top-tier white collar jobs, such as managers and professionals, tend to be occupied by males (especially white males), and highly skilled and/or educated persons with an advantaged background. Statistics demonstrate that this demographic enjoys high wages, high career prospects, and high unionisation rates (Castells, op. cit., pp. 243-260).

It should be noted that, with informatisation, tertiary service industries related to ICT were also generally expanded. However, the increase of employment in the tertiary service sector did not come with an increase in wages for workers overall. This is due to the form of labour in the tertiary service industry; generally part-time work and simple jobs, excepting a small number of management positions. Moreover, due to the limits of labour productivity (i.e., an employee's inability to work indefinitely), the service industry cannot ensure above a certain level of income. Therefore, the polarised occupational structures in agriculture and manufacturing, and the expansion of the tertiary service sector jobs, have deepened the decline of the middle-income class and increased the polarisation of wealth (The Economist, 2014, pp. 7-8; Goos et al, 2014, pp. 2509-2510).

Additionally, disparity in wealth can be observed due to the information gap. Access to and utilisation of information during this era of rapid expansion in informatisation is possible through appropriate education and training. However, the opportunity for such education or training has not been equally granted to all people. In other words, the socially disadvantaged such as the elderly, the disabled, low-educated persons, and women had limited access to or use of the essential information from the beginning; often unable to receive sustainable learning and training in ICT. The information gap slowly increased the possibility that the socially disadvantaged become excluded from entering the labour market, or dismissed due to low levels of competition as labour market flexibility became predominant. People in possession of advanced technology and information, on the other hand, were already ahead when entering the labour market, and even had significant chances to rise in position after entering the labour market (Shin, 2013, pp. 115-116; Cho, 2001, pp. 537-538). When fierce competition for survival was spurred by labour market flexibility, people who were more skilled and knowledgeable became the subjects for reinvestment and up-to-date training, thus strengthening the competitiveness of enterprises. This became cyclic, guaranteeing aforesaid favoured people positions of respect and high income (Choi, 2014, pp. 7-9, 14-16). During the rapid informatisation process, the information gap led to divergence in opportunities (employment) and results (income) of economic activity. As this process is repeated continuously, the resulting deepening polarisation of wealth and the income gap has become increasingly conspicuous and problematic (Kang et al, 2002, pp. 116-123).

4. Informatisation and the Welfare State

So far, social change and its side effects have been discussed, including the inequality that has emerged from informatisation since the second-half of the twentieth century. Here, the methods by which the welfare state has dealt with these inequality issues caused by informatisation are examined. In addition, several approaches as trialled by welfare states to intervene with the above issues are considered.

4.1 Transformation of the Welfare State and Informatisation

The golden age of the welfare state, which flourished in some parts of Europe after the Second World War, was admired by rich Western countries. However, people's hope for quick advancement in this direction was shaken to the core when the world experienced oil shock in the early 1970s. The Western welfare state has been criticised in regards to its legitimacy as a welfare state, and the phrase 'the crisis of the welfare state' became widely known. As a result of the earlier criticisms and problematic issues surrounding foundling welfare states, it was not until the 1980s that many countries began envisioning a new welfare state through transformation of the status quo (Park, 2000, p. 196).

Through self-reflection on an international scale and the many discussions about the crisis of the welfare state, it became understood that 'high welfare, high burden' was the basic principal behind the dysfunctionality of the western welfare state. Two key reasons for this lack of functionality can be pinpointed. Firstly, during the 1970s, there was the continually increasing public social spending due to the aging population and levels of unemployment that had already triggered the economic crisis. Western welfare states feared the depletion of national finances due to excessive public social spending, which was proving to be a critical limitation of the outward expansion of the welfare state. Secondly, the previous centralised and complicated bureaucratic formality of the welfare state had failed to adequately respond to the increasing and changing welfare needs of citizens, which was the limitation of the inward rationality of the welfare state (Kim, 2012, p. 652).

As aforementioned, this period runs parallel with the era of various inequalities caused by the rapid informatisation process. There were social problems such as the digital divide, social exclusion, job insecurity, unemployment, the income gap, wealth polarisation, and fragmentation problems in the labour market caused by changes in industrial and job structure, all of which became prevalent during the informatisation process and could be seen as the results of market failure during this period. Thus, the realisation that these socioeconomic situations needed to be 'solved' or 'rectified' became widespread, as did the issues surrounding the necessity for the intervention of the welfare state.

Indeed, it seems obvious that the welfare state has, over time, tried to actively identify solutions to problems caused by informatisation, as opposed to the less evolved approach taken during the industrialisation era. In regards to the effects of the informatisation process, the new welfare state primarily needed to overcome internal limitations (financial crises) and external limitations (economic crises) as encountered in the previous welfare state. Moreover, adequate secondary responses to welfare needs were required in order to meet the demands of the times. The welfare state attempted to establish speedier and more professional welfare, in which the necessary and appropriate services were delivered in the right place and at right time to those experiencing social risks (Caputo, 1998, p. 5). In other words, during the second-half of the twentieth century, history shows that the welfare state was finally forced to meet such public demands. The aim was to provide quantitatively and qualitatively superior public social services through improvement of efficiency in public social spending.

Under the emerging new welfare state, these diverse public social services had to be managed under an integrated public social service system. Thus, the concentrated power of the central welfare organisation was outsourced to professional and specialised sub-agencies, who were able to identify and incorporate public social services in response to the needs appearing in the field. It was partially through trial and error that selective welfare services were developed for the socially unprivileged, as well as universal welfare services for ordinary citizens.

4.2 Perspectives on the Intervention of the Welfare State

Now some of the perspectives on the intervention of the welfare state in order to address inequality problems that arose from the information process are briefly looked at.

The welfare state had to concentrate on the implementation of information welfare. This came to be generally labelled 'welfare of informatisation.' In the informatisation process, the digital divide was often cited as the fundamental problem. Universal access to information needed to be secured, thus reducing or eliminating information inequality. This is the essence of the first perspective. A strong emphasis is put on the improvement of ICT access opportunities to eliminate the information gap that exists due to region, income, age, gender, social status, etc. Such improvement is implemented via financial support, education, training, and more. In other words, the welfare state must encourage citizens to participate in and benefit from informatisation. This perspective gives priority to universal access of the welfare state, regarding access to and usage of information as a welfare right, and ensuring at least the minimum of information welfare for all citizens (Lee, 2000, pp. 254-257).

The welfare state has to practice welfare through informatisation of welfare. This idea embodies the second perspective, in which informed public social services are channelled through the informatisation of welfare. From this perspective, 'informatisation of welfare,' is defined as the improvement in efficiency of public social service management, the establishment of public social service delivery systems, the settlement of social services management systems, and the securing of opportunities for social participation. This perspective stresses that the welfare state has to remove the ineffective elements of welfare administration and welfare facilities through the use of ICT. In addition, its advocates posit that the welfare state must provide prompt services to meet the needs of various clients through the informatisation of welfare, superseding temporal and spatial constraints (Jeong & Kim, 2004, pp. 68-72).

Third, there exists a perspective on e-welfare. This describes the welfare state's need to provide public social services through active intercommunication via the Internet. E-welfare is defined as the exchange and delivery of social welfare information and public social service information through public social service network systems. Furthermore, the welfare state is required to pursue the improvement of public social services and its integration, systematic cost reduction, quality improvement through the evaluation of public social services, and the identification of public social services required by citizens through using ICT. Ultimately, from this viewpoint, the welfare state will be able to establish a universal public social service system by providing customised public social services (Jeong, 2008, p. 54). To this end, connectivity, communication, and networking of public social service are emphasised. More specifically expressed; via public social services, when clients, social workers, and welfare professionals are organically connected (connectivity) through a cooperative system, when information regarding the selection and evaluation of clients and social workers is exchanged through active communication (communication), and when all processes are systematically networked, the welfare state can eventually provide superior public social services.

Lastly, there is a perspective on u-welfare. That is, the welfare state has to provide more intelligent public social services through ubiquitous technology (Lee, 2009, pp. 180-182). Ubiquity implies uninterrupted connectivity to the network, including communication whenever and wherever possible. Therefore, in a ubiquitous society, human and computers can become one 'organism,' so that people can connect with anyone, anywhere, at any time, via computers. This is an idyllic intelligence-based society in which people can enjoy any service regardless of time and space (Kang, 2004, pp. 151-160).[20] From this perspective, the welfare

---

[20] The goal of the ubiquitous society is focused on universality, user-orientation, and uniqueness. The ubiquitous society aspires to user-friendliness and barrier-free interfaces, so that the elderly or the disabled without Internet experience can easily work through the ubiquitous devices, thus participating in the overall social environment. The ubiquitous society is about moving away from the provider-oriented and con-

state must directly or indirectly combine ubiquitous technology with the social welfare sector, so that clients can be provided all the above advantages. This viewpoint argues that u-welfare can stabilise the convergence of public social services and the provisions of intelligent personalised public social services.

4.3 Trialling the Intervention of the Welfare State

The welfare state was, in fact, able to take advantage of the informatisation process for the intervention of various inequality issues. As a result, the welfare state ended up providing more appropriate, reasonable and efficient public social services to citizens (Korea Institute for Health and Social Affairs (KIHSA) & Ministry of Health and Welfare (MHW), 2001, pp. 3-4). Here, changes in the practice of the welfare state orchestrated to move with the development of ICT are explored in three areas: Management, delivery and demand.

1) Informatisation and Management of Public Social Services

First, informatisation has improved welfare efficacy through computerisation and automation. It made various public social services available to and comprehensive for recipients. As a matter of fact, when providing public social services in order to solve problematic socioeconomic situations, the comprehensive exchanges of information and joint activity are often needed because social welfare sectors such as social insurance, public assistance, and social welfare administration are closely linked. Informatisation enables real-time networking, so that active information-sharing and effective role allocation among the various welfare sectors and public social service providers are possible. Consequently,

---

sumer oriented social system. This transformation of the social system reflects the needs of ICT users, ensuring that relevant information reaches the consumer in the information society. In addition, the ubiquitous society pursues the development of individual creativity and new services encourage the development of new applications which connect man with man, man with objects, and objects with objects. Ubiquitous technologies are currently used for welfare purposes, and it is predicted that they will continue to be used in the future (through IPTV, UCC, location-based services, smart phones, etc.).

informatisation prevents the welfare state from wasting time and expenses as occurred in the previous system. Among the mishaps informatisation helps avoid are duplicate processing of information, diminished speed in responsiveness, and diminished effectiveness in providing public social services (Kim, Ibid., pp. 666-667).[21]

Second, ICT ultimately secured the link between various public social services online and offline, resulting in high-quality public social services for a larger number of clients. Comprehensive mobile counselling systems are representative examples. Through these systems, clients can be provided counselling services online anonymously and individually. Also, public social service providers can improve upon counselling services, taking advantage of the accumulated data, much of which is being received in real time.[22]

Third, informatisation boosted citizen participation in various social areas through the development of networking. After countless cyber welfare communities were created, the interest in and attention of welfare issues rapidly began to grow. People became more proactive, taking part in lively discussions and debates on welfare issues, as well as participating in organised social activities run online. Cyberspace is now a foundation for better communication and interaction between the underprivileged, including the disabled, elderly, unemployed, youth, women, and low-income earners. It also gives the chance for average citizens to interact with each other and the above minority groups. The positive outcome of all this is that social distances can be reduced and solidarity

---

21 For example, the elderly often have welfare needs for social services such as health services, nursing services, and counselling services. In order to satisfy their welfare needs, various social services must be provided in conjunction. Therefore, related information is shared between welfare organisations to better provide thorough individual-oriented social services. In the process of identifying demand and providing social services, when devices such as tablet computers and smart phones are provided, and the Broadband Convergence Network (BCN) is established, social workers can search for information from a database of community centres or related agencies, taking advantage of such information in real time. Social workers and related professionals can collaborate organically via email exchange, messages, and relevant files.

22 In youth mobile centres, twenty-four hour counselling services are available to address family problems, school maladjustment, and Internet addiction. There are offered through the bulletin boards of home pages, message services, and telephones. In addition, social services for family violence, sexual abuse, drug addiction, etc., all of which are required to ensure anonymity, are provided effectively via mobile and online counselling services.

(as well as a heightened understanding of issues surrounding the disadvantaged) can be increased in society as a whole.

It seems clear that informatisation has contributed to the promotion of social integration. Above all, social welfare experts can also participate in and sometimes lead discussions online regarding alternative approaches within the welfare system. This allows citizens to more keenly recognise accurate information on public policies (especially social policy) and participate in the formation and direction of progress (Jeong & Kim, op. cit., p. 66).

2) Informatisation and Delivery of Public Social Services

First, one of the biggest problems of social welfare administration is the lack of efficacy within the public social service delivery system. In fact, when looking at public social service delivery processes as created by welfare-related governmental authorities, applications for welfare benefits vary too much in format and criteria. This generates a lot of confusion and inconvenience for welfare benefit applicants and relevant administrative agencies.[23] As a part of the informatisation process, the automatisation and standardisation of the welfare delivery process can help increase the efficacy of the overall public social service delivery system, also minimising delivery costs.

Second, doubts have been often expressed, online and offline, as to whether various welfare benefits financed by taxes properly cater to people in need. Many public social programs have been established or modified to overcome and prevent social risks in accordance with the

---

23 In regards to the delivery process of public social services in Korea, there have been many complaints because the eligibility of beneficiaries are not established quickly and welfare benefits are provided in a tardy manner. In fact, in 2011, 292 public welfare programs were implemented and distributed in several ministries. Each public welfare program and each ministry had different criteria for the eligibility of beneficiaries, as well as different calculation methods for household incomes. As a typical example, looking at the type of criteria for the eligibility of welfare beneficiaries, there exists almost 41 criteria. For example, the requirement for one type of welfare benefit might range between 100%, 120%, and 180% of the minimum living cost for families with four persons (1.49 million won in 2012), while the requirement for another type of welfare benefit might range between 30%, 50%, and 70% of the average household income. These different criteria are too complex, especially because public welfare programs are introduced pro re nata from time to time ("Tattered Welfare", 2012).

continuous changes in the socioeconomic environment. At the same time, welfare practices in the field have also been amended or supplemented to ensure the successful running of welfare programs. During the process of adoption and modification of these programs in the system, the loss and/or duplication of welfare benefits have occurred with significant frequency. Furthermore, illegal supply and demand of welfare benefits has reduced the effectiveness of public social services.[24] In this regard, informatisation has contributed to ensure the transparency in supply and management of public social services through computerisation, standardisation, and automatisation of the identification. This has aided in more accurate selection of welfare recipients, as well as tracking their progress.[25]

Third, informatisation aids the quick detection of each individual's characteristics, needs, and skillsets, enabling placements in public social service programs that meet their specific welfare needs. Above all, the underprivileged are able to receive personalised public social services in the right place and time through the Internet and social networking services. For example, RFID (Radio Frequency Identification) has proved a useful instrument to provide a variety of public social services for children, the disabled, the elderly, etc. In the case of young children, their location can be monitored and confirmed through an RFID chip. Visually impaired people can also be provided real-time navigation through an RFID chip imbedded inside their cane and footpaths. For the hearing impaired without use of their legs, an RFID chip attached to the wheelchair can inform their routes and location. In the case of the elderly, because health information is often collected and delivered via the

24 Welfare benefits are sometimes provided to people making false claims. According to the Ministry of Employment and Labor, the number of false unemployment benefit recipients was 27,390 people in 2011; about 1,400 people more than the 25,992 false unemployment benefit recipients in 2009 ("Illegal Pay-outs", 2014).

25 The Korean government created combined social welfare management. Currently, two combined social welfare management networks exist. One is the Social Welfare Management Network for Management and Integration, in which 'management and integration' refers to social welfare benefits and social welfare recipients of central and local governments. The other is the Social Welfare Management Network, which is linked to all government social security systems (Happiness e-um) based on the assignments of each ministry (16 ministries; 293 public social welfare programs) (Homepage of Korea Health and Welfare Information Service, http://edu.khwis.or.kr/index.jsp).

sensor in the RFID, when people are in a bad state of health, caregivers, medical staff, social workers, and hospitals can be notified promptly to deal with the given situation ("The Travel of Visually", 2013).[26]

3) Informatisation and Demand of Public Social Services

As public social services have taken several measures to respond to the information gap and related issues, the welfare state has begun to consider citizens' basic needs for access and utilisation of ICT. Therefore, as a top priority, the welfare state has expanded opportunities for diverse types of ICT education and training in public administrative organisations or public institutions for all citizens. In particular, the underprivileged, such as the elderly, disabled, those with a low-income, and the unemployed (who would normally have difficulty accessing and using ICT) are often able to participate in education and training for ICT at little or no cost. In addition, the welfare state often financially supports the underprivileged (depending on their income level) in paying for telecom services (such as Internet usage fees, mobile phone fees, etc.). As a result, the new welfare requirements for access to and use of ICT has reformed and given new direction to the existing education and public policies; especially social policy.

Additionally, information has made it possible to select public social services according to individual preferences and needs. Every citizen can search for their eligibility for various types of public social services online, often using mobile phones and apps. Many people opt to research and apply for public social services without the help of social workers through the aforementioned methods, eliminating the need to attend time-consuming appointments.[27] In recent years, as digital convergence

---

26 In addition, the Ministry of Information and Communication promoted an active USN-based (Ubiquitous Sensor Network-based) Speed Control System for traffic safety, installing them around Kindergartens and the elementary schools. ("The Ministry of Information", 2007) The Ministry of Health and Welfare and the National Health Insurance Corporation have been promoting the introduction of an electronic management system for homecare services using RFID (Radio-Frequency Identification) since the second-half of 2008 ("The National Health", 2011).

27 In Korea, an e-voucher system has been utilised since 2007 to assist in-care services for the disabled, care services for the elderly, and maternity services for pregnant women (Homepage of Korea Health and Welfare Information Service, http://edu.khwis.or.kr/in-

technologies became more highly developed, the use of public social services have also become available through touchscreens in public places, IPTVs at home, and, of course, smart phones in nearly any given location.

5. Summary

In chapter three, first the historical meaning of informatisation in the second-half of the twentieth century was observed. According to the arguments of Bell, Toffler, and Castells, reflecting on the representative features related to information and technology, it is reasonable to consider the current era as new and disparate from the previous era.

Secondly, numerous changes in economy, politics, and social culture caused by informatisation were examined through the results of previous studies. From an economic standpoint, the ICT industry and ICT-related industries continue to rapidly develop and reach into uncharted territory. These changes led to an increase in employment of skilled ICT workers and the flexibility of the relationship between labour and capital. Additionally, informatisation has contributed to economic growth through accumulating and providing information as a new production factor. Interest and investment in human capital and social capital have been major catalysts for the intimate relationship between informatisation and economic growth.

In the political arena, informatisation has led to electronic media becoming political instruments and a part of political strategies. It has also brought about social network movements and social network politics. It was established that the development of the Internet and mobile communications enable people to participate in the formation of political agendas and political decision-making processes without the constraints of time and space. Additionally, the development of e-government, e-governance, and e-democracy led to the improvement of transparency and efficiency of administration and political decision-making processes.

---

dex.jsp).

Looking at elements of social culture, informatisation contributing to a new relationship between work life and family life was examined. Informatisation heightens the demand for knowledge and technology labour, and reduces time and space constraints in economic activity. These changes increasingly enable women to reconcile family and work, and to distance themselves from the traditional role division between men and women. Additionally, in the informatisation process, the activation of intercommunication encouraged the expression, thoughts and opinions of the 'I' through various platforms and media. These changes in communication, resulting in the building of new social relationships, enables heightened participation in community meetings and discussions on social issues. Furthermore, informatisation has brought about extensive changes in our daily lives. At the workplace, home, school, etc., ICT has become an indispensable instrument.

Thirdly, inequalities that arise due to informatisation were briefly discussed, including social exclusion of the underprivileged in political and social participation due to their lack of access or knowledge of ICT. The development of ICT also prompted changes in occupational structure, leading to segmentation between workers more or less skilled in ICT. Workers who could not adjust to new ICT environments suffered job insecurity and unemployment. Ultimately, it was observed that social problems such as the information gap, social exclusion, segmentation in the labour market, job insecurity, and unemployment, has led to the income gap, and finally polarisation of wealth.

Lastly, the welfare state's responses to these hitherto uncharted types of inequalities were observed via four perspectives: The implementation of information welfare, the informatisation of welfare, e-welfare, and u-welfare. The intervention of the welfare state to address inequality problems that arise from the information process were briefly discussed. In addition, changes in the welfare state orchestrated to move alongside the development of ICT were explored in three areas: Management, delivery and demand. In management of the public social services, it was shown that informatisation has improved welfare efficacy through computerisation and automation. ICT ultimately secured the link between various public social services online and offline, resulting in higher quality public social services for a larger number of clients. Also, informatisation boosted citizen participation in various social areas (especially welfare) through networking. In delivery of the public social service, the automatisation and standardisation of the welfare delivery process helped increase the efficacy of the overall public social service delivery system, also minimising delivery costs. Additionally, informatisation has contributed to transparency in supply and management of public social services through computerisation, standardisation, and automatisation. This has aided in a more accurate selection of welfare recipients.

Chapter IV

Hypotheses and Method of Analysis

Chapter IV Hypotheses and Method of Analysis

Drawing on the mechanisms of informatisation and the development of the welfare state as presented in chapter three, this chapter seeks to establish hypotheses and operational definitions. The adopted methods of analysis and the explanations of variables are thereafter presented to prove the hypotheses.

1. Hypotheses of the Study

In this section, several hypotheses are explored to uncover the causal relationship between informatisation and the development of the welfare state.

1.1 Hypotheses for the Causal Relationship between the ICT Industry and the Welfare State

First, the following two hypotheses are formulated to ascertain the causal relationship between the ICT industry and the development of the welfare state.

1. *The development of the ICT industry increases public social spending.*
2. *The development of the ICT industry increases income inequality.*

The first hypothesis is established by examining the impact of the ICT industry on public social spending. First, it is irrefutable that the development of the ICT industry generates positive results, among which is job creation in ICT and ICT-related industrial sectors. It also improves productivity through computerisation, automation and flexibility, enhances labour quality due to autonomy and creativity, and increases globalised intercommunication through information networks (Kim et al, 1996, pp. 57-61; LG Communicatopia Institute, 1999, p. 337). Such tangible results allow many countries to increase their national income and achieve economic growth (Jin & Jo, 2012, pp. 89-90; Rauland & Bauer, 2011, p. 1081).

The increase of national income leads to the improvement of life quality, and the increase of national wealth leads to an abundance of welfare resources. Free communication through information networks can be an eye-opening experience, causing citizens to ponder the welfare state, motivating them to make educated assessments regarding life quality and the population's need for welfare programs. Such exposure undoubtedly contributes largely to the increase of positive opinions and attitudes in regards to advanced welfare states. It follows that, if authorities take heed of people's opinions and requirements prior to the establishment of a welfare state, it is more likely that a higher share of government spending will be dedicated to public welfare.

However, the development of the ICT industry does not yield solely positive results. One observable phenomenon is, in the event of rapid changes in the external environment caused by ICT, uncertainty and instability in the labour market can ensue. Labour market flexibility, commonly seen to come hand-in-hand with the ICT industry, can threaten job and/or income stability, also destroying mutual confidence in existing labour-management relations. Most importantly, the training involved in learning new skills in ICT is a major stressor for some employees, especially if they belong to a disadvantaged demographic. If these workers are unable to overcome the associated obstacles with new technology, they often end up unemployed and/or below the poverty line (Jeong et al, 1996, pp. 151-166, 214-229). Conversely, these consequences are yet another trigger by which the public's awareness for the need of public welfare may be increased, yielding delayed but some potentially positive results from a negative environment in the labour market.

Weighing up the positive and negative consequences of the ICT industry, it may seem obvious that the development of the ICT industry does indeed increase public social spending. However, further angles must be examined before conclusions can be drawn. The nature of the ICT industry naturally leads to creativity and autonomy. Moreover, communication networks prompt economic openness and economic exchanges (i.e., globalisation), rendering it necessary that every competitive country possess world-class ICT. Triggered by the desire to create the most cutting-edge technologies on the open market, aggressive investment increases follow. This process is natural in the development of an industry, but when entrepreneurs and investors focus only on dominating the domestic and/or foreign market, they often lose regard for those who are behind in the race; a scenario which can lead to a reduction in public social spending.

All above factors considered, the aim of the first hypothesis is to uncover, through empirical means, whether there exists a definitive causal relationship between the development of the ICT industry and public social spending, and whether the impact of any such relationship is positive or negative.

The second hypothesis is established by examining the impact of the ICT industry on income inequality. The development of the ICT industry demands adaptation on the behalf of employees through training and learning in the field of ICT. Workers who are able to adapt smoothly can survive the labour market and achieve a higher income. However, as aforementioned, maladjusted workers often end up experiencing unemployment and poverty. There are certain demographics in particular that are vulnerable to this phenomenon, such as lesser-educated people, low-wage earners, the elderly, the disabled, etc., all of whom have a lesser chance of surviving and/or succeeding in the new world and labour market (Park, 2004, pp. 120-122; Seo, 2008, pp. 571-574). These are among the issues that could gradually deepen income inequality among workers.

Despite this, it is not necessarily the cases that all disadvantaged minorities are unable to adapt to new ICT in work environments. Certain factors may yet proffer them some opportunities in the labour market. Historically, the development of the ICT industry changed the emphasis from physical labour to intellectual labour in many arenas. This was achieved through computerised, automated production processes, as well as the diversification of employment patterns. Examples of this are telecommuting and call centre services for telemarketing or e-commerce (Kim et al, op. cit., pp. 87-88). If socially disadvantaged people or existing excluded workers are able to become competent in such ICT-related jobs, there is hope yet for their continued employment and quality of life.

All above factors considered, the aim of the second hypothesis is to uncover, through empirical means, whether there exists a definitive causal relationship between the development of the ICT industry and income inequality, and whether the impact of any such relationship is positive or negative.

1.2 Hypotheses for the Causal Relationship between ICT Usage and the Welfare State

Second, the following two hypotheses are formulated to ascertain the causal relationship between ICT usage and the development of the welfare state.

1. *The use of ICT increases public social spending.*
2. *The use of ICT increases income inequality.*

The first hypothesis is established by examining the impact of ICT usage on public social spending. First of all, it is indisputable that the use of ICT yields many positive results. Through the acquisition and sharing of information, ICT contributes to the rapid spread of information. The expansion of knowledge and information can improve life quality and increase diversity of lifestyles (Kim et al, Ibid., pp. 92-94). For example, if there is an emergency during the holidays or in the middle of the night, people are able to search quickly for the nearest available medical centre via the Internet. This can hold true even if an accident occurs in a remote place, given the person in question has a device with Internet access. Likewise, patients in need of convenient and useful services, such as twenty-four-hour telephone medical referral services, benefit a great deal from the expansion and accessibility of public health care services. In some cases, availability of information can be the difference between life and death; or indeed the difference between treatable injuries and irrevocable disabilities. In a welfare state, all costs for these types of services are covered by public social spending.

As free intercommunication, the Internet makes it easy to give feedback and take part in public and political affairs, regardless of where you live - a fact that often directly and indirectly affects policy decisions (Yang & Kim, 2002, pp. 156-160). This is especially evident in the case of welfare issues, where criticism, opinions and policy alternatives conceived by the public and media are easily posted and observed on the Internet; the result of which is often eventually reflected in the government's welfare policies. For instance, when the mother and her daughters committed suicide (as mentioned at the beginning of this study),[28] various media pounced on the incident and the news was shared many times over, spreading rapidly throughout cyberspace. Given the circumstances of the event, it is not surprising that people rushed to share their opinions on the status quo of the existing social welfare services for socially disadvantaged people. There was an avalanche of criticism regarding lack of social welfare services and information thereof in South Korea, resulting in efforts by the government to improve the existing system. Needless to say, this is one positive outcome to arise from a deeply tragic event.

The social problems that can arise due to the use of ICT must also be examined. Some of these negative side effects include smart phone addiction, Internet addiction, and computer addiction; all brought on by a

[28] Please see the page 1 of this study.

lack of self-restraint when using ICT. Some of these phenomena have even led to crime and increased social exclusion (Lee, 2003, pp. 10-20).[29] Another dilemma associated with the rise of ICT is the 'digital divide' phenomenon, which widens the gap between the underprivileged and privileged. This is due to the ability (or lack thereof) to utilise and/or access the appropriate devices and information that help people rise within hierarchies, affecting their social status, income, power, and so on (Seo, 2000, pp. 78-80; 2001, pp. 17-31). Many study results show that the aged, poor, and disabled have less access to information and less ability to implement the information of which they are aware, resulting in lower income levels and higher poverty rates (U, 2003, pp. 375-379). It seems obvious that, as ICT usage rises, so do hitherto unanticipated social problems; hence the need for increased government involvement to find solutions and increase public social spending.

If the government operates efficiently in certain regards, a country may yet yield positive results and avoid the aforementioned pitfalls. For example, when ICT is provided at a low cost to the wider population, along with easily accessible ICT-related education and training, the underprivileged have a heightened chance of accessing the labour market, enabling them to participate more actively in productive activities. Given the proper conditions, the long-term result is that their employment rate and income increases, while public social spending decreases.

Another positive aspect of ICT integration into public welfare is the increased efficiency of welfare administration. The welfare and digital administrative system are structured so that the management of welfare receipt and the delivery of welfare services are computerised and automated. This type of systematic administrative system is achieved in

---

29 In South Korea, the Ministry of Science, ICT and Future Planning and The National Information Society Agency conduct a yearly 'Internet Addiction Survey,' after which they announce the results. The results reveal that 7% of those surveyed are classified in the 'high risk of Internet addiction' group, whose excess use of wired and/or wireless Internet can lead to withdrawal symptoms (when the technology is unavailable to them) and impaired functionality in daily life. The Ministry of Science, ICT and Future Planning, in conjunction with a total of eight other agencies, ensures that the Korean government takes measures to prevent and solve this addiction problem. This is done by establishing Internet addiction prevention/response centres, and improving counselling/treatment services ("Internet and Smart Phone", 2014; "Smart Phone Addiction", 2014).

a timely manner and beneficial for people in need. Also, because there is more control over administrative mishaps such as doubling up on monetary benefits or giving benefits to unintended recipients, public social spending can be reduced. Similarly, in the event that a primary social risk is realised (poverty, old age, industrial accidents, illness, unemployment, etc.,) the rapid and accurate response built into the computerised, automated electronic system can prevent secondary risks coming to pass. For instance, if the main breadwinner loses their job, the primary response must be rapid identification of the problem (i.e., unemployment). In this case, ICT allows for expediency, ensuring that unemployment benefits and job-training opportunities are provided relatively quickly. This does not only benefit the breadwinner, but helps to protect their entire family, as well as avert the various social problems that are caused by unemployment and poverty. A prompt response achieved through the digital administrative system will also help avert future problems for the government caused by the snowball effect, thus decreasing public social spending in the long run.

All above factors considered, the aim of the first hypothesis is to uncover, through empirical means, whether there exists a definitive causal relationship between ICT usage and public social spending, and whether the impact of any such relationship is positive or negative.

The second hypothesis is established by examining the impact of ICT on income inequality. In the past, people relied upon 'help-wanted' advertisements through classical media such as newspapers, radio, and television, all of which are limited in time and space. ICT, on the other hand, encourages active information acquisition and sharing, allowing information to spread at an exponential rate and guaranteeing more freedom of career choice. Through active intercommunication, the Internet sheds light on existing labour jobs that would otherwise remain hidden to potential applicants. This method of labour supply can contribute to the incitement of the labour market, thus reducing unemployment and maintaining or increasing the level of income.

As previously mentioned, however, if ICT access is either difficult or impossible, the opposite results can transpire. Those with a lower level of education or income start off at a disadvantage, finding it difficult to rise in rank within their company or perhaps even secure a job in the first place. This is due to their lack of wealth and lesser level of knowledge in regards to ICT. As a result, certain demographics are often forced to suffer a lower social status, a lower income, and disempowerment. If this dilemma becomes cyclic, especially within families and even communities, the outcome is perpetually unequal social stratification and social structure (Yun, 2000, pp. 88-100).

Taking all above factors into account, the aim of the first hypothesis is to uncover, through empirical means, whether there exists a definitive causal relationship between ICT usage and income inequality, and whether the impact of any such relationship is positive or negative.

1.3 Hypotheses for the Causal Relationship between the E-government and the Welfare State

Finally, the following hypothesis is presented to identify the causal relationship between the development of the e-government and the welfare state.

The development of the e-government increases public social spending.

This hypothesis is established by examining the relationship between several features that appear during the development of e-governments, as well as the possible impact of those features (and relationships thereof) on public social spending.

In the public domain, the introduction and spread of ICT has already occurred in most countries around the world (UNDESA, 2010, p. 3). The development of the e-government ensures transparency and promptness of administration, as well as citizen participation in decision making processes (Kim et al, op. cit., pp. 94-97; Jo, 2008, pp. 95-96). E-governments, in which online services are provided and ICT is actively used in the public sector, allow welfare administration to be implemented systematically through a computerised, automated delivery system. Efficiency and effectiveness can also be improved, because the digital welfare service delivery system prevents the phenomena of mistakenly omitting welfare services, supplying welfare services too many times, or supplying amounts too large or small. Furthermore, the e-government helps prevent the necessity of learning through mere trial and error, aids the formulation and implementation of new welfare policies, and spreads awareness of the government's welfare policy goals (Park et al, 2011, pp. 55-63). Therefore, the most appropriate and reasonable public social spending is actualised, resulting in the improvement of welfare standards for citizens.

If online public spaces are open for people to discuss welfare issues, the most appropriate alternatives can be considered and decided upon for welfare service recipients and providers (OECD, 2001, pp. 67-82; Yang & Kim, 2002, pp. 180-181; Jo, 2012, pp. 45-46). As issues are taken into account in more detail, previously hidden welfare needs may be exposed, resulting in the occurrence of a sharp increase in welfare spending in the short term.

Despite the short-term effects, however, such interactive devices do prevent the increase of excessive social spending in the long term. This is due to the avoidance of the negative effects that occur in situations where welfare services are not provided at the appropriate level, via the appropriate method, and to the appropriate people within the current political climate.

Taking all above factors into account, the aim of the first hypothesis is to uncover, through empirical means, whether there exists a definitive causal relationship between the e-government and public social spending, and whether the impact of any such relationship is positive or negative.

2. Operational Definitions for the Analysis

When analysing the impact of ICT development on public social spending and income inequality, the concept of informatisation and the welfare state are operationally defined as follows.

2.1 The Operational Definition of Informatisation

In the previous chapter, informatisation was defined as the process of increasingly commodifying information as a means of production, consumption, transportation, and investment. In light of this definition, informatisation can be observed in the following three areas: The ICT industry, ICT usage, and ICT in the public sector.

Many countries have seen rapid development in the ICT industry and ICT-related industries (Jeong, 2005, pp. 102-107; Jeong & Park, 2010, p. 77-78; Park, 2012, pp. 17-19). Investment in ICT, production and export of equipment, import and consumption of equipment, and the number of employees in this area, are all highly indicative of the level of development the ICT industry has reached. It is safe to say, then, that the development of the ICT industry reflects the level of informatisation in society.

As for ICT usage, ICT's advance is impossible without the continuity of consumption. Changes in most areas of ICT usage continue to occur with rapidity and the number of people utilising this technology has increased at an exponential rate. Today, ICT is being actively utilised in almost every area of modern society; including social lives, family lives, and the workplace. Whether or not they are aware of the fact, most people are heavily dependent on the Internet. Networking, receiving and sending emails, viewing, posting and sharing news and events; it is taken for granted that all these activities now heavily depend on the Internet. Indeed, it is becoming impossible to contemplate schools, companies and homes functioning to optimal capacity without the Internet. Therefore, ICT usage can directly reflect the degree of informatisation in society. For research purposes, it is highly important to ascertain the amount of Internet usage, rates of mobile subscription, and number of PCs in homes and work environments.

It is also clearly evident that ICT has been introduced to the public sector in many countries. Governments that actively build ICT infrastructure tend to incorporate ICT services into decision-making processes and support education and training through said infrastructure. These are the governments most likely to see informatisation increase in level of complexity and speed of development.

In order to effectively conduct this analysis, and taking the above official and societal indicators into consideration, the concept of infomatisation is operationally defined as 'the development of the ICT industry, increase of ICT usage, and introduction and increase of ICT in the public sector.'

2.2 The Operational Definition of the Welfare State

In the previous chapter, it is established that the welfare state is responsible for ensuring civilian minimal living standards. To conduct this analysis comprehensively, the concept of the welfare state must also be operationally defined. Although there are a range of factors indicative of the development of the welfare state, public social spending and income inequality are the focus for the purposes of this study, the reasons for which are revealed in the following passage.

Public social spending is required in order to meet the basic needs for those who are most vulnerable to social risks. Even if a country is not suffering a crisis, such as a great depression or oil shock, public social spending continues to increase more or less over time. When a welfare state is not undergoing a socioeconomic crisis, on the other hand, the priority becomes the augmentation of public social budgets, thus minimising the negative after-effects of social problems and avoiding social unrest.

Being that inequality is closely associated with wage, it is the state's first priority to solve this imbalance. It could be said that this is the most essential factor within capitalist societies. Because social polarisation caused by income inequality can endanger frictionless social integration and social cohesion, the welfare state attempts to mitigate polarisation through redistributive policies. Such efforts executed in the name of welfare result in more effective equal distribution within the state.

Therefore, for the purposes of this analysis, the concept of the welfare state is operationally defined as 'a change in public social spending and income inequality.'

3. Method of the Analysis

The following analytical methods are used in this study in order to analyse the impact of informatisation on the development of the welfare state.

First, simple cross-sectional regression is adopted to detect the impact of independent variables on dependent variables from the point on the cross sections. This analysis examines whether an association exists between informatisation and public social spending, or an association between informatisation and inequality. The consideration of time change is excluded in this first step in order to establish results at single points in time.

Next, a pooled time-series cross-section regression analysis method (hereafter pooled TSCS) is implemented to observe any relationship between dependent variables and independent variables during the chosen timespan. In this study, this model is adopted to discover whether informatisation influences the development of the welfare state positively or negatively in the long term. Adhering to the 'de facto Beck-Katz standard,' which is a method of pooled TSCS analysis established by Nathaniel Beck and Jonathan N. Katz, an OLS regression on the pooled TSCS data is performed, adding a lagged dependent variable[30] as well as unit and period dummies to the battery of right-hand side variables,

---

30 Here, in the case of a lagged dependent variable, a five-year lagged dependent variable is included instead of a one-year lagged dependent variable, because of the coefficient estimate distortion caused by the autocorrelation error of the dependent variable (Achen, 2000, pp. 24-25; Huber & Stephens, 2001a, p. 65).

after which the 'panel corrected standard errors' (PCSE) can be calculated (Beck & Katz, 1995, p. 645). Furthermore, in order to gain reliable results, Thomas Pluemper, Vera E. Troeger, and Philip Manow's suggestion is considered as a comparison model. He argues that, in order to identify a theoretical perspective, when observing the degree of the independent variables' effect on the levels of the dependent variables (level effect), country dummy, time dummy, and a lagged dependent variable should not be included in the equation in order to avoid biased estimate results (Pluemper et al., 2005, pp. 330-334).

Third, an error correction model (ECM) and an vector error correction model (VECM) with country fixed effects are performed, in which independent variables are included as the types of first differences (changes) and lagged levels are included in the right side of equation. These analytical models are convenient for discovering the impact of independent variables on dependent variables simultaneously in the long term and short term (Iversen & Cusack, 2000, p. 330). The decision to use first differences instead of levels for the dependent variables, and the inclusion of country fixed effects in the ECM and VECM specification, shifts the perspective from the 'pooled' model to the 'within-effects' model. This shift means changes in independent variables can be used to predict changes in dependent variables 'within' a given unit (country), instead of predicting differences between units (countries) (Busemeyer, 2008, p. 13). This model is useful when expecting a difference between long and short-term effects. As aforementioned, the relationship between informatisation and public social spending or informatisation and inequality can change over time, so the relationship may be observed to change positively or negatively depending on the timeframe.

Fourth, the first difference model is employed to capture the impact of short-term changes in independent variables on short-term changes in dependent variables (Busemeyer, Ibid., p. 13; Min & Choi, 2009, pp. 151-156). This model can reconfirm the results of ECM and VECM, showing the relationship between informatisation and public social spending, and the relationship between informatisation and inequality, when excluding lagged dependent variables on the right side of equation.

Lastly, a panel vector autoregressive (PVAR) captures the response of a dependent variable to the other variables' shock (Min & Choi, 2014, pp. 241-242). This model is applied to observe the response of changes in dependent variables to changes in independent variables in the short term. All variables are utilised with the form of first differences. In addition, this analytical technique eliminates group heterogeneity through the Helmert transformation process, solving autocorrelation issues by once again applying system GMM (generalized method of moments) estimation. Therefore, this model can more accurately show informatisation's relationship with both public social expenditure and inequality in the short term.

4. Definitions and Measurement of Variables

This section deals with the definitions and sources of variables used in this analysis.

4.1 Dependent Variables

1) Public Social Expenditure

The OECD has released social expenditure statistics every year since 1980. In 2014, it also released the OECD Social Expenditure Data Set for the current 34 OECD countries (Adema et al, 2011, p. 8). This data set was created based on the common aspects of the welfare system according to international standards, and has since been used to compare the political economy of welfare states at a macroeconomic level (Obinger & Wagschal, op. cit., p. 334; Jahn, op. cit., p. 143).

In order to determine the amount of effort put into welfare and the welfare preferences of each country, this study takes advantage of the OECD's definitions of social expenditure and public social expenditure. The OECD defines social expenditure thus:

> The provision by public and private institutions of benefits to, and

> financial contributions targeted at, households and individuals in order to provide support during circumstances which adversely affect their welfare, provided that the provision of the benefits and financial contributions constitutes neither a direct payment for a particular good or service nor an individual contract or transfer (OECD, 2007, p.6).

Adopting this definition, cash benefits, social services and tax breaks designed with social welfare in mind can all be regarded as social benefits.

Not surprisingly, the OECD is not the only organisation to release a social data set. So has the IMF (International Monetary Fund), the ILO (International Labour Organisation), and the EU (European Commission). Compared to SOCX (OECD's Social Expenditure Database) and the SSI (ILO's Social Security Inquiry), the scope of Euro Statistics (Eurostat) is narrower because it focuses on support that is allocated to individuals, thus omitting some of the spending on public health and/or active labour market programs. The OECD Social Expenditure Data Set based on the OECD's definitions is much less restrictive because it includes government subsidies towards the cost of the employment of previously unemployed persons (OECD, Ibid., p. 8; Bae, et al, 2008, p.200).

<Table 4.1> OECD Social Expenditure Data Set

<table>
<tr><td rowspan="2">Construction</td><td rowspan="2">General government expenditure</td><td rowspan="2">Social insurance benefits</td><td colspan="2">Private expenditure</td><td colspan="2">Tax</td></tr>
<tr><td>Statutory salaries</td><td>Voluntary benefits</td><td>Direct and indirect taxes, social insurance fee</td><td>TBSPs (+)</td></tr>
<tr><td rowspan="5">Type of statistics</td><td colspan="2">Public social expenditure</td><td colspan="2">Private social expenditure</td><td colspan="2" rowspan="5"></td></tr>
<tr><td colspan="4">Total social expenditure</td></tr>
<tr><td colspan="2" rowspan="3">Net social expenditure</td><td colspan="2">*</td></tr>
<tr><td colspan="2">**</td></tr>
<tr><td colspan="2">***</td></tr>
</table>

1) The above table was reconstructed by the author of this study.

2) Tax: Direct and/or indirect taxes paid by transfer income earners.

3) TBSPs (Tax Breaks for Social Purposes): Reductions, exemptions, deductions or postponement of taxes.

* Tax>TBSPs, ** Tax=TBSPs, *** Tax<TBSPs.

Source: Go, Kyounghwan et al. (2009). 2007 Social Spending Trends in Korea and Income Security Systems for Retired Persons in OECD countries. *Korea Institute for Health and Social Affairs Policy Paper*, p. 35.

As seen in the above table, the OECD Social Expenditure Data Set is constructed using data on general government expenditure, social insurance benefits of public social expenditure, taxes, statutory salaries and the voluntary benefits of private social expenditure. The distinction between public and private social protection is established on the basis of whoever controls the relevant financial flows; that is, public institutions or private bodies. Public social expenditure is social spending with financial flows controlled by the general government, taking into account different levels of government and social security funds. All social benefits not provided by the general government are classed as private social expenditure (Willem et al, op. cit., p. 93).

Public social expenditure in the OECD Social Expenditure Data Set includes spending for social insurance (pension, unemployment, health, workmen's accident compensation, nursing care), social services (care for the elderly, incapacity-related benefits, health and medical care, family care, active labour market policies), and social assistance (medicaid, social aids, benefits for veterans) (Go et al, 2009, p. 72).

2) Income Inequality

Income inequality is one the most significant variables when measuring the efficacy of welfare efforts in various political economies. However, the number of studies on income inequality is limited due to a lack of time-series data. The LIS (Luxemburg Income Study) has been the data commonly used for international comparisons of income inequality. Because this data covers a limited number of years and only covers developed western countries, however, LIS' income inequality data set has several limitations as time-series data for international comparative studies.

Other commonly used data includes the World Bank's World Income Inequality Data Set (WIID), which was accumulated by Klaus Deininger and Lyn Squire (Deininger & Squire, 1996, pp. 565-591). However, this data set also has limitations preventing a thorough view of income inequality. The coverage is sparse and unbalanced; with fewer observations than 700 countries a year in the most widely used versions of the data set. Although Africa, Latin America and Asia are continents in dire need of continued research, Klaus Deininger and Lyn Squire did not measure the inequality of many of these areas frequently enough. The United States, Great Britain, Bulgaria, India and Taiwan are among the few countries for which Klaus Deininger and Lyn Squire provide observations over long periods of time (almost annually in most cases) (Galbraith & Kum, 2004, p.2).

To compensate for these limitations, the Estimated Household Income Inequality Data Set (EHII) was compiled. This data draws from the inequality data (UTIP-UNIDO) produced by the University of Texas Inequality Project (UITP). UTIP-UNIDO is the measure of pay inequality in manufacturing based on industrial statistics published annually by the Industrial Development Organisation of the UN (UNDIO). UNDIO has accrued approximately 3,200 observations over 36 years (1963-1999), and additionally utilises source data, the accuracy and consistency of which are much more likely to be reliable, both through time and across countries (Galbraith & Kum, Ibid., p. 3, 4).

However, because UNDIO does not include income inequality data, the Estimated Household Income Inequality Data Set (EHII) was reworked by the University of Texas Inequality Project. They achieved this by correlating UNDIO data with the parallels between econometrics and wage inequality in manufacturing, income inequality and other exogenous variables (including the manufacturing employment share of the population, data dummy, etc.)[31] The EHII data set is much more com-

[31] There are conceptual differences between wage inequality and income inequality, but they are nevertheless related. Wage is the largest single element in income in most countries, and manufacturing pay is a significant component of all payment types.

prehensive than Klaus Deininger and Lyn Squire's data set, especially as the EHII data set is consistently adjusted to reflect household income inequality (Galbraith & Kum, Ibid., p. 4).

4.2 Independent Variables

Time-series data, which are released by the International Telecommunication Union (ITU), are used as the main independent variables to shed light on the development of the ICT industry and its usage. The ITU, which is the United Nation's specialised agency for ICT, is recognised globally as the leading provider of timely and comprehensive telecommunication/ICT statistics and trends.[32]

The annual investments in telecommunication, exports of telecommunication equipment, imports of telecommunication equipment, and the number of full-time telecommunication staff are among the most important sources of independent variables to reveal development within the ICT industry. In order to conduct a comparative analysis, these variables have to be standardised when considering differences among countries. Annual investments in telecommunication, exports of telecommunication equipment, and imports of telecommunication equipment are calculated as a percentage of the GDP. The number of full-time telecommunication staff is standardised by the total labour force.[33] In addition, in order to observe how open the market is for tele-

Low-wage (and largely unqualified) workers in manufacturing are fungible for low-wage (and similarly unqualified) workers in services and agriculture, and vice versa. Therefore, changes in inequality within the manufacturing industry will tend to mirror changes in inequality in the structure of people's pay overall (Galbraith & Kum, 2004, p. 4, 9, 17).

32 The World Telecommunication/ICT Indicators Database on CD-ROM and the online ITU contains time-series data for the years 1960, 1965, 1970 and annually from 1975 to 2012 for more than 150 telecommunication/ICT statistics (ITU, 2010).

33 Total labour force comprises people ages 15 and older who fit the International Labor Organization's definition of the economically active population; that is, all people who supply labour for the production of goods and services during a specified period. This definition includes both the employed and the unemployed. While national practices vary in treatment of such groups as the armed forces and seasonal or part-time workers, in general, the labour force includes the armed forces, the unemployed, and first-time job-seekers; while excluding homemakers, and other unpaid caregivers and workers in the informal sector (World Bank, 2015).

communication equipment, openness of information is calculated by adding exports of telecommunication equipment to imports of telecommunication equipment as a percentage of the GDP.[34] Thus calculated, the openness of information is also utilised as an independent variable in the analyses.

Internet users, mobile cellular subscriptions, and the number of computers designated for personal use are among the most significant sources of independent variables to reveal the amount and rate of ICT usage. The following table shows the definition and source of these variables.

<Table 4.2> **Definition of Variables & Data Sources: Variables Related to the ICT Industry and ICT Usage**

Variable name	Definition	Source
Internet user rates	Rate of internet users for the past one year's total population.	ITU
Personal computer numbers	Number of PC owners per 100 persons.	ITU
Mobile cellular phone subscriptions	Mobile cellular phone subscribers per 100 persons.	ITU
Total annual investment in telecommunication sector (%)	The gross annual investment in telecom (including fixed, mobile and Internet services) for acquiring property and networks. (The annual investments in telecommunication are calculated as a percentage of the GDP).	ITU & World Bank
Imports-telecommunication equipment (%)	Import of electrical apparatus for line telephony and line telegraphy, transmission apparatus for radio-telephony, radio-telegraphy, radio-broadcasting and television, reception apparatus for radio-telephony and radio-telegraphy, parts and accessories suitable for principal use. (Imports of telecommunication equipment is calculated as a percentage of the GDP).	ITU & World Bank
Exports-telecommunication equipment (%)	Export of electrical apparatus for line telephony and line telegraphy, transmission apparatus for radio-telephony, radio-telegraphy, radio-broadcasting and television, reception apparatus for radio-telephony and radio-telegraphy, parts and accessories suitable for principal use.	ITU & World Bank

34 This calculation is performed by the author.

	(Exports of telecommunication equipment is calculated as a percentage of the GDP).	
Total full-time telecommunication staff (%)	Total number of full-time staff employed by telecommunication network operators in the country for the provision of public telecommunication services (including fixed, mobile and internet services). (The number of full-time telecommunication staff is calculated as a percentage of total labour force).	ITU & World Bank
Information openness (%)	The outward or inward orientation of a given country's economy in telecommunication equipment trade. (Information openness is calculated by exports of telecommunication equipment plus imports of telecommunication equipment as percentage of the GDP).	ITU & World Bank

* The above table was constructed by the author of this study.

Source: International Telecommunication Union (ITU). (2010). World Telecommunication/ICT Indicators Database (CD). Geneva: Author; Homepage of World Bank, http://data.worldbank.org.

Independent variables indicative of the development of the e-government are taken from time-series data which is released by the Division for Public Administration (hereafter DPADM) and the Development Management of the Department of Economic and Social Affairs of the United Nations (hereafter UNDESA). The e-government survey of 193 countries conducted by DPADM and UNDESA (which has remained biennial since 2008) includes the e-government development index, the web measure index (otherwise known as the online service index), the telecommunication infrastructure index, the human capital index, the e-participation index, and e-government rankings from years 2002, 2003, 2004, 2005, 2008, 2010, 2012, 2014 (UNDESA, 2014, p.4).

The E-Government Development Index is a method by which the Internet and World Wide Web (WWW) are measured for provision of information, products and services. It also measures the level of telecommunications and human capital infrastructure development within a country. The Infrastructure Index is a composite weighted average index of five primary indices (the number of internet users, PCs, telephone circuits, mobile phone subscribers, and broadband Internet subscribers) based on fundamental infrastructural indicators. These indicators are sufficient to define a country's capacity in regards to ICT infrastructure. The human capital index is a composite of the adult literacy rate and the combined primary, secondary and tertiary gross enrolment ratio, with two thirds weight given to the adult literacy rate and one third to the gross enrolment ratio.[35] The Web Measure Index is the level of sophistication of a state's online presence. This index is based on a four-stage model, the stages of which are: Emerging information services, enhanced information services, transactional services and the connected approach (Alshomrani, op. cit., p. 412). The e-participation index comprises quality and efficacy of information and services as provided by a country for the purpose of engaging its citizens in public-policy making through the use of e-government programs (UNDESA, 2010, pp. 109-124).

The UN surveyed and evaluated the development of e-governments through indices that are collectively represented in the following table (National Information Society Agency, 2010, p. 1):

<Table 4.3> UN E-government Development Index

Evaluation Index	Category		Constituent Element
E-government development index	Web measure index	Step 1: Emerging information services	The existence of official websites, the provision of links to central government websites.
		Step 2: Enhanced information services	Providing online information about public policies (including the latest data on various policies).
		Step 3: Interactive information services	Providing interactive and user-friendly online services, such as sending mobile phone messages, WAP/PDA access, security devices, electronic signatures.

35 The data for the adult literacy rate and the gross enrolment ratio was drawn primarily from the United Nations Educational, Scientific and Cultural Organization (UNESCO) and supplemented with data from the United Nations Development Program (UNDP) (UNDESA, 2008, p.17).

		Step 4: Transactional services	Providing a variety of options and online services, such as online civil applications, bidding, credit card payments, tax payments, passport/license renewal functions.
		Step 5: Connected approach	Providing links on official websites that lead to other websites for other government departments etc., local government and non-administrative organisations, the publication of the expiration date regarding complaints-handling, providing official online civil participation.
	ICT infrastructure index	The mean of standardised five index values	The number of internet users, PCs, telephone circuits, mobile phone subscribers, broadband Internet subscribers. (All above indexes are calculated per 100 persons).
	Human capital index	The weighted average of two index values	Adult literacy rates, enrolment rates.
Online participation index	Information providing	Online access and use of key information about public policies.	
	Policy participation	Availability of real-time online discussions about public policies.	
	Policy decisions	Civil involvement in public policy decision-making processes, results feedback, the sharing of decisions on certain issues with citizens.	

* The above table was reconstructed by the author of this study.

Source: National Information Society Agency. (2010). *2010 UN E-Government Evaluation; Global Informatisation Policy Resource,* p. 1. Seoul: Author.

4.3 Control Variables

In the next section, variables related to the development of the welfare state selected for this study are briefly outlined.

1) Corruption Perception Index

The corruption perception index (CPI) is an aggregate indicator that ranks countries in terms of the degree to which corruption is perceived to exist among public officials and politicians. The CPI has been published by Transparency International annually since 1995 (TI, 2010, p.1; Lee, 2011, pp. 118-119).

The criteria of corruption is determined by assessing the following conditions: The extent to which an executive is held accountable for their use of funds, the extent to which they are held accountable for the results of their actions by the electorate, legislature and judiciary, and the extent to which public employees in executive positions are required to account for their use of resources, their administrative decisions, and results achieved (TI, op. cit., p. 1-2). A country/territory's score indicates the perceived level of public sector corruption. The scale consists of 0 - 10, where 0 means a country is perceived as highly corrupt and 10 means a country is perceived as very ethical (TI, 2011, p.1).

2) Trade Union Density

Trade union density is calculated using Labour Force Statistics put out by the OECD. Trade union density is the ratio of the number of wage earners who are trade union members to the total number of wage earners. Wherever possible, density is calculated using survey data, except in the case of non-active and self-employed members, where administrative data is adapted accordingly (OECD, 2014, p.1). Data are expressed in percentages.

3) Economic Openness

The Penn World Table Version 7.1 was released by the Center for International Comparisons of Production, Income and Prices at the University of Pennsylvania in 2012. The Penn World Table provides data on the economic openness for 189 countries/territories over some or all of the years between 1950 and 2010 (Center for International Comparisons of Production, Income and Prices at the University of

Pennsylvania, 2012). The Penn World Table is also used as a source of information regarding economic openness for the purposes of this study.

Exports plus imports (or total trade) divided by the current GDP is the formula by which the present state of economic openness is calculated in any given country. Export and import figures are presented in national currencies in the World Bank and United Nations data archives (Ahn, 2004, p. 10).

4) Urban Population Rates

Urban population refers to people living in urban areas as defined by national statistics offices. That is, the percentage of the total population who can be considered to be living in an urban environment. It is calculated using World Bank population estimates and urban ratios from the United Nations World Urbanization Prospects (WB, 2014). Data concerning urban population rates are drawn from the World Bank for the purposes of this analysis.

5) GDP per Capita

GDP is the gross value of an economy (the sum of all resident producers in the economy) plus product taxes (minus any subsidies not included in the value of the products). This calculation does not account for depreciation or fabricated assets, nor does it recognise depletion and degradation of natural resources. GDP per capita is the gross domestic product divided by the midyear population (WB, 2014). For the purposes of this study, statistics concerning GDP per capita are also drawn from the World Bank. The data is presented in current U.S. dollars.

6) Total Unemployment Rates

The unemployment rate is defined by the number of unemployed persons as a percentage of the labour force, in which the labour force is defined as the number of the unemployed plus those in paid positions plus self-employed individuals. Unemployed persons are defined as those who have reported to the government that they lack employment, they are available to fill a work position, and they have taken active steps in the last four weeks that might help them procure work.

The ILO Guidelines specify what actions count as active steps to find work; including answering vacancy notices, visiting factories, visiting construction sites and other places of work, placing advertisements in the press, and registering with labour offices. The ILO unemployment rates differ from rates derived from registered unemployed databases at labour offices. The latter rates are often taken from databases published in individual countries.[36] For certitude and accuracy, this study takes total unemployment rates from the OECD's data set only.

7) Political Rights and Civil Liberties

Freedom House assesses the real-world rights and freedoms enjoyed by individuals, rather than governments or government performance per se. It publishes an annual global report on political rights and civil liberties, composed of numerical ratings and descriptive texts for 195 countries and 14 territories (FH, 2014, p.1).

The Freedom House assigns a country or territory two ratings; one for political rights and one for civil liberties. These ratings are based on total scores accrued via questions related to political rights and civil liberties. The final rating indicates the degree of freedom in the aforementioned arenas. A score between 1 and 7 is settled upon yearly, wherein 1 represents the greatest degree of freedom and 7 represents smallest degree of freedom (FH, Ibid., p.3).

Data concerning political rights and civil liberties, which are published by the Freedom House annually, is drawn upon for the purposes of this study.

---

36 Data on registered unemployment have limited international comparability, as the rules for registering at labour offices vary from country to country. Although all OECD countries use the ILO Guidelines for measuring unemployment, the unemployment levels tend to be affected by changes in operational definitions, survey design and the survey conduct used in national labour force surveys. Despite such limits, the unemployment rates are of good international comparability and fairly consistent over time (OECD, 2013, p. 14).

<Table 4.4> **Definition of Variables & Data Sources: Variables Related to the Welfare State's Development**

Variable name	Definition	Source
Corruption perceptions index	The perceived level of public sector corruption.	TI
Trade union density	The trade union members divided by the total number of wage and salary earners.	OECD
Economic openness	Exports plus imports as a percentage of the current GDP.	Penn World Table
Urban population	The urban population percentage of the total population.	World Bank
GDP per capita	The gross domestic product divided by midyear population.	World Bank
Total unemployment	The number of unemployed persons as a percentage of the labour force.	OECD
Political rights	The real-world rights enjoyed by individuals.	Freedom House
Civil liberties	The real-world liberties enjoyed by individuals.	Freedom House

* The above table was constructed by the author of this study.

Source: Homepages of each organisation.

5. Summary

In this chapter, hypotheses, operational definitions, analysis methods, and variables are presented in order to perform analyses. For clarity and quick reference, a summation is outlined below.

First, several hypotheses are established. The first hypothesis is 'the development of the ICT industry increases public social spending.' This is proposed in order to examine the impact of the ICT industry on public social spending. The second hypothesis is 'the development of the ICT industry increases income inequality.' This is established to discover the impact of the ICT industry on income inequality. The third hypothesis is 'the use of ICT increases public social spending.' This is proposed to examine the impact of ICT usage on public social spending. The fourth hypothesis is 'the use of ICT increases income inequality.' This is presented to discover the impact of ICT on income inequality. The final hypothesis is 'the development of the e-government increases public social spending.' This is examined to uncover the relationship between the development of the e-government and the welfare state.

Second, the terms 'welfare state' and 'informatisation' are operationally defined. The welfare state is operationally defined as 'a change in public social spending and a decrease of income inequality.' The concept of infomatisation is operationally defined as 'the development of the ICT industry, increase of ICT usage, and introduction and increase of ICT in the public sector.'

Third, several analytical methods to be used in this study are introduced. Thereafter, variables are presented to enable the analyses to be conducted. These include dependent variables, such as public social expenditure and estimated household income inequality, independent variables related to the ICT industry, ICT usage and the e-government, and control variables such as the urban population rate, GDP per capita, total unemployment rates, trade union density, the corruption perception index, political rights, civil liberties, and economic openness.

Chapter V

The Development of the ICT Industry and Welfare State

Chapter V The Development of the ICT Industry and Welfare State

Chapter five analyses the relationship between the development of the ICT industry and the welfare state using variables as presented in the previous chapter. The analysis is performed with the 34 OECD countries as analysis objects and time-series data from 1985 to 2010, spanning a total period of 26 years.

Descriptive statistics are employed in order to understand the general characteristics of the variables, followed by correlation analyses to uncover any statistical relationships between the variables. Thereafter, simple cross-sectional regressions are conducted, which can show the effect of the development of ICT industry on the development of the welfare state via a cross-sectional point. Finally, several pooled TSCS analyses are performed in order to investigate the causal relationship between dependent variables and independent variables. Independent variables are standardised so that they can be compared appropriately among countries. Control variables are managed differently depending on what is appropriate for each analysis model. Missing values are not handled in descriptive statistics, correlation analyses, and simple cross-sectional regressions, but are handled in some pooled TSCS analyses.[37]

[37] For the first difference analysis, an error correction model analysis, a vector error correction model analysis and panel vector autoregressive analysis, missing values are calculated by the moving average (with a window of five years), in order to conduct the analyses.

Hypotheses

1. *The development of the ICT industry increases public social spending.*
2. *The development of the ICT industry increases income inequality.*

Variables

Dependent variables: Public Social Expenditure, Estimated Household Income Inequality Independent variables: Total Annual Investment in Telecommunication, Total Full-time Staff in Telecommunication, Imports - Telecommunication Equipment, Exports - Telecommunication Equipment, Information Openness

Control variables: Urban Population Rate, GDP per Capita, Total Unemployment Rates, Trade Union Density, Corruption Perception Index, Political Rights, Civil Liberties, Economic Openness

1. General Characteristics of Variables

1.1 Descriptive Statistics of the 34 OECD Countries

In descriptive statistics, original values are used without adulteration of those values. Historically, time-series data is separated into segments of two periods in order to observe changes over time in more detail. Those periods of time are before 2000, and after 2000.

The following table shows the results of descriptive statistics variables. Here, the mean and standard deviation are calculated to the second decimal place, providing more than sufficient accuracy when looking at and explaining changes over time.

<Table 5.1> **General Characteristics of Variables**

	The Entire Period			Pre - 2000			Post - 2000		
Variable	Observation	Mean	Std. Dev.	Observation	Mean	Std. Dev.	Observation	Mean	Std. Dev.
Public Social Expenditure	789	19.38	6.43	422	18.67	6.93	367	20.19	5.71
Estimated Household Income Inequality	651	36.97	4.92	431	36.48	5.19	220	37.93	4.21
Investment	732	0.62	0.31	481	0.64	0.29	251	0.60	0.34
Staff	598	0.56	0.81	336	0.54	0.18	262	0.58	1.21
Import	729	0.43	0.39	425	0.30	0.27	304	0.61	0.46
Export	682	0.60	1.19	379	0.37	0.77	303	0.88	1.52
Information Openness	681	1.04	1.47	378	0.68	0.94	303	1.49	1.85

* The values represent the mean and the standard deviation of each variable in the 34 OECD countries during 1985 - 2010.

Where changes in public social welfare spending as one dependent variable are observable, the mean increases slightly between the 1990s and 2000s. Taking a closer look at growth rates, the mean increases from 18.67 (standard deviation: 6.93) in the period before 2000, to 20.19 (standard deviation: 5.71) in the period after 2000. Where income inequality is the dependent variable, the mean is 36.48 in the period before 2000 (standard deviation: 5.19). In the period after 2000, the mean increases slightly to 37.93 (standard deviation: 4.21).

Looking at the independent variables, the mean of the total annual investment in telecommunication (%) is 0.64 in the period before 2000 (standard deviation: 0.29). In the period after 2000, the mean decreases slightly to 0.60 (standard deviation: 0.34). Total full-time telecommunication staff (%) increases to 0.54 in the period before 2000 (standard deviation: 0.18). In the period after 2000, the mean increases slightly to 0.58 (standard deviation: 1.21). In the case of the import of telecommunication equipment (%), the mean is 0.30 in the period before 2000 (standard deviation: 0.27). In the period after 2000, the mean increases by nearly two times, to 0.61 (standard deviation: 0. 46). In the case of the export of telecommunication equipment (%), the mean is 0.37 in the period before 2000 (standard deviation: 0.77). In the period after 2000, the mean also increases by nearly two times, to 0.88 (standard deviation: 1.52). The mean of information openness (%) shows a third case of an almost doubled increase, from 0.68 (standard deviation: 0.94) to 1.49 (standard deviation: 1.85) in the same periods.

1.2 Descriptive Statistics by Country

1) Charting the Changes in Variables

Normally, before analysing the data, a trend graph of each variable based on the time-series data of the 34 OECD countries is analysed. Considering the abundance of other data within this study, however, such graphs are omitted on account of space consideration.

2) Mean Value Analyses

The mean of each variable is analysed during the period 1985-2010. Here, for the sake of clarity, the differences in the mean value of each dependent variable and independent variable are presented for each country in the format of figures as well as text. The level of each variable is often judged by different authorities, resulting in a radically different range of ranking systems. When terms such as and similar to 'upper group,' 'middle group,' 'lower group' and 'substandard' are used, they must therefore be seen as approximations. Such classifications are necessarily used, however, as the purpose of this section is to examine the differences shown between each of the variables of OECD countries during the analysis period.

(1) Comparisons of Dependent Variables

❶ Public Social Expenditure

Here, the mean value of public social expenditure is compared between countries from 1985 to 2010. As seen in the figure below, the mean value of public welfare expenditure in Sweden is 30.20%, France is 27.93%, Finland is 26.70%, Denmark is 26.70%, Austria is 26.60%, Belgium is 26.30%, and Germany is 25.57%. These countries, dedicating above 25% of their budgets to public social expenditure, are at the frontier of public welfare advancement. It is probably not insignificant that, with the exception of Austria, Belgium and Germany, all these countries are located in Northern Europe.

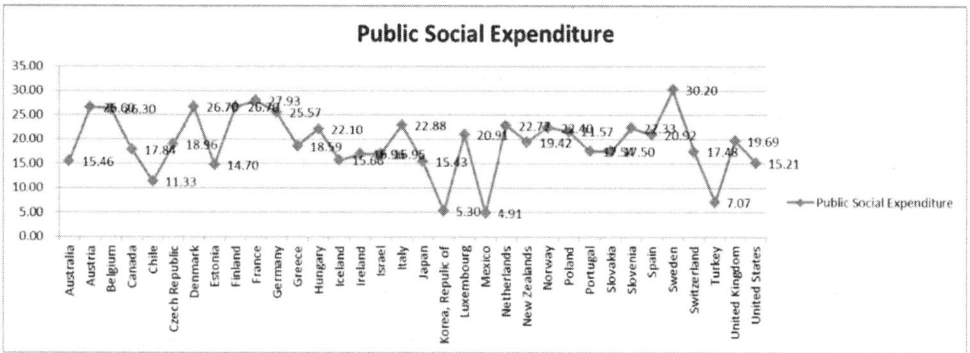

* The values represent the annual average of public social expenditure in the 34 OECD countries during 1985-2010.

<Figure 5.1> **Public Social Expenditure from 1985 to 2010**

The next eight in the ranks are Italy (22.88%), the Netherlands (22.77%), Norway (22.40%), Slovenia (22.33%), Hungary (22.10%), Poland (21.57%), Spain (20.92%), and Luxembourg (20.91%). It is also significant to note that these are all European countries.

In the low range in regards to the mean value of public social expenditure are Japan (15.43%), the United States (15.21%), Estonia (14.70%), and Chile (11.33%), all of whom designate about 10% to 15% of public social spending to total GDP. Countries whose mean value falls at less than 10% are Turkey, South Korea, and Mexico; at 7.07%, 5.30%, and 4.91% respectively. These countries belong to the lowest group in levels of public social expenditure.

One of the eminent features of these results is that the Czech Republic, Slovakia, Hungary, and Poland show high levels of public social expenditure. These are countries that share the common experience of a socialist system over the mid-to-late twentieth century. Therefore, it is fair to suggest that relatively high levels of public social expenditure can be the aftermath of a socialist system.

In addition, it is worthwhile pointing out the disparity between the first country and the last in terms of public social spending. As the front runner, Sweden reaches 30.20%, while Mexico reaches a mere 4.91% in last place. The difference of mean values between these countries in regards to public social expenditure is a surprising 25.29%, meaning Sweden's percentage is almost six times greater than that of Mexico's.

❷ Household Income Inequality

The mean value of each OECD country's household income inequality (Estimated Household Income Inequality: EHII) from 1985 to 2010 can be explained as follows:

EHII, a type of Gini Scale, was devised by UTIP to determine household income inequality rankings on a scale of 1 to 100, in which 1 indicates the lowest level of household income inequality and 100 indicates the highest level of household income inequality. Among OECD countries, no country surpasses 48.06 in ranking. Nevertheless, as the evidence stands, there is considerable disparity of household income inequality between OECD countries. Countries with the lowest household income inequality include the Czech Republic (27.55) and Sweden (29.49), with household income inequality ranking at less than 30. These are followed by other countries with a relatively low ranking (and therefore low household income inequality), including Slovenia, Denmark, Switzerland, Iceland, Finland, Germany, Luxembourg, Norway, and Estonia, all of which receive rankings of between 30 and 35.

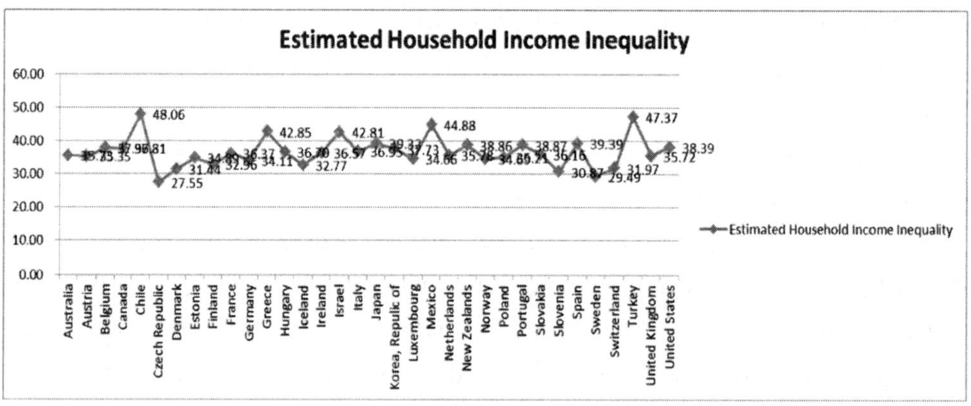

* The values represent the annual average of Estimated Household Income Inequality in the 34 OECD countries during 1985-2010.

<Figure 5.2> Household Income Inequality from 1985 to 2010

A ranking of above 40 can be considered high in regards to household income inequality among OECD countries. These include Chile (48.06), Turkey (47.37), Mexico (44.88), Greece (42.85), and Israel (42.81). The difference between Chile (with the highest level of household income inequality at 48.06) and the Czech Republic (with the lowest level of household income inequality at 27.55) reveals a significant gap of 20.51.

❸ Public Social Spending and Household Income Inequality

Looking at public social spending alongside household income inequality, it seems that countries ranking at the highest end in levels of public social spending have low levels of household income inequality. Conversely, it is apparent that countries with high levels of household income inequality tend to engage in much less public social spending. However, there are several exceptions, so judgment must be passed with reservation in regards to the links between high levels of public social spending and low levels of household income inequality.

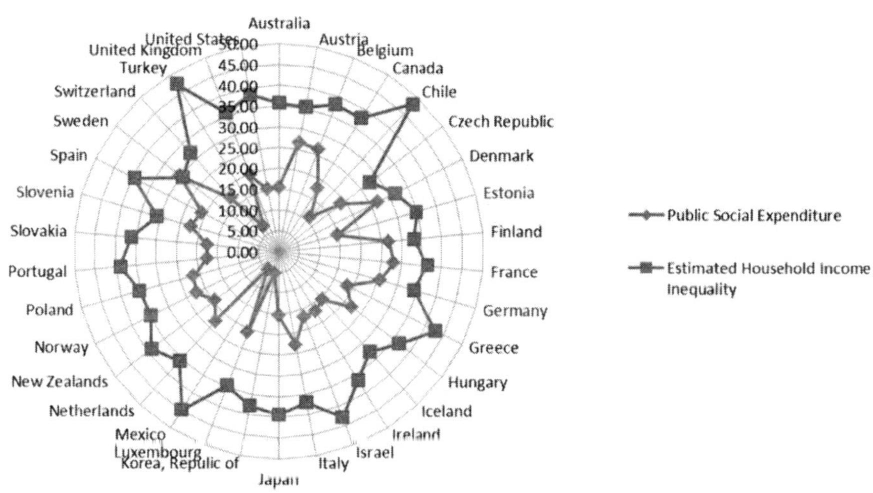

* The values represent the annual average of public social expenditure and estimated household income inequality in the 34 OECD countries during 1985-2010.

<Figure 5.3> **Public Social Expenditure and Household Income Inequality from 1985 to 2010**

(2) Comparison of Main Independent Variables

Here follows a comparison of the indices used in this analysis as independent variables representing the ICT industry's development in different countries.

❶ Total Annual Investment in Telecommunication (%)

In the case of total annual investments in telecommunication, there appear to be significant variations between countries. At the highest end, the Czech Republic invested 1.09% of the GDP to total annual investment in telecommunication, and South Korea invested 1.01%, both of which are considerable amounts. Also dedicating generous amounts to telecommunication were Slovenia (0.91%), Hungary (0.89%), Estonia (0.81%), and Australia (0.81%). Many other countries also showed large investments of over 0.50% of the total GDP towards telecommunication per year.

Moving down the scale a little, Sweden invested 0.49%, the Netherlands invested 0.49%, Mexico invested 0.48%, Denmark invested 0.46%, France invested 0.45%, and Iceland invested 0.44%. Countries who allocated the smallest amounts to telecommunication were Belgium (0.42%), Turkey (0.42%), the United States (0.41%) and Luxembourg (0.39%).

There is a 0.7% difference between the Czech Republic's investment in telecommunication (which was the highest among all OECD countries), and Luxembourg, (which was the lowest among all OECD countries), revealing almost two times the difference between the two. The following figure exemplifies that the level of the investment in the ICT sector varies considerably among countries.

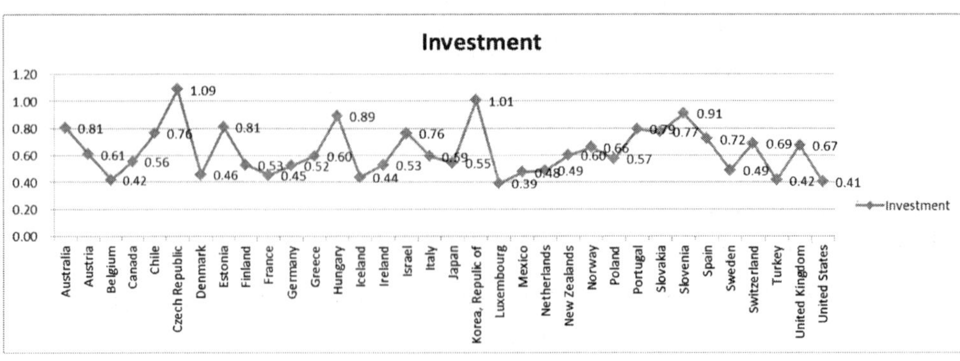

* The values represent the annual average of total annual investment in telecommunication in the 34 OECD countries during 1985-2010.

<Figure 5.4> Total Annual Investment in Telecommunication (%)

❷ Total Full-time Telecommunication Staff (%)

Between 1985 and 2010, taking a look at the percentage of full-time employees in the telecommunication area of the total labour force, the annual average is revealed to be overwhelmingly high in both the Japan (1.31%) and Australia (0.93%).

Besides Japan and Australia, countries showing the highest percentage of people in the telecommunication sector are Ireland (0.86%), Norway (0.81%), Iceland (0.74%), and the United States (0.73%). In countries like Finland, the United Kingdom, Denmark, Sweden, Belgium, Luxembourg, France, Germany, Canada, and Switzerland, the annual average of full-time employment in the ICT-related labour market is between 0.55% and 0.69%.

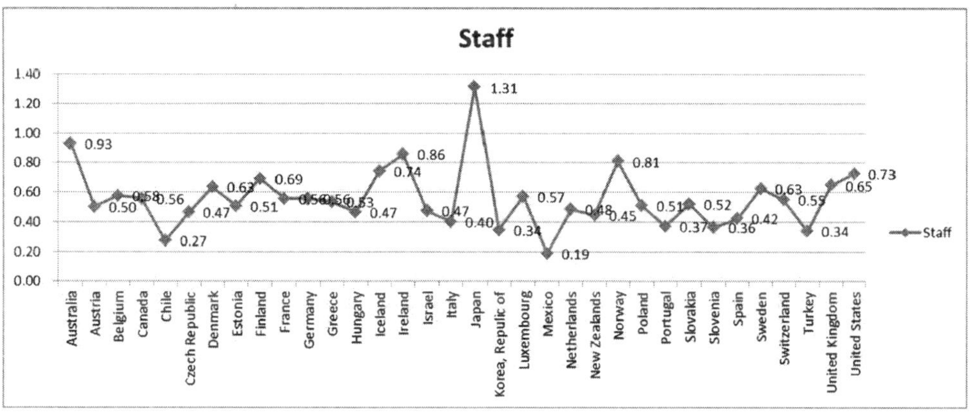

* The values represent the annual average of total full-time telecommunication staff in the 34 OECD countries during 1985-2010.

<Figure 5.5> **Total Full-time Telecommunication Staff (%)**

Compared to the relatively prosperous aforementioned countries, there is a significant decrease in percentages in countries such as Greece (0.53%), Slovakia (0.52%), Poland (0.51%), Estonia (0.51%) and Austria (0.50%). Then are the countries at the lowest end of the scale, including South Korea (0.34%), Turkey (0.34%), Chile (0.27%), and Mexico (0.19%).

As shown in the figure above, the disparity between percentages of ICT workers in OECD countries is substantial. The difference between Japan and Mexico, for example, is about 1.12%. This result clearly indicates a large difference in the sizes of ICT-related labour markets.

❸ Imports - Telecommunication Equipment (%)

Looking at the average annual imports of telecommunication equipment, Estonia and Luxembourg spent 1.50% of the total GDP annually during the period 1985-2010. This is an amount overwhelmingly higher than any other OECD country. Hungary came in third at 1.16%, followed by the Czech Republic at 0.72 %.

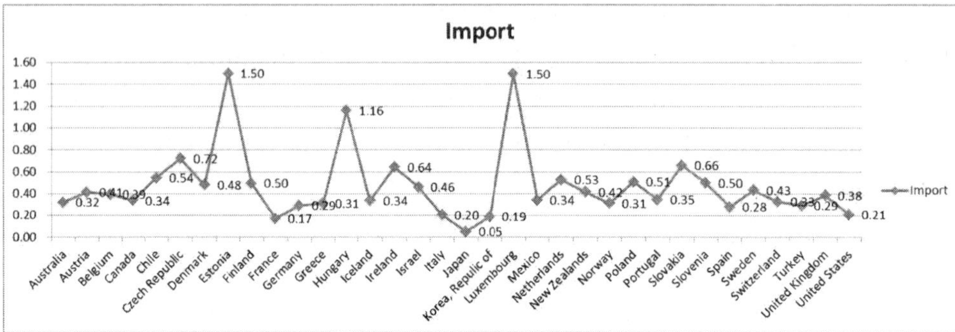

* The values represent the annual average of import of telecommunication equipment in the OECD 34 countries during 1985-2010.

<Figure 5.6> Imports: Telecommunication Equipment (%)

Countries such as Slovakia, Ireland, Chile, the Netherlands, Poland, Slovenia and Finland allocated an average of about 0.66% to 0.50% to the import of telecommunication annually, which is also a relatively high value. In addition, Denmark, Israel, Sweden, New Zealand and Austria spent in the vicinity of 0.48% to 0.41% of the total GDP annually. This is, again, not a significantly lesser amount.

The group of countries dedicating a lesser amount to telecommunication import includes Turkey (0.29%), Germany (0.29%), Spain (0.28%), the United States (0.21%), Italy (0.20%), South Korea (0.19%), and France (0.17%). The lowest spender is Japan, dedicating an average of 0.05% annually to the import of telecommunication equipment.

As the figure clearly demonstrates, although the disparity between the highest ranking countries (Estonia and Luxembourg) and Japan is large, numbers do not vary significantly between countries such as South Korea, France, Italy, etc. Considering the available data, it would be reasonable to conclude that a high import of telecommunication equipment directly reflects a high level of ICT development within the same country.

❹ Exports - Telecommunication Equipment (%)

Looking at the average annual exports of telecommunication equipment, the worth of goods transported from Estonia is 3.21% of the total GDP. This is the only country seen to be exporting telecommunication equipment above the value of 3%. Finland and Hungary show 2.97% and 2.83% respectively. Sweden (1.74%) and Israel (1.64%) also rank in the top group, with a large amounts worth of annual exports. Because it is likely that the average amount of annual exports reflect the development of the ICT industry in countries, it is fair to speculate that Estonia, Finland, Hungary Sweden, Israel and Luxembourg are the most developed countries in the ICT sector. Countries such as Ireland, South Korea, Mexico, the United Kingdom, and Canada show 1.02% to 0.45% of the total GDP, meaning that these countries also belong on the frontier.

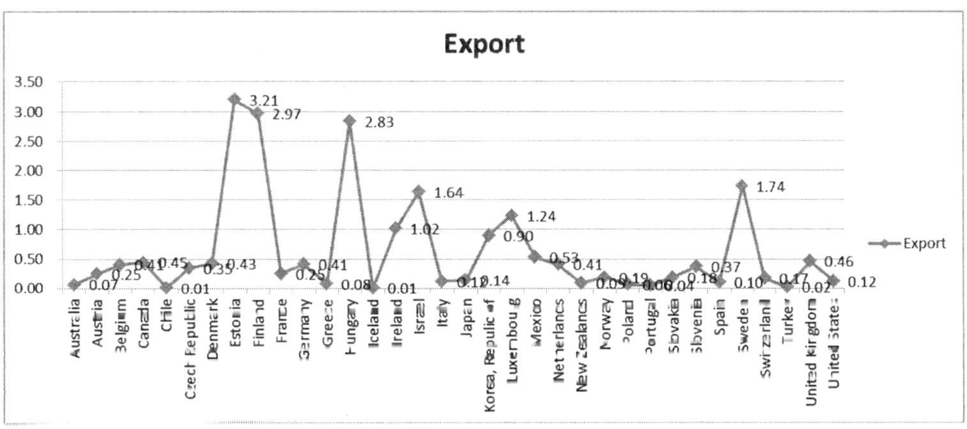

* The values represent the annual average of exports of telecommunication equipment in the 34 OECD countries during 1985-2010.

<Figure 5.7> **Exports: Telecommunication Equipment (%)**

❺ Information Openness (%)

Information openness is the sum of ICT imports and ICT exports divided by the GDP. Estonia and Hungary (4.71% and 4.09% respectively) reveal the highest percentage among OECD countries. Finland (3.47%), Luxembourg (2.74%), Israel (2.19%), Sweden (2.17%), Ireland (1.66%), South Korea (1.09%), and the Czech Republic (1.07%) are also leading countries in information openness.

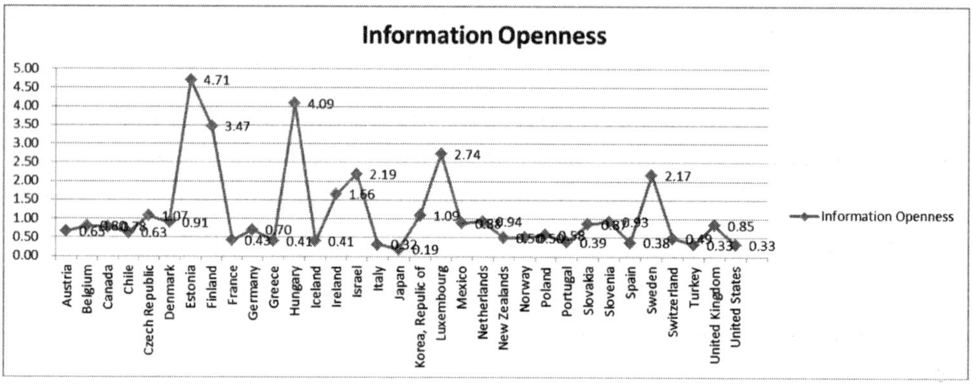

* The values represent the annual average of information openness in the 34 OECD countries during 1985-2010.

<Figure 5.8> Information Openness (%)

Sliding down the scale, Switzerland, France, Australia, Iceland, Greece, Portugal, and Spain show values below 0.50%. The countries with the least amount of information openness are Turkey, the United States, Italy, and Japan.

(3) Comparison of Main Control Variables

The analysis in this chapter uses control variables whose effects on the development of the welfare state have been verified in previous studies. These control variables include urban population rates, GDP per capita, total unemployment rates, trade union density, the corruption perception index, political rights, civil liberties, and economic openness. Explanations for these variables are omitted on account of space consideration.

2. Correlation Analysis

Here, a correlation analysis is performed via a pairwise deletion. Looking at the results of the correlation analysis, public social expenditure and household income inequality have a negative (-) correlation.

<Table 5.2> **Results of Correlation Analysis**

	Public Social Expenditure	Estimated Household Income Inequality	Investment	Staff	Import	Export	Information Openness
Public Social Expenditure	1						
(Sig.)	0.0000						
Estimated Household	-0.5573	1					
Income Inequality (Sig.)	0.0000	0.0000					
Investment	-0.1668	-0.0266	1				
(Sig.)	0.0000	0.5158	0.0000				
Staff	0.0718	-0.4325	-0.0335	1			
(Sig.)	0.0893	0.0000	0.4241	0.0000			
Import	0.0703	-0.0735	0.1313	-0.0299	1		
(Sig.)	0.0670	0.0752	0.0006	0.4750	0.0000		
Export	0.1058	-0.1560	-0.0165	-0.0063	0.6072	1	
(Sig.)	0.0069	0.0002	0.6791	0.8850	0.0000	0.0000	
Information Openness	0.1007	-0.1458	0.0212	-0.0132	0.7656	0.9760	1
(Sig.)	0.0102	0.0006	0.5954	0.7606	0.0000	0.0000	0.0000

Correlations between public social expenditure and imports of telecommunication equipment, exports of telecommunication equipment, total full-time telecommunication staff, and information openness all show plus (+) signs; while the correlation between public social expenditure and total annual investments in telecommunication show minus (-) signs. If a plus sign is present when interpreting the results of a correlation analysis, it can be construed that there exists a positive correlation between variables. If a minus sign is present, the interpretation is reversed and a negative correlation exists between variables. Therefore, because imports of telecommunication equipment, exports of telecommunication equipment, total full-time telecommunication staff, and information openness reveal high values, the values of public social expenditure within the given countries are also high. Conversely, because the values of total annual investments in telecommunication are high, the values of public social expenditure within the given countries are low.

Correlations between income inequality and total annual investments in telecommunication, total full-time telecommunication staff, imports of telecommunication equipment, exports of telecommunication equipment, and information openness, all show minus signs. To interpret these results, because there exists high values of total annual investments in telecommunication, total full-time telecommunication staff, imports of telecommunication equipment, exports of telecommunication equipment, and information openness, the values of income inequality is low. It can therefore be said that they share negative correlations.

3. Causality Analysis of ICT Industry Development, Public Social Spending and Income Inequality

With the information uncovered thus far, it is now possible to conduct a causality analysis of ICT industry development, public social spending, and income inequality. This analysis begins on the assumption that causal relationships between dependent and independent variables, as well as relationships between dependent and control variables, are linear, i.e., the model is linear in its parameters.

3.1 Causality Analysis of ICT Industry Development and Public Social Spending

First, to analyse the causal relationship between ICT industry development and public social spending, several pooled TSCS analyses are conducted using public social expenditure as the dependent variable, independent variables related to ICT industry development, and numerous control variables related to welfare state development.[38]

38 To achieve a more normal distribution and increase the efficacy of the analysis' performance, GDP per capita as a control variable is computed via a natural log using log transformation.

Hypothesis

The development of the ICT industry increases public social spending.

1) Testing the Assumptions of Linear Regression and Analysis Modelling

Prior to conducting the pooled TSCS analysis, whether or not the pooled data meet the basic assumptions of OLS must first be confirmed. This validation can be met via the following testing processes:

(1) The existence of multicollinearity: If the independent variables are too strongly collinear, the analysis results may be biased. Therefore, each value of the Variance Inflation Factor (hereafter VIF) is controlled below 4 in all regressions. (2) The existence of the random effect or fixed effect: The F test and Hausman test are conducted to determine the effects existing due to omitted variables. (3) The existence of autocorrelation: The Wooldridge test is conducted in order to observe whether there exists autocorrelation in residuals. (4) The existence of heteroskedasticity: Heteroskedasticity means that the residuals have constant variance in every unit and at every time. The Modified Wald test is performed to confirm heteroskedasticity.[39] The results of each test are omitted on account of space consideration.

2) Simple Cross-sectional Regression Analyses

First, the simple cross-sectional regression analyses are performed, with the expectation of a significant difference in the impact of the ICT industry's development between the cross-sectional and over time dimensions. The years chosen for analyses are 1996 and 2005, which have relatively few missing values and can represent the 1990s and the 2000s respectively. The equation is as follows:

---

39 The Breusch and Pagan Lagrangian multiplier test is used to observe contemporaneous correlation. However, it is impossible to conduct the test due to the missing values. Contemporaneous correlation usually appears in comparative analyses across countries, so it is taken for granted that it will be utilised in studies. This assumption is understandable because the existence of contemporaneous correlation does not influence the results as does the estimated coefficient and causal significance.

$$PSE_{it} = \alpha + \beta 1X1_{it} + \beta 2X2_{it} + \cdots + e_{it}$$

(PSE: Public Social Expenditure, x1, x2, ... : Variables related to the ICT industry and previously discussed relevant variables related to the development of the welfare state, i: country, t: time, e: residuals)

The following two tables present the results of cross-sectional regressions for public social spending. [40] In 1996 (see Table 5.3), there are no significant variables related to the ICT industry's development, as shown in the results.

<Table 5.3> Results of Simple Cross-sectional Regression Analyses for Year 1996

	Simple Cross-sectional Analysis for Public Social Expenditure: 1996				
	1 INVESTMENT Modell	2 STAFF Modell	3 IMPORT Modell	4 EXPORT Modell	5 INFO-OPENNESS Modell
Dependent Variable			Public Social Expenditure		
			Independent Variables		
Investment	-1.339 (-4.385)				
Staff		1.724 (-6.883)			
Import			5.988 (-10.12)		
Export				1.562 (-2.134)	
Information openness					1.791 (-2.101)
			Control Variables		
GDP per capita	4.379* (-2.278)	4.576** (-2.071)	5.445** (-2.332)	4.613** (-1.976)	4.816** (-1.965)
Economic openness	0.0253 (-0.0411)	0.025 (-0.0412)	0.00901 (-0.0493)	0.0185 (-0.0417)	0.0126 (-0.0432)
Urban population rates	0.0425 (-0.118)	0.0361 (-0.118)	0.0153 (-0.123)	0.0239 (-0.118)	0.0152 (-0.119)
Civil liberties	-1.061 (-1.815)	-0.753 (-1.733)	-0.506 (-1.774)	-0.706 (-1.678)	-0.58 (-1.689)
Trade unemployment rates	0.718** (-0.276)	0.728** (-0.271)	0.742** (-0.264)	0.669** (-0.281)	0.659** (-0.279)
Constant	-31.28 (-26.04)	-35.04 (-22.02)	-42.57 (-24.77)	-33.37 (-21.87)	-35.14 (-21.57)
Observations	27	27	27	27	27
R-squared	0.547	0.547	0.553	0.557	0.561
Standard errors in parentheses					
*** p<0.01, ** p<0.05, * p<0.1					

40 In the case of the simple cross-sectional regressions of year 1996, Estonia, Hungary, Iceland, Israel, Luxembourg, Slovakia, and Slovenia are excluded due to missing values, so only 27 countries are utilised in the analyses. In the case of the simple cross-sectional regressions during year 2005, only 25 countries are used in the analysis for INVESTMENT Model 2, excluding Chile, Finland, Ireland, Israel, the Netherlands, Norway, Slovenia, the United Kingdom, and the United States. In the analysis of STAFF Model 2, only 28 countries are included, while Ireland, Israel, the Netherlands, Norway, Poland, and the United States are excluded.

However, in 2005 (see Table 5.4), investment shows a strong negative significance, with an estimated coefficient of –20.69 and 99% probability (*** $p < 0.01$). Conversely, import and information openness show a positive significance, with an estimated coefficient of +6.113 (** $p < 0.05$) and of +0.830 (** $p < 0.1$), respectively. The other two variables (staff and export) do not show significant results.

<Table 5.4> **Results of Simple Cross-sectional Regression Analyses for Year 2005**

	Simple Cross-sectional Analysis for Public Social Expenditure:				
	1 INVESTMENT Model2	2 STAFF Model2	3 IMPORT	4 EXPORT Model2	5 INFO-OPENNESS Model2
Dependent Variable			Public Social		
			Independent		
Investment	-20.69*** (-6.257)				
Staff		-9.667 (-5.758)			
Import			6.113** (-2.684)		
Export				0.859 (-0.537)	
Information openness					0.830* (-0.465)
			Control		
GDP per capita	5.407*** (-1.599)	8.371*** (-1.785)	6.848*** (-1.396)	6.654*** (-1.458)	6.739*** (-1.447)
Economic openness	-0.0238 (-0.0145)	-0.00257 (-0.0158)	-0.0307* (-0.0176)	-0.0119 (-0.015)	-0.0151 (-0.0153)
Urban population rates	-0.0817 (-0.0898)	-0.0951 (-0.0826)	-0.0582 (-0.0673)	-0.0536 (-0.0702)	-0.0556 (-0.0695)
Civil liberties	-5.902*** (-1.769)	-4.071** (-1.878)	-2.338 (-1.718)	-3.298* (-1.71)	-3.140* (-1.701)
Trade unemployment rates	0.772*** (-0.26)	0.805** (-0.322)	0.894*** (-0.249)	0.915*** (-0.261)	0.917*** (-0.259)
Constant	-15.46 (-18.22)	-53.54*** (-18.38)	-49.88*** (-16.01)	-45.86*** (-16.49)	-46.99*** (-16.39)
Observations	25	28	34	34	34
R-squared	0.77	0.676	0.647	0.616	0.624
Standard errors in parentheses					
*** p<0.01, ** p<0.05, * p<0.1					

3) Panel-corrected Standard Errors (PCSE) Model Analyses

If the pooled TSCS data violates the basic assumptions of OLS (as aforementioned, it does in this case), many students suggest using the PCSE model (in the case of existing heteroscedasticity and contemporaneous correlation), including a lagged dependent variable (in the case of existing autocorrelation), and including country dummy and time dummy (in the case of an existing fix effect in unobserved variables). In the analyses of this study, the basic model is established using the PCSE model absent a lagged dependent variable, country dummy and time dummy according to Pluemper et al's suggestion. Next, a comparison model is established using the PCSE model, which includes a lagged dependent variable, country dummy and time dummy, according to Beck & Katz's suggestion. The basic model and comparison model can be affirmed as follows:

Pluemper's model (Basic model): $PSE_{it} = \alpha + \beta 1X1_{it} + \beta 2X2_{it} + \cdots + e_{it}$

Beck & Katz's model (Comparison model):

$$PSE_{it} = \alpha + \beta 0PSE_{it-5} + \beta 1X1_{it} + \cdots + \sum \beta_i\, countrydummy_{it} + \sum \beta_{ik}\, timedummy_{kit} + e_{it}$$

(PSE: Public Social Expenditure, x1, x2, ... : Variables related to the ICT industry and previously discussed relevant variables related to the development of the welfare state, i: country, t: time, e: residuals)

When analysing the basic model and comparison model, three periods of time are represented: The entire period (from 1985 to 2010), the period before year 2000, and the period after year 2000. There are several reasons for these divisions of the analysis period. First, several countries, recognised as ICT powerhouses have been at the frontier of the development of the ICT industry because of Internet usage and the encouragement thereof since the 1990s. However, studies of the positive correlations between economic growth and ICT development indicate that most OECD countries have been investing in the ICT industry in earnest since the 2000s (Vu, 2009, p. 3, 31-33; Colecchia & Schreye, 2001, p.3). Second, although there has been significant international interest in the e-government since the mid-1990s, this focus greatly increased internationally and domestically as the world moved into the 2000s. During this time, most OECD countries redoubled efforts to improve digital services and its usage in the public arena (OECD, 2009, p.3). Therefore, in all regression results, Model 1 indicates the results of the entire period, Model 2 indicates the results of pre-2000 and Model 3 indicates the results of post-2000.

As seen in Table 5.5 below, investment only shows a significant result in the Beck & Katz model. Investment Model 5 (pre-2000), with an estimated coefficient of 0.862 and 99% probability (***p<0.01), reveals a positive relationship between public social expenditure and investment in telecommunication equipment. However, there is no significant relationship between public social expenditure and investment in other periods and models. In the case of staff (see Table 5.6), only during the same period (pre-2000) of the Beck & Katz model can a significant negative relationship between public social expenditure and ICT staff be seen, with an estimated coefficient of - 3.871 and 99% probability (***p<0.01). Looking at import and export in ICT, export shows negative significance in the same period (pre-2000) of the Beck & Katz model, while import does not show any significance. The estimated coefficient is - 0.352 and 95% probability (**p<0.05). However, the relationship between pubic social expenditure and information openness shows weak negative significance in period pre-2000 (with an estimated coefficient of - 0.289 and 95% probability (**p<0.05)) as well as post-2000 (with an estimated coefficient of - 0.138 and 90% probability (*p<0.1)) in the Beck & Katz model.

<Table 5.5> Results of PCSE Model Analyses for Investment

	Pluemper Model			Beck & Katz Model		
	1	2	3	4	5	6
	INVESTMENT Model1	INVESTMENT Model2	INVESTMENT Model3	INVESTMENT Model4	INVESTMENT Model5	INVESTMENT Model6
Dependent Variable	Public Social Expenditure					
	Independent Variables					
Public social expenditure (5 lagged level)				0.159***	-0.118	-0.0385
				(-0.0511)	(-0.0975)	(-0.0494)
Investment	0.222	-0.347	0.0251	0.257	0.862***	0.0631
	(-0.335)	(-0.966)	(-0.508)	(-0.192)	(-0.325)	(-0.196)
	Control Variables					
GDP per capita	2.731***	1.607*	2.911***	-0.234	0.199	-1.133
	(-0.432)	(-0.931)	(-0.541)	(-0.525)	(-0.84)	(-0.81)
Corruption Perception Index	0.300*	0.640**	0.369	-0.0033	0.00587	0.0945
	(-0.178)	(-0.3)	(-0.239)	(-0.117)	(-0.142)	(-0.15)
Urban population rates	-0.0915***	-0.0432	-0.0976**	0.184***	0.125	0.154**
	(-0.0294)	(-0.0475)	(-0.0397)	(-0.0575)	(-0.238)	(-0.0725)
Political rights	-1.869***	3.533***	2.261***	0.0109	-0.0121	0.383
	(-0.453)	(-0.925)	(-0.796)	(-0.313)	(-0.521)	(-0.656)
Civil liberties	0.0226	1.473**	0.0597	0.320*	1.296*	0.496***
	(-0.323)	(-0.724)	(-0.44)	(-0.167)	(-0.776)	(-0.168)
Trade union density	0.0964***	0.0984***	0.0828***	0.0754***	-0.0218	0.127***
	(-0.0154)	(-0.0269)	(-0.018)	(-0.0239)	(-0.0517)	(0.0258)
Total unemployment rates	0.473***	0.527***	0.561***	0.187***	0.378***	0.0962**
	(-0.0665)	(-0.132)	(-0.0858)	(-0.0382)	(-0.057)	(-0.0413)
Economic openness	-0.00363	0.00571	-0.00526	-0.0268***	-0.022	-0.0211**
	(-0.00458)	(-0.00943)	(-0.00508)	(-0.00706)	(-0.0162)	(-0.00876)
Constant	-6.852	3.092	6.916	-0.961		12.65
	(-4.488)	(-9.764)	(-5.691)	(-9.373)		(-14.17)
Observations	355	116	239	338	112	226
R-squared	0.823	0.785	0.814	0.979	0.995	0.987
Number of country	33	32	33	33	29	32
Standard errors in parentheses						
*** p<0.01, ** p<0.05, * p<0.1						

<Table 5.6> Results of PCSE Model Analyses for Staff

	Pluemper Model			Beck & Katz Model		
	1 STAFF Model1	2 STAFF Model2	3 STAFF Model3	4 STAFF Model4	5 STAFF Model5	6 STAFF Model6
Dependent Variable	Public Social Expenditure					
	Independent Variables					
Public social expenditure				0.137***	-0.12	-0.053
(5 lagged level)				(-0.0497)	(-0.0921)	(-0.0493)
Staff	0.0589	-3.123	0.0476	0.018	-3.871***	0.0154
	(-0.0417)	(-2.263)	(-0.0393)	(-0.0191)	(-1.224)	(-0.0133)
	Control Variables					
GDP per capita	2.601***	1.811**	2.786***	-0.169	0.188	-0.71
	(-0.4)	(-0.817)	(-0.478)	(-0.509)	(-0.778)	(-0.753)
Corruption Perception Index	0.316*	0.736**	0.386*	-0.0238	0.0173	0.135
	(-0.168)	(-0.309)	(-0.225)	(-0.117)	(-0.129)	(-0.157)
Urban population rates	-0.105***	-0.0459	-0.101***	0.189***	0.339*	0.170**
	(-0.0277)	(-0.0457)	(-0.0339)	(-0.0603)	(-0.193)	(-0.0722)
Political rights	-2.216***	-3.529***	-3.951***	0.0396	0.16	0.477
	(-0.453)	(-0.844)	(-0.773)	(-0.345)	(-0.295)	(-0.679)
Civil liberties	0.032	1.445*	0.156	0.358**	1.460**	0.545***
	(-0.305)	(-0.743)	(-0.392)	(-0.17)	(-0.597)	(-0.177)
Trade union density	0.0860***	0.106***	0.0704***	0.0818***	0.0385	0.123***
	(-0.0166)	(-0.027)	(-0.0191)	(-0.0235)	(-0.0566)	(-0.025)
Total unemployment rates	0.462***	0.551***	0.540***	0.177***	0.326***	0.133***
	(-0.0586)	(-0.122)	(-0.075)	(-0.0354)	(-0.0496)	(-0.0364)
Economic openness	-0.00156	0.00532	-0.00365	-0.0273***	-0.0221	-0.0246***
	(-0.00419)	(-0.00943)	(-0.00442)	(-0.00718)	(-0.0187)	(-0.00867)
Constant	-3.952	-4.5	-4.627	-1.323		6.833
	(-4.039)	(-7.812)	(-4.892)	(-9.369)		(-13.39)
Observations	362	116	246	345	112	233
R-squared	0.824	0.783	0.819	0.978	0.995	0.986
Number of country	33	32	33	33	29	32
Standard errors in parentheses						
*** p<0.01, ** p<0.05, * p<0.1						

<Table 5.7> Results of PCSE Model Analyses for Import

	Pluemper Model			Beck & Katz Model		
	1 IMPORT Model1	2 IMPORT Model2	3 IMPORT Model3	4 IMPORT Model4	5 IMPORT Model5	6 IMPORT Model6
Dependent Variable	Public Social Expenditure					
	Independent Variables					
Public social expenditure				0.169***	-0.138	-0.00968
(5 lagged level)				(-0.0445)	(-0.0993)	(-0.0504)
Import	0.231	1.377	0.131	-0.141	0.0106	-0.306
	(-0.262)	(-1.746)	(-0.333)	(-0.208)	(-0.396)	(-0.198)
	Control Variables					
GDP per capita	2.552***	1.964**	2.611***	-0.820*	0.379	-2.055***
	(-0.394)	(-0.877)	(-0.48)	(-0.499)	(-0.96)	(-0.617)
Corruption Perception Index	0.342**	0.578*	0.422**	0.00694	0.0606	0.271*
	(-0.158)	(-0.313)	(-0.213)	(-0.115)	(-0.141)	(-0.154)
Urban population rates	-0.0948***	-0.0468	-0.0901***	0.119**	0.191	0.0793
	(-0.0265)	(-0.0468)	(-0.0325)	(-0.0494)	(-0.242)	(-0.0535)
Political rights	-1.862***	-3.323***	-3.377***	-0.0228	0.1	0.445
	(-0.425)	(-0.831)	(-0.784)	(-0.298)	(-0.479)	(-0.563)
Civil liberties	0.0814	1.444**	0.0885	0.267*	1.319*	0.432***
	(-0.288)	(-0.729)	(-0.366)	(-0.158)	(-0.71)	(-0.159)
Trade union density	0.0921***	0.0982***	0.0733***	0.0561**	0.0357	0.0974***
	(-0.0151)	(-0.027)	(-0.017)	(-0.0237)	(-0.0602)	(-0.0238)
Total unemployment rates	0.432***	0.563***	0.512***	0.170***	0.374***	0.122***
	(-0.0572)	(-0.12)	(-0.0738)	(-0.0353)	(-0.0576)	(-0.0385)
Economic openness	-0.00334	-0.00132	-0.00496	-0.0361***	-0.00624	-0.0346***
	(-0.00444)	(-0.0129)	(-0.00458)	(-0.00841)	(-0.0258)	(-0.00867)
Constant	-4.863	-6.834	-4.348	12.18	-7.85	
	(-3.993)	(-8.216)	(-4.9)	(-8.594)	(-21.2)	
Observations	397	113	284	380	109	271
R-squared	0.797	0.793	0.789	0.972	0.995	0.981
Number of country	33	32	33	33	29	32
Standard errors in parentheses						
*** p<0.01, ** p<0.05, * p<0.1						

<Table 5.8> Results of PCSE Model Analyses for Export

	Pluemper Model			Beck & Katz Model		
	1 EXPORT Model1	2 EXPORT Model2	3 EXPORT Model3	4 EXPORT Model4	5 EXPORT Model5	6 EXPORT Model6
Dependent Variable	Public Social Expenditure					
	Independent Variables					
Public social expenditure				0.188***	-0.169*	0.0162
(5 lagged level)				(-0.045)	(-0.0882)	(-0.0514)
Export	-0.00055	-0.112	-0.0258	-0.176	-0.352**	-0.182
	(-0.0875)	(-0.302)	(-0.121)	(-0.108)	(-0.139)	(-0.117)
	Control Variables					
GDP per capita	2.309***	1.572*	2.509***	-0.77	0.0732	-1.922***
	(-0.392)	(-0.832)	(-0.477)	(-0.499)	(-0.918)	(-0.602)
Corruption Perception Index	0.374**	0.647**	0.438**	0.00902	0.0292	0.287*
	(-0.16)	(-0.313)	(-0.214)	(-0.116)	(-0.128)	(-0.154)
Urban population rates	-0.0982***	-0.0471	-0.0903***	0.123**	0.106	0.0762
	(-0.0269)	(-0.0493)	(-0.0324)	(-0.0488)	(-0.232)	(-0.0532)
Political rights	-1.964***	-3.518***	-3.324***	-0.0667	0.0148	0.41
	(-0.429)	(-0.834)	(-0.785)	(-0.304)	(-0.411)	(-0.565)
Civil liberties	0.0486	1.435*	0.104	0.266*	1.250*	0.444***
	(-0.288)	(-0.761)	(-0.357)	(-0.159)	(-0.668)	(-0.161)
Trade union density	0.0952***	0.111***	0.0742***	0.0575**	0.00321	0.102***
	(-0.0153)	(-0.0352)	(-0.0174)	(-0.0238)	(-0.0506)	(-0.0238)
Total unemployment rates	0.416***	0.519***	0.504***	0.163***	0.296***	0.127***
	(-0.0582)	(-0.127)	(-0.0736)	(-0.0352)	(-0.0514)	(-0.0376)
Economic openness	-0.00371	0.00311	-0.00399	-0.0347***	-0.00668	-0.0329***
	(-0.00435)	(-0.0105)	(-0.00446)	(-0.00846)	(-0.024)	(-0.00861)
Constant	-1.901	-2.678	-3.465	10.86		26.53***
	(-3.918)	(-7.69)	(-4.805)	(-8.593)		(-10.05)
Observations	395	111	284	378	107	271
R-squared	0.807	0.792	0.794	0.973	0.995	0.981
Number of country	33	32	33	33	29	32
Standard errors in parentheses						
*** p<0.01, ** p<0.05, * p<0.1						

<Table 5.9> Results of PCSE Model Analyses for Information Openness

	Pluemper Model			Beck & Katz Model		
	1 INFO-OPENNESS Model1	2 INFO-OPENNESS Model2	3 INFO-OPENNESS Model3	4 INFO-OPENNESS Model4	5 INFO-OPENNESS Model5	6 INFO-OPENNESS
Dependent Variable	Public Social Expenditure					
	Independent Variables					
Public social expenditure				0.184***	-0.171*	0.0102
(5 lagged level)				(-0.045)	(-0.0902)	(-
Information openness	0.0213	-0.0291	-0.00885	-0.125	-0.289**	-
	(-0.0742)	(-0.287)	(-0.1)	(-0.0799)	(-0.124)	(-
	Control Variables					
GDP per capita	2.379***	1.583*	2.522***	-0.79	0.272	-
	(-0.395)	(-0.843)	(-0.484)	(-0.499)	(-0.94)	(
Corruption Perception Index	0.359**	0.632**	0.436**	0.00504	0.0331	0.285*
	(-0.161)	(-0.318)	(-0.215)	(-0.116)	(-0.120)	(-
Urban population rates	0.102***	-0.0489	-0.0905***	0.125**	0.121	0.0773
	(-0.0267)	(-0.0492)	(-0.0325)	(-0.0489)	(-0.231)	(-
Political rights	-1.959***	-3.579***	-3.320***	-0.0524	0.0948	0.421
	(-0.429)	(-0.841)	(-0.787)	(-0.302)	(-0.399)	(-
Civil liberties	0.0677	1.496*	0.105	0.264*	1.295**	0.440***
	(-0.29)	(-0.768)	(-0.357)	(-0.159)	(-0.646)	(-
Trade union density	0.0961***	0.110***	0.0740***	0.0567**	0.0115	0.101***
	(-0.0152)	(-0.0342)	(-0.0173)	(-0.0238)	(-0.0515)	(-
Total unemployment rates	0.419***	0.514***	0.603***	0.161***	0.301***	0.122***
	(-0.0585)	(-0.128)	(-0.0733)	(-0.0353)	(-0.0516)	(-
Economic openness	-0.00352	0.0036	-0.00413	-0.0346***	0.000994	-
	(-0.00439)	(-0.0102)	(-0.00455)	(-0.00845)	(-0.0252)	(-
Constant	-2.391	-2.604	-3.551			
	(-3.949)	(-7.76)	(-4.849)			
Observations	394	110	284	377	106	271
R-squared	0.806	0.787	0.794	0.973	0.995	0.981
Number of country	33	32	33	33	29	32
Standard errors in parentheses						
*** p<0.01, ** p<0.05, * p<0.1						

4) Error Correction Model (ECM) and Vector Error Correction Model (VECM) Analyses

If a non-stationary time-series data is regressed, the resulting regression with a high R^2 may be a spurious regression. Therefore, unit root tests and co-integration tests can be performed as pre-tests, in order to avoid 'spurious regression' situations. If the dependent variable and independent variable are co-integrated, an error correction model analysis can be conducted to observe the transitory effects and long-term permanent effects (Iversen & Cusack, op. cit., p. 330). If the two series are non-stationary but co-integrated, an error correction model analysis can be performed. If more than two series are non-stationary but co-integrated, a vector error correction model can be conducted at the end (Gujaratie, 2011, p. 231, 267). The equations of these models can be shown as follows:

$$\Delta PSE_{it} = \alpha + \beta_1 \cdot PSE_{it-1} + \sum \beta^j \cdot X^j_{it-1} + \sum \beta^j_\Delta \cdot X^j_{it-1} + e_t$$

$$\Delta PSE_{it} = \alpha + \beta_1 \cdot PSE_{it-1} + \sum \beta^j \cdot X_1{}^j_{it-1} + \sum \beta^j \cdot X_2{}^j_{it-1} \dots + \sum \beta^j_\Delta \cdot X_1{}^j_{it-1} + \sum \beta^j_\Delta \cdot X_2 X^j_{it-1} \dots + e_t$$

(PSE: Public Social Expenditure, x1, x2, ... : Variables related to the ICT industry and previously discussed relevant variables related to the development of the welfare state, Δ: first difference, i: country, t: time, e: residuals)

In the above equations, parameters for lagged independent level variables (X_{t-1}) show the lasting effect of the one-off changes in those variables, while parameters for change variables (△X) measure the passing effect of the one-off changes in those variables. The long-term permanent effect of the independent variables can be calculated by dividing the parameter for the lagged level of each variable by the negative of the lagged dependent level variable ($\beta^j/-\beta_1$). If an independent variable exhibits only transitory effects; that is, if only the parameter for its first difference is different from zero, the dependent variable will eventually revert back to its original level, unless the independent variable changes continuously (Iversen & Cusack, op. cit., p. 330).

In addition, it is helpful to perform the Granger causality test in order to verify whether the independent variable is necessary to explain the dependent variable. Via this method, inappropriate variables can be excluded in the analysis model and the validity of conducting regression analyses can be confirmed in advance.[41]

First, it can be observed through graphs that the pooled time-series cross-section data has trends over time.[42] This means the data can be non-stationary and contain unit roots. The result of the Breitung unit-root test and the Im-Pesaran-Shin unit-root test show that all variables have unit roots and are non-stationary. However, when they are first differenced, these variables can also be stationary and absent unit roots. Second, the results of Westerlund's error-correction-based co-integration tests show whether there are co-integrations between the dependent variable and independent variables (Westerlund & Edgerton, 2007, p. 187).[43] This means that the relationship between the dependent variable and independent variables are linear, although all variables are non-stationary and serial correlations. Third, the results of the Granger causality test confirm the causal relationship between the dependent variable and independent variables.[44] Lastly, if heteroskedasticity is found in each

---

41 Generally, causality between X (independent variable) and Y (dependent variable), if any, must be determined externally, by appealing to some theory or via some kind of experimentation (Gujaratie, 2011, p. 270). Koop's argument also deserves a mention here: '…with time-series data we can make slightly stronger statements about causality simply by exploiting the fact that time does not run backward! That is, if event A happens before event B, then it is possible that A is causing B. However, it is not possible that B is causing A. In other words, events in the past can cause events to happen today. Future events cannot.' (Koop, 2005, p.187).

42 Please see graphs in the figures in the appendix.

43 When performing the co-integration test, the option of lag 1 is added in each analysis, because the series data are based on a series of consecutive years. The results of the Pesaran (2004) CD test show a strong cross-section independence, although the results are omitted on account of space consideration. Furthermore, as shown in the aforementioned unit-root tests, the pool time-series cross-section data has a strong serial correlation. Therefore, it is more appropriate to interpret the robust p-value via the bootstrap option.

44 For each country, the Granger causality test is conducted with first difference variables, including the option of lag 5. The results show that two-way Granger causality exists in each relationship between the dependent variable and independent variables. However, this study focuses not the impact of public social spending on ICT industry development, but on the impact of ICT industry development on public social spending. All these results are added in the appendix on account of space consideration.

pooled regression, a panel-corrected standard error model according to Beck & Katz's suggestion is employed in order to perform ECM and VECM, including country dummy in the models (Iversen & Cusack, op. cit., p. 332).[45]

As shown in Table 5.10 as follows, the results of ECM analyses show significance in all variables. Investment and import have a negative effect on public social spending in the short term, while staff has a positive effect in the short term. In the long term, staff, export, and information openness show weak negative associations with public social expenditure. The long-term permanent effect of staff is -0.22. That is, for each percentage point that staff grows, the long-term equilibrium level of public social spending declines by 0.22. The permanent effect for export is -3.57. In other words, for each percent that export declines, the long-term target equilibrium for public social expenditure increases by approximately 3.57. In the case of information openness, the long-term permanent effect of information openness is -2.21. Here, for each percentage point that staff goes up, the long-term equilibrium level of public social expenditure declines by 2.21.

In the case of VECM analyses (see Table 5.11), the results show similar phenomena to those of the ECM analysis. Most variables show a negative impact on public social expenditure in the short term and long term. Only import shows positive significance in the long term. However, according to the results, import also has a negative effect in the short term. The long-term permanent effect of staff is approximately -2.75. That is, for each percentage that staff increases, the long-term equilibrium level of public social spending declines by 2.75. The permanent effect for import is 5.22. To further clarify, for each percent import increases, the long-term target equilibrium for public social expenditure increases by approximately 5.22. In the case of export, the long-term permanent effect of export is about -2.39. The long-term permanent effect of information openness is approximately -1.59.

---

45 Estonia, Slovakia and Slovenia are not included in the ECM and VECM model analyses.

<Table 5.10> Results of ECM Analyses

	ECM with Country FE				
	1 INVESTMENT Model	2 STAFF Model	3 IMPORT Model	4 EXPORT Model	5 INFO-OPENNESS Model
Dependent Variable	△Public social expenditure				
	Independent Variables				
Public social expenditure (Lagged level)	-0.0137*** (-0.00409)	-0.0124*** (-0.00402)	-0.0148*** (-0.00443)	-0.0102*** (-0.00391)	-0.0104*** (-0.00404)
△Investment	-0.260* (-0.156)				
Investment (Lagged level)	-0.0371 (-0.0331)				
△Staff		0.190** (-0.0878)			
Staff (Lagged level)		-0.0472*** (-0.0182)			
△Import			-0.756*** (-0.221)		
Import (Lagged level)			0.00279 (-0.0369)		
△Export				-0.0893 (-0.113)	
Export (Lagged level)				-0.0365** (-0.0144)	
△Information openness					-0.129 (-0.085)
Information openness (Lagged level)					-0.0230** (-0.0114)
Constant	0.422*** (-0.0778)	0.418*** (-0.0685)	0.413*** (-0.0696)	0.342*** (-0.0651)	0.353*** (-0.0662)
Observations	775	775	775	775	775
R-squared	0.387	0.39	0.397	0.397	0.395
Number of country	31	31	31	31	31
Standard errors in parentheses *** p<0.01, ** p<0.05, * p<0.1					

<Table 5.11> Results of VECM Analyses

	VECM with Country FE				
	1 INVESTMENT Model	2 STAFF Model	3 IMPORT Model	4 EXPORT Model	5 INFO-OPENNESS Model
Dependent Variable	ΔPublic social expenditure				
	Independent Variables				
Public social expenditure (Lagged level)	-0.0158*** (-0.00567)	-0.0151** (-0.00601)	-0.0140** (-0.00545)	-0.0168*** (-0.00563)	-0.0159*** (-0.00564)
ΔInvestment	-0.372** (-0.18)				
Investment (Lagged level)	-0.0356 (-0.0376)				
ΔStaff		0.181** (-0.0809)			
Staff (Lagged level)		-0.0415** (-0.0169)			
ΔImport			-1.083*** (-0.288)		
Import (Lagged level)			0.0731* (-0.0438)		
ΔExport				0.0403 (-0.115)	
Export (Lagged level)				-0.0401** (-0.016)	
ΔInformation openness					-0.0286 (-0.0921)
Information openness (Lagged level)					-0.0253* (-0.0132)
	Control Variables				
ΔGDP per capita	0.0924 (-0.277)	0.124 (-0.268)	-0.112 (-0.281)	0.151 (-0.269)	0.176 (-0.268)
GDP per capita (Lagged level)	0.0792*** (-0.0276)	0.0764*** (-0.0284)	0.0409 (-0.0297)	0.0866*** (-0.0277)	0.0864*** (-0.0285)
ΔEconomic openness	-0.0117** (-0.00472)	-0.0122*** (-0.00462)	-0.00765* (-0.00454)	-0.0117** (-0.00465)	-0.0103** (-0.00462)
Economic openness (Lagged level)	-0.00175*** (-0.000562)	-0.00135** (-0.000538)	-0.00259*** (-0.000613)	-0.000688 (-0.000582)	-0.000942 (-0.00059)
ΔCivil liberties	0.00731 (-0.02)	0.00699 (-0.0196)	0.0117 (-0.0198)	0.00664 (-0.0199)	0.00679 (-0.02)
Civil liberties (Lagged level)	0.0322** (-0.0149)	0.0279* (-0.0147)	0.0288* (-0.015)	0.0273* (-0.0149)	0.0283* (-0.015)
ΔPolitical rights	-0.0193 (-0.022)	-0.0149 (-0.021)	-0.0179 (-0.0215)	-0.014 (-0.0217)	-0.014 (-0.0217)
Political rights (Lagged level)	-0.012 (-0.0137)	-0.0091 (-0.013)	-0.0208 (-0.0138)	-0.00969 (-0.0135)	-0.0106 (-0.0136)
Constant	-0.292 (-0.224)	-0.277 (-0.232)	0.0712 (-0.254)	-0.416* (-0.229)	-0.413* (-0.237)
Observations	775	775	775	775	775
R-squared	0.406	0.407	0.416	0.412	0.408
Number of country	31	31	31	31	31
Standard errors in parentheses *** p<0.01, ** p<0.05, * p<0.1					

5) First Difference Model Analyses

The first difference model analysis can detect the impact of short-term changes in independent variables on short-term changes in the dependent variable (Busemeyer, op. cit., p. 13).[46] This analysis is performed to determine the impact of short-term changes in the ICT industry on short-term changes in public social expenditure. The equation consists of

---

46 Estonia, Slovakia and Slovenia are not included in the first difference model analyses. In the case of the civil liberties variable, after the first difference, 3 were added to all values in order to perform the analysis appropriately.

first differences of all variables.

$$\Delta PSE_i = \beta_1 \Delta x_{1_i} + \beta_2 \Delta x_{2_i} \ldots + \Delta e_i$$

(PSE: Public Social Expenditure, x1, x2, ... : Variables related to the ICT industry and previously discussed relevant variables related to the development of the welfare state, Δ: first difference, i: country, e: residuals)

As shown in Table 5.12 and Table 5.13, during the period post-2000, investment shows a weak negative significance, with an estimated coefficient of -0.722 and 95% probability (**p<0.05). During the period pre-2000, export and information openness also show a weak negative relationship with public social expenditure. Interestingly, import shows a negative significance in all periods, and more negative significance in the period pre-2000, with an estimated coefficient of -4.352 and 99% probability (***p<0.01). Conversely, only staff has a weak positive short-term impact on the change of public social expenditure for the entire period, with an estimated coefficient of +0.143 and 95% probability (**p<0.05).

<Table 5.12> Results of First Difference Model Analyses 1

	First Difference Model								
	1 INVESTMENT Model1	2 INVESTMENT Model2	3 INVESTMENT Model3	4 STAFF Model1	5 STAFF Model2	6 STAFF Model3	7 IMPORT Model1	8 IMPORT Model2	9 IMPORT Model3
Dependent Variable	△Public social expenditure								
	Independent Variables								
△Investment	-0.242	-0.433	-0.722**						
	(-0.207)	(-0.334)	(-0.291)						
△Staff				0.143**	0.184	0.0407			
				(-0.0705)	(-0.804)	(-0.0671)			
△Import							-0.535**	-4.352***	-0.601**
							(-0.226)	(-0.645)	(-0.277)
	Control Variables								
△GDP per capita	0.211	0.404	0.207	0.366	0.331	0.639*	0.217	0.769*	0.545
	(-0.276)	(-0.429)	(-0.371)	(-0.273)	(-0.428)	(-0.347)	(-0.27)	(-0.411)	(-0.338)
△Economic openness	-0.0162***	-0.0213***	-0.0104*	-0.0160***	-0.0211***	-0.00759	-0.0134***	0.0118*	-0.00861
	(-0.00404)	(-0.00531)	(-0.00605)	(-0.00401)	(-0.00534)	(-0.006)	(-0.0041)	(-0.00701)	(-0.00597)
△Corruption Perception Index	0.206	-0.0853	0.28	0.215	-0.0313	0.358*	0.247*	0.0882	0.382**
	(-0.15)	(-0.222)	(-0.192)	(-0.147)	(-0.219)	(-0.191)	(-0.146)	(-0.209)	(-0.189)
△Urban population rates	0.0556**	-0.0301	0.200***	0.0432*	-0.023	0.193***	0.0590***	-0.0269	0.208***
	(-0.0227)	(-0.0311)	(-0.0337)	(-0.0237)	(-0.0308)	(-0.0378)	(-0.0226)	(-0.0291)	(-0.0339)
△Civil liberties	-0.0122	-0.0183	-0.0124	-0.0103	-0.0114	-0.00939	0.00847	0.00941	0.0156
	(-0.0221)	(-0.0276)	(-0.0383)	(-0.022)	(-0.0273)	(-0.0386)	(-0.0219)	(-0.0261)	(-0.0384)
Constant	0.150**	0.205**	0.0783	0.140**	0.183**	0.0566	0.141**	0.175**	0.0727
	(-0.069)	(-0.0858)	(-0.119)	(-0.0683)	(-0.0844)	(-0.119)	(-0.0682)	(-0.0802)	(-0.119)
Observations	775	434	341	775	434	341	775	434	341
R-squared	0.039	0.043	0.149	0.043	0.039	0.135	0.045	0.132	0.146
Number of country	31	31	31	31	31	31	31	31	31
Standard errors in parentheses *** p<0.01, ** p<0.05, * p<0.1									

<Table 5.13> Results of First Difference Model Analyses 2

	First Difference Model					
	10 EXPORT Model1	11 EXPORT Model2	12 EXPORT Model3	13 INFO-OPENNESS Model1	14 INFO-OPENNESS Model2	15 INFO-OPENNESS Model3
Dependent Variable	△Public social expenditure					
	Independent Variables					
△Export	-0.0805	-0.500***	0.0485			
	(-0.0818)	(-0.141)	(-0.0961)			
△Info-openness				-0.0969	-0.579***	-0.0141
				(-0.0653)	(-0.127)	(-0.0757)
	Control Variables					
△GDP per capita	0.292	0.306	0.562	0.285	0.378	0.605*
	(-0.27)	(-0.421)	(-0.346)	(-0.27)	(-0.417)	(-0.343)
△Economic openness	-0.0143***	-0.0119**	-0.00771	-0.0137***	-0.00615	-0.0072
	(-0.00421)	(-0.00584)	(-0.00604)	(-0.00421)	(-0.00614)	(-0.006)
△Corruption Perception Index	0.261*	0.0321	0.361*	0.264*	0.0621	0.374*
	(-0.147)	(-0.217)	(-0.191)	(-0.147)	(-0.215)	(-0.191)
△Urban population rates	0.0586***	-0.0203	0.200***	0.0591***	-0.0207	0.203***
	(-0.0227)	(-0.0301)	(-0.0343)	(-0.0227)	(-0.0299)	(-0.0343)
△Civil liberties	-0.00969	-0.00978	-0.00894	-0.00946	-0.00667	-0.00954
	(-0.022)	(-0.0268)	(-0.0386)	(-0.022)	(-0.0266)	(-0.0386)
Constant	0.138**	0.187**	0.0585	0.139**	0.185**	0.0563
	(-0.0684)	(-0.0832)	(-0.119)	(-0.0683)	(-0.0824)	(-0.119)
Observations	775	434	341	775	434	341
R-squared	0.039	0.066	0.134	0.04	0.083	0.134
Number of country	31	31	31	31	31	31
Standard errors in parentheses *** p<0.01, ** p<0.05, * p<0.1						

6) Panel Vector Autoregressive (PVAR) Model Analysis

Panel vector autoregressive (PVAR) model analysis includes group heterogeneity in the equation. In other words, this analysis eliminates group heterogeneity by using the Helmert transformation process[47] and solves the autocorrelation issue by applying system GMM estimation. The PVAR model analysis shows the response of one variable to another variable's shock.[48] Therefore, public social expenditure's response to change in ICT industry variables can be shown in the short term. The model can be affirmed in the equation below. Because pooled time-series cross-section data is non-stationary, first differences of all variables are used in the analysis.

47 Helmert transformation is also referred to as 'forward mean-difference'..

48 According to the results of the AIC (Akaike Information Criterion), the BIC (Bayesian Information Criteria), and the HQIC (Hannan and Quinn Information Criterion), the option of lag 3 is added in each analysis. Estonia, Slovakia and Slovenia are not included in the first difference model analyses. In the case of the civil liberties variable, after the first difference, 3 were added to all values in order to perform the analysis appropriately.

$$\Delta PSE_{it} = \alpha + \beta_1 \Delta PSE_{it-1} + \beta_2 \Delta PSE_{it-2} + \cdots + \beta_p \Delta PSE_{it-n} + \beta_1 \Delta X_{1_{it-1}} + \beta_2 \Delta X_{1_{it-2}} + \cdots + \beta_p \Delta X_{1_{it-n}} + \cdots + \beta_1 \Delta X_{2_{it-1}} + \beta_2 \Delta X_{2_{it-2}} + \cdots + \beta_p \Delta X_{2_{it-n}} + \mu_i + e_i$$

(PSE: Public Social Expenditure, x1, x2, ... : Variables related to the ICT industry and previously discussed relevant variables related to the development of the welfare state, Δ: first difference, i: country, t: time, p: lag, μ: group heterogeneity, e: residuals)

The following tables and figures show the results of the PVAR analyses. Specifically, in each of the figures, a highlighted arrow indicates three integral graph lines which shed light on the essence of this study. The pre-coded PVAR program shows the response of public social expenditure to ICT industry variables' shock; starting from the first point in time to the next six points in time. The figures are drawn according to the results of orthogonalized IRF (Impulse Response Function) through the Monte Carlo loop. Each figure showing relationships between a dependent variable and independent variables consists of three graphs based on a confidence interval of 95% between the lower graph line and the upper graph line. The middle graph line can be interpreted as impulse-response function at the end.

Looking at the case of investment (see Table 5.14), the results show a change from a decreasing effect (-0.0013) to an increasing effect (-0.0009) at the fourth point in time (see the highlighted part of Table 5.14). This change can be better observed through the aforementioned integral graph lines under the arrow in Figure 5.1. Therefore, it can be said that the response of public social expenditure to investment's shock is negative and every negative shock effect is maintained strongly for up to four years, after which the effect becomes progressively and weaker.

In the case of staff, the response of public social expenditure to staff's shock is not certain or constant. As shown in Table 5.15, the negative effect and positive effect alternate every two years. However, the values of the negative effects are much higher than those of the positive effects up until the fifth year. These alternations continue until the sixth year, when the positive effect becomes stronger, with the value of 0.1172. The converse impact staff has on public social expenditure is clear from the graph lines under the arrow in Figure 5.2, which is repeated and ends with positive effect.

Taking a look at import (see Table 5.16), the response of public social expenditure to import's shock is negative. With time, this negative effect becomes a little stronger (from -0.0004 to -0.0032). These results are shown in Figure 5.3 below. The middle graph line of the figure drops sharply from the first point to the fifth point, after which it remains stable until the sixth point. Next, export also shows negative effects (see Table 5.17 and Figure 5.5). The negative response of public social expenditure to export's shock is stronger with time. Similarly, in the case of information openness, the results show negative effects over time (see Table 5.18 and Figure 5.6).

<Table 5.14> Results of Panel Vector Autoregressive Model Analyses for Investment

Impulse-responses of variable in varname to the shock in column variable								
	△Investment							
Variables	Shock	Order	△Public social expenditure	△GDP per capita	△Economic openness	△Political rights	△Civil liberties	△Investment
△Public social expenditure	0	1	0.0130	0.0000	0.0000	0.0000	0.0000	0.0000
	1	1	0.0192	-0.0005	-0.0030	-0.0011	-0.0009	0.0000
	2	1	0.0246	-0.0004	-0.0053	-0.0028	-0.0018	-0.0006
	3	1	0.0270	-0.0011	-0.0075	-0.0053	-0.0029	-0.0011
	4	1	0.0274	-0.0017	-0.0087	-0.0068	-0.0035	-0.0013
	5	1	0.0260	-0.0025	-0.0092	-0.0073	-0.0036	-0.0009
	6	1	0.0231	-0.0035	-0.0086	-0.0070	-0.0033	-0.0002
△GDP per capita	0	2	0.0011	0.0033	0.0000	0.0000	0.0000	0.0000
	1	2	0.0013	0.0040	-0.0002	-0.0009	-0.0006	-0.0002
	2	2	0.0015	0.0046	-0.0002	-0.0016	-0.0011	-0.0006
	3	2	0.0013	0.0043	0.0000	-0.0021	-0.0015	-0.0009
	4	2	0.0011	0.0036	0.0003	-0.0016	-0.0012	-0.0010
	5	2	0.0007	0.0026	0.0006	-0.001	-0.0009	-0.0010
	6	2	0.0003	0.0013	0.0011	-0.0003	-0.0005	-0.0008
△Economic openness	0	3	0.0080	-0.0809	0.2699	0.0000	0.0000	0.0000
	1	3	0.0101	-0.1009	0.4495	0.1149	0.0598	0.0243
	2	3	0.0201	-0.0880	0.5338	0.2306	0.1312	0.0408
	3	3	0.0241	-0.0599	0.5395	0.3325	0.1865	0.0407
	4	3	0.0212	-0.0354	0.4980	0.3288	0.1735	0.0250
	5	3	0.0161	-0.0108	0.4302	0.2778	0.1423	0.0058
	6	3	0.0109	0.0188	0.3283	0.2243	0.1152	-0.0065
△Political rights	0	4	0.0111	0.0554	-0.0680	0.2964	0.0000	0.0000
	1	4	-0.0014	-0.0185	-0.0292	-0.0628	-0.0339	-0.0274
	2	4	-0.0203	-0.0380	0.0190	-0.0935	-0.0436	-0.0287
	3	4	-0.0053	-0.0055	0.0141	-0.0287	-0.0041	-0.0092
	4	4	0.0004	0.0153	-0.0183	0.0625	0.0386	0.0026
	5	4	-0.0005	0.0124	-0.0295	0.0368	0.0107	-0.0016
	6	4	-0.0039	-0.0015	-0.0081	-0.0230	-0.0218	-0.0074
△Civil liberties	0	5	0.0031	0.0010	-0.0122	0.1174	0.2782	0.0000
	1	5	-0.0267	-0.0114	-0.0630	0.0116	-0.0646	-0.0107
	2	5	0.0033	-0.0079	0.0278	-0.0351	-0.0433	-0.0221
	3	5	-0.0116	-0.0154	0.0147	-0.0358	-0.0111	-0.0060
	4	5	-0.0005	0.0105	-0.0044	0.0227	0.0215	0.0016
	5	5	-0.0012	0.0123	-0.0234	0.0314	0.0147	0.0026
	6	5	-0.0018	0.0063	-0.0178	-0.0054	-0.0097	-0.0020
△Investment	0	6	-0.0001	-0.0001	-0.0002	-0.0003	0.0000	0.0029
	1	6	-0.0001	-0.0004	0.0003	-0.0013	-0.0001	0.0052
	2	6	-0.0001	-0.0006	0.0012	-0.0022	-0.0001	0.0068
	3	6	0.0001	-0.0005	0.0020	-0.0030	0.0000	0.0078
	4	6	0.0003	-0.0001	0.0025	-0.0029	0.0003	0.0081
	5	6	0.0006	0.0004	0.0026	-0.0027	0.0004	0.0077
	6	6	0.0008	0.0008	0.0026	-0.0025	0.0004	0.0067

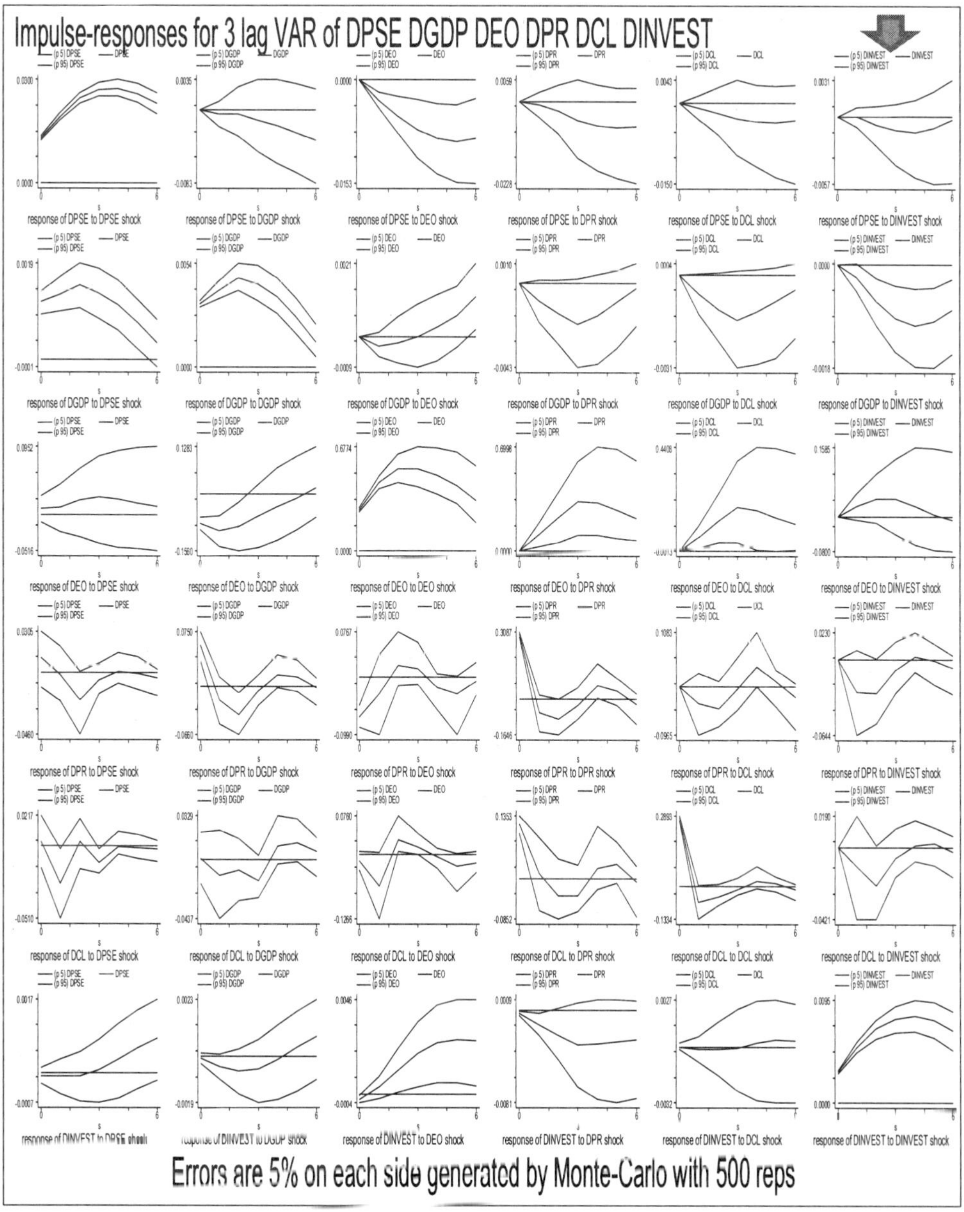

* DPSE: △Public Social Expenditure, DGDP: △GDP per Capita, DEO: △Economic Openness, DPR: △Political Rights, DCL: △Civil Liberties, DINVEST: △Investment.

<Figure 5.9> Graphs of Panel Vector Autoregressive Model Analyses for Investment

<Table 5.15> Results of Panel Vector Autoregressive Model Analyses for Staff

Impulse-responses of variable in varname to the shock in column variable								
	△Staff							
Variables	Shock	Order	△Public social expenditure	△GDP per capita	△Economic openness	△Political rights	△Civil liberties	△Staff
△Public social expenditure	0	1	0.0213	0.0000	0.0000	0.0000	0.0000	0.0000
	1	1	-0.0003	-0.0061	0.0093	-0.0143	-0.0060	-0.0176
	2	1	0.0447	0.0005	-0.0055	-0.0005	-0.0001	0.0014
	3	1	-0.0321	-0.0136	0.0220	-0.0357	-0.0127	-0.0426
	4	1	0.1028	0.0110	-0.0274	0.0253	0.0137	0.0263
	5	1	-0.1319	-0.0314	0.0555	-0.0780	-0.0292	-0.0964
	6	1	0.2699	0.0412	-0.0893	0.1041	0.0468	0.1172
△GDP per capita	0	2	0.0027	0.0035	0.0000	0.0000	0.0000	0.0000
	1	2	0.0022	0.0039	0.0003	-0.0017	-0.0011	-0.0001
	2	2	0.0020	0.0044	0.0007	-0.0026	-0.0017	-0.0002
	3	2	0.0012	0.0040	0.0011	-0.0033	-0.0020	-0.0003
	4	2	0.0010	0.0037	0.0014	-0.0022	-0.0012	-0.0004
	5	2	0.0011	0.0028	0.0016	-0.0011	-0.0007	0.0000
	6	2	-0.0005	0.0015	0.0025	-0.0007	-0.0004	-0.0004
△Economic openness	0	3	-0.1463	-0.0799	0.2783	0.0000	0.0000	0.0000
	1	3	-0.1953	-0.0676	0.4616	0.1439	0.0835	-0.0192
	2	3	-0.0898	-0.0143	0.5237	0.3116	0.1812	0.0113
	3	3	-0.1349	0.0138	0.5727	0.3826	0.2199	-0.0474
	4	3	0.0869	0.0642	0.4738	0.4344	0.2089	0.0742
	5	3	-0.2771	0.0084	0.5598	0.1897	0.0918	-0.1079
	6	3	0.4002	0.1452	0.2403	0.4096	0.1827	0.2418
△Political rights	0	4	0.1993	0.0866	-0.0910	0.3136	0.0000	0.0000
	1	4	-0.0266	-0.0503	-0.0119	-0.1121	-0.0759	0.0209
	2	4	-0.1816	-0.0697	0.0549	-0.1453	-0.0673	-0.0378
	3	4	0.1218	0.0222	-0.0370	0.0261	0.0301	0.0812
	4	4	-0.1964	-0.0057	0.0683	-0.0009	0.0386	-0.1444
	5	4	0.5113	0.1013	-0.2043	0.2507	0.0903	0.2505
	6	4	-0.8655	-0.1651	0.3040	-0.4229	-0.2032	-0.4367
△Civil liberties	0	5	0.0756	0.0257	-0.0236	0.1323	0.2793	0.0000
	1	5	0.0053	-0.0212	-0.0599	-0.0063	-0.0831	0.0225
	2	5	-0.0801	-0.0264	0.0486	-0.0662	-0.0584	-0.0223
	3	5	0.0197	-0.0062	-0.0014	-0.0169	0.0021	0.0368
	4	5	-0.0802	0.0058	0.0310	0.0037	0.0278	-0.0606
	5	5	0.2386	0.0557	-0.0994	0.1304	0.0546	0.1083
	6	5	-0.3564	-0.0638	0.1153	-0.1751	-0.0898	-0.1844
△Staff	0	6	0.1336	0.0112	-0.0447	0.0266	-0.0015	0.0888
	1	6	-0.1186	-0.0399	0.0474	-0.0907	-0.0564	-0.0328
	2	6	0.2371	0.0242	-0.0807	0.0577	0.0042	0.1610
	3	6	-0.4709	-0.0889	0.1735	-0.2234	-0.0939	-0.2284
	4	6	0.7500	0.1457	-0.2703	0.3580	0.1604	0.3896
	5	6	-1.3399	-0.2277	0.4734	-0.5629	-0.2252	-0.7186
	6	6	2.2960	0.4261	-0.8282	1.0553	0.4455	1.1912

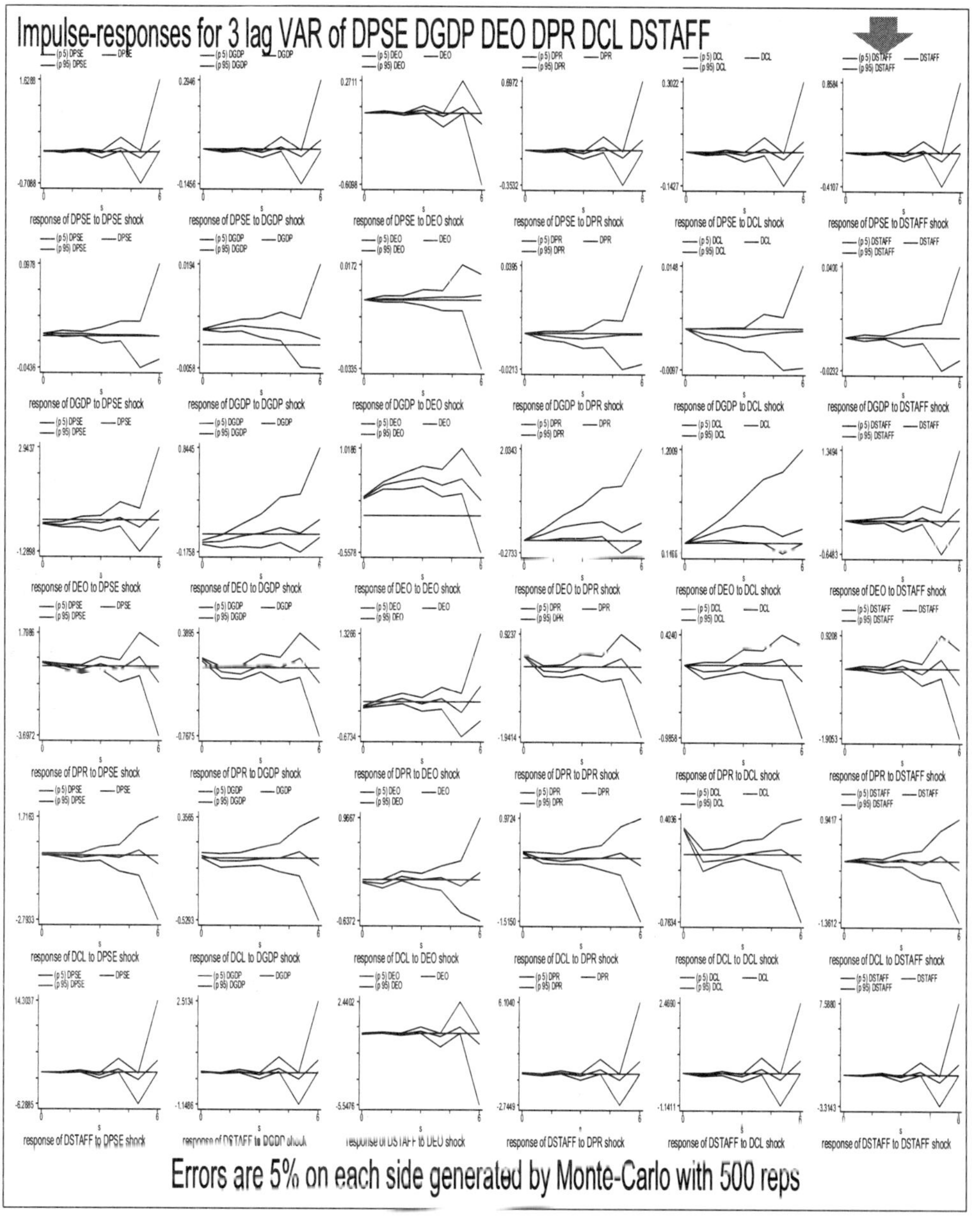

* DPSE: △Public Social Expenditure, DGDP: △GDP per Capita, DEO: △Economic Openness, DPR: △Political Rights, DCL: △Civil Liberties, DSTAFF: △Staff.

<Figure 5.10> Graphs of Panel Vector Autoregressive Model Analyses for Staff

<Table 5.16> Results of Panel Vector Autoregressive Model Analyses for Import

Impulse-responses of variable in varname to the shock in column variable

	△Import							
Variables	Shock	Order	△Public social expenditure	△GDP per capita	△Economic openness	△Political rights	△Civil liberties	△Import
△Public social expenditure	0	1	0.0159	0.0000	0.0000	0.0000	0.0000	0.0000
	1	1	0.0161	-0.0100	-0.0046	-0.0046	-0.0035	-0.0004
	2	1	0.0240	-0.0079	-0.0058	-0.0047	-0.0032	-0.0019
	3	1	0.0210	-0.0160	-0.0101	-0.0093	-0.0052	-0.0023
	4	1	0.0249	-0.0118	-0.0095	-0.0049	-0.0016	-0.0031
	5	1	0.0196	-0.0167	-0.0118	-0.0064	-0.0028	-0.0032
	6	1	0.0197	-0.0124	-0.0094	-0.0022	0.0002	-0.0032
△GDP per capita	0	2	0.0056	0.0069	0.0000	0.0000	0.0000	0.0000
	1	2	0.0023	0.0026	-0.0021	-0.0039	-0.0029	0.0002
	2	2	0.0045	0.0056	-0.0016	-0.0045	-0.0034	-0.0005
	3	2	0.0009	0.0010	-0.0031	-0.0076	-0.0051	-0.0003
	4	2	0.0030	0.0039	-0.0014	-0.0042	-0.0024	-0.0006
	5	2	-0.0003	-0.0001	-0.0023	-0.0046	-0.0030	-0.0005
	6	2	0.0007	0.0013	-0.0006	-0.0015	-0.0009	-0.0006
△Economic openness	0	3	0.2046	0.2086	0.2373	0.0000	0.0000	0.0000
	1	3	0.0620	0.0047	0.3279	-0.1321	-0.1101	0.0696
	2	3	0.1193	0.0825	0.4439	-0.1445	-0.1204	0.0877
	3	3	-0.0122	-0.0784	0.4078	-0.2513	-0.1708	0.1196
	4	3	0.0549	0.0345	0.4142	-0.1186	-0.0593	0.1208
	5	3	-0.0615	-0.0869	0.2741	-0.1283	-0.0753	0.1161
	6	3	-0.0335	-0.0191	0.1914	-0.0195	0.0008	0.1003
△Political rights	0	4	0.1234	0.1633	0.0661	0.2718	0.0000	0.0000
	1	4	-0.0455	-0.0689	-0.0463	-0.0665	-0.0493	-0.0267
	2	4	-0.0635	-0.0656	-0.0173	-0.0717	-0.0347	-0.0091
	3	4	-0.0030	0.0004	0.0033	-0.0165	0.0096	0.0074
	4	4	0.0348	0.0477	0.0198	0.0683	0.0547	0.0070
	5	4	0.0142	0.0225	-0.0044	0.0247	0.0003	-0.0077
	6	4	-0.0085	-0.0076	-0.0115	-0.0323	-0.0324	-0.0071
△Civil liberties	0	5	0.0779	0.0918	0.0561	0.1087	0.2790	0.0000
	1	5	-0.1064	-0.1043	-0.0547	-0.0166	-0.0889	-0.0183
	2	5	0.0789	0.0979	0.0322	0.0215	-0.0049	-0.0099
	3	5	-0.1065	-0.1324	-0.0341	-0.0745	-0.0349	0.0207
	4	5	0.0929	0.1282	0.0481	0.0890	0.0693	0.0001
	5	5	-0.0651	-0.0815	-0.0406	-0.0484	-0.0407	0.0064
	6	5	0.0709	0.0969	0.0284	0.0520	0.0345	-0.0067
△Import	0	6	-0.0053	-0.0062	-0.0013	-0.0003	0.0000	0.0027
	1	6	-0.0035	-0.0034	0.0002	0.0032	0.0028	0.0043
	2	6	-0.0045	-0.0046	0.0002	0.0047	0.0042	0.0062
	3	6	-0.0019	-0.0011	0.0018	0.0076	0.0059	0.0070
	4	6	-0.0032	-0.0027	0.0011	0.0051	0.0038	0.0076
	5	6	-0.0011	-0.0001	0.0023	0.0047	0.0038	0.0077
	6	6	-0.0015	-0.0008	0.0018	0.0023	0.0023	0.0076

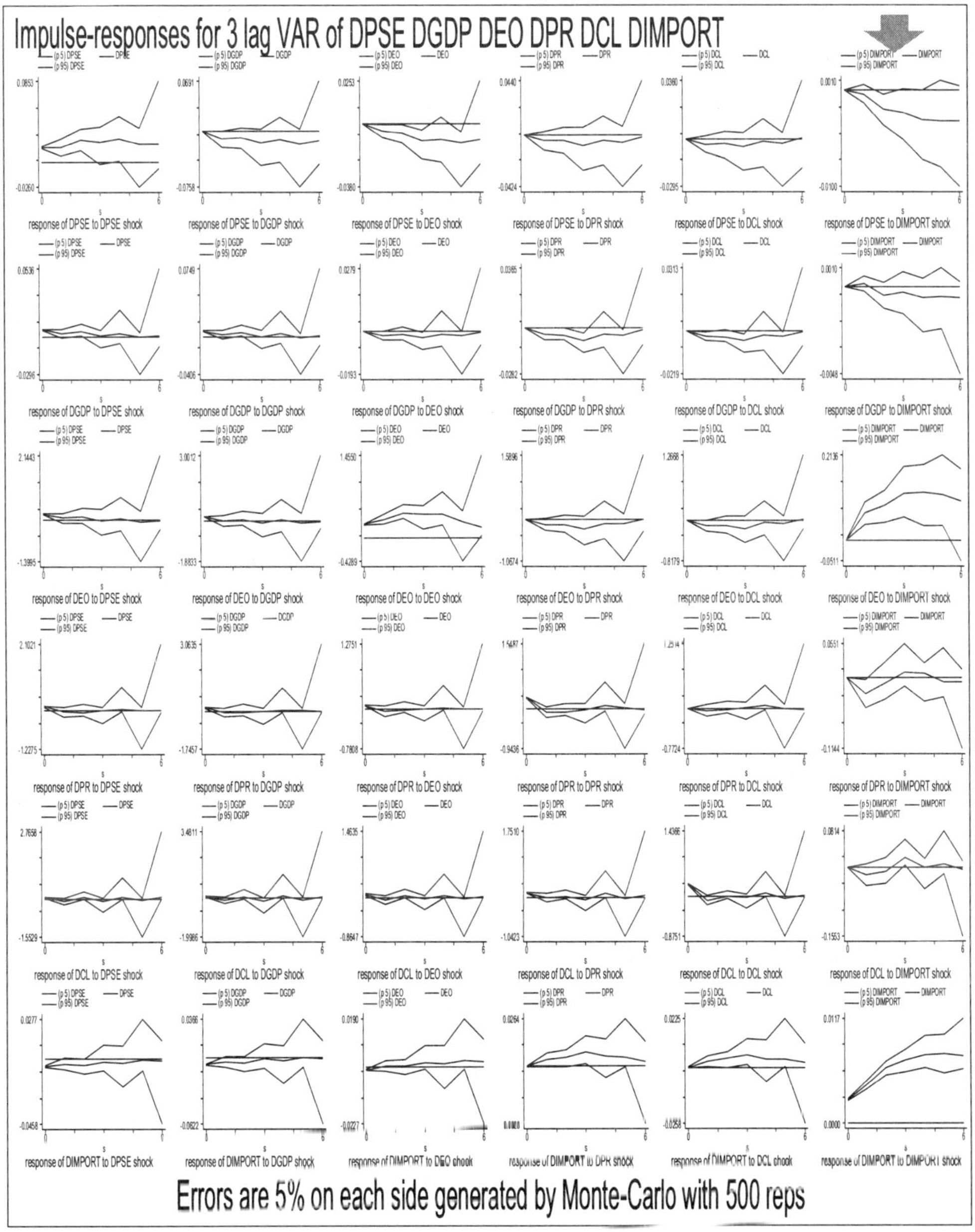

* DPSE: △Public Social Expenditure, DGDP: △GDP per Capita, DEO: △Economic Openness, DPR: △Political Rights, DCL: △Civil Liberties, DIMPORT: △Import.

<Figure 5.11> **Graphs of Panel Vector Autoregressive Model Analyses for Import**

<Table 5.17> Results of Panel Vector Autoregressive Model Analyses for Export

Impulse-responses of variable in varname to the shock in column variable

△Export

Variables	Shock	Order	△Public social expenditure	△GDP per capita	△Economic openness	△Political rights	△Civil liberties	△Export
△Public social expenditure	0	1	0.0128	0.0000	0.0000	0.0000	0.0000	0.0000
	1	1	0.0192	0.0015	-0.0026	0.0001	-0.0003	-0.0020
	2	1	0.0249	0.0025	-0.0046	-0.0010	-0.0009	-0.0037
	3	1	0.0275	0.0016	-0.0066	-0.0031	-0.0018	-0.0051
	4	1	0.0282	0.0008	-0.0078	-0.0045	-0.0024	-0.0061
	5	1	0.0270	-0.0001	-0.0081	-0.0047	-0.0022	-0.0066
	6	1	0.0243	-0.0010	-0.0075	-0.0038	-0.0015	-0.0065
△GDP per capita	0	2	0.0012	0.0058	0.0000	0.0000	0.0000	0.0000
	1	2	0.0013	0.0049	-0.0003	-0.0026	-0.0018	0.0001
	2	2	0.0015	0.0049	-0.0002	-0.0041	-0.0028	0.0002
	3	2	0.0014	0.0034	-0.0001	-0.0056	-0.0035	0.0002
	4	2	0.0013	0.0033	0.0004	-0.0042	-0.0022	0.0003
	5	2	0.0010	0.0022	0.0007	-0.0031	-0.0017	0.0002
	6	2	0.0007	0.0008	0.0013	-0.0020	-0.0011	0.0003
△Economic openness	0	3	0.0340	-0.0670	0.2218	0.0000	0.0000	0.0000
	1	3	0.0499	-0.0860	0.3965	0.0499	0.0258	0.0270
	2	3	0.0615	-0.0700	0.5001	0.0966	0.0572	0.0469
	3	3	0.0661	-0.0405	0.5358	0.1270	0.0775	0.0587
	4	3	0.0640	-0.0218	0.5113	0.1160	0.0681	0.0654
	5	3	0.0572	-0.0077	0.4443	0.0841	0.0508	0.0702
	6	3	0.0466	0.0097	0.3474	0.0534	0.0383	0.0737
△Political rights	0	4	-0.0002	0.2204	0.0019	0.3048	0.0000	0.0000
	1	4	-0.0004	-0.0945	-0.0309	-0.0982	-0.0679	-0.0078
	2	4	-0.0181	-0.1010	-0.0060	-0.0934	-0.0434	-0.0002
	3	4	-0.0021	-0.0120	0.0061	-0.0258	0.0096	0.0047
	4	4	0.0000	0.0759	0.0059	0.0943	0.0719	0.0021
	5	4	-0.0028	0.0334	-0.0141	0.0326	-0.0002	-0.0053
	6	4	-0.0021	-0.0244	-0.0061	-0.0437	-0.0423	-0.0037
△Civil liberties	0	5	0.0017	0.0519	0.0203	0.1187	0.2790	0.0000
	1	5	-0.0280	-0.0066	-0.0451	0.0158	-0.0680	-0.0144
	2	5	0.0074	-0.0157	0.0138	-0.0275	-0.0396	-0.0004
	3	5	-0.0087	-0.0468	0.0071	-0.0438	-0.0129	0.0058
	4	5	-0.0018	0.0312	0.0059	0.0291	0.0301	0.0040
	5	5	-0.0020	0.0268	-0.0071	0.0215	0.0108	-0.0006
	6	5	-0.0016	0.0119	-0.0095	-0.0007	-0.0088	-0.0024
△Export	0	6	-0.0009	-0.0061	0.0005	-0.0011	0.0002	0.0052
	1	6	-0.0017	-0.0072	0.0015	0.0017	0.0030	0.0098
	2	6	-0.0018	-0.0066	0.0029	0.0051	0.0060	0.0134
	3	6	-0.0016	-0.0048	0.0043	0.0088	0.0085	0.0158
	4	6	-0.0012	-0.0045	0.0056	0.0090	0.0083	0.0172
	5	6	-0.0005	-0.0040	0.0070	0.0082	0.0078	0.0176
	6	6	0.0002	-0.0026	0.0079	0.0075	0.0075	0.0170

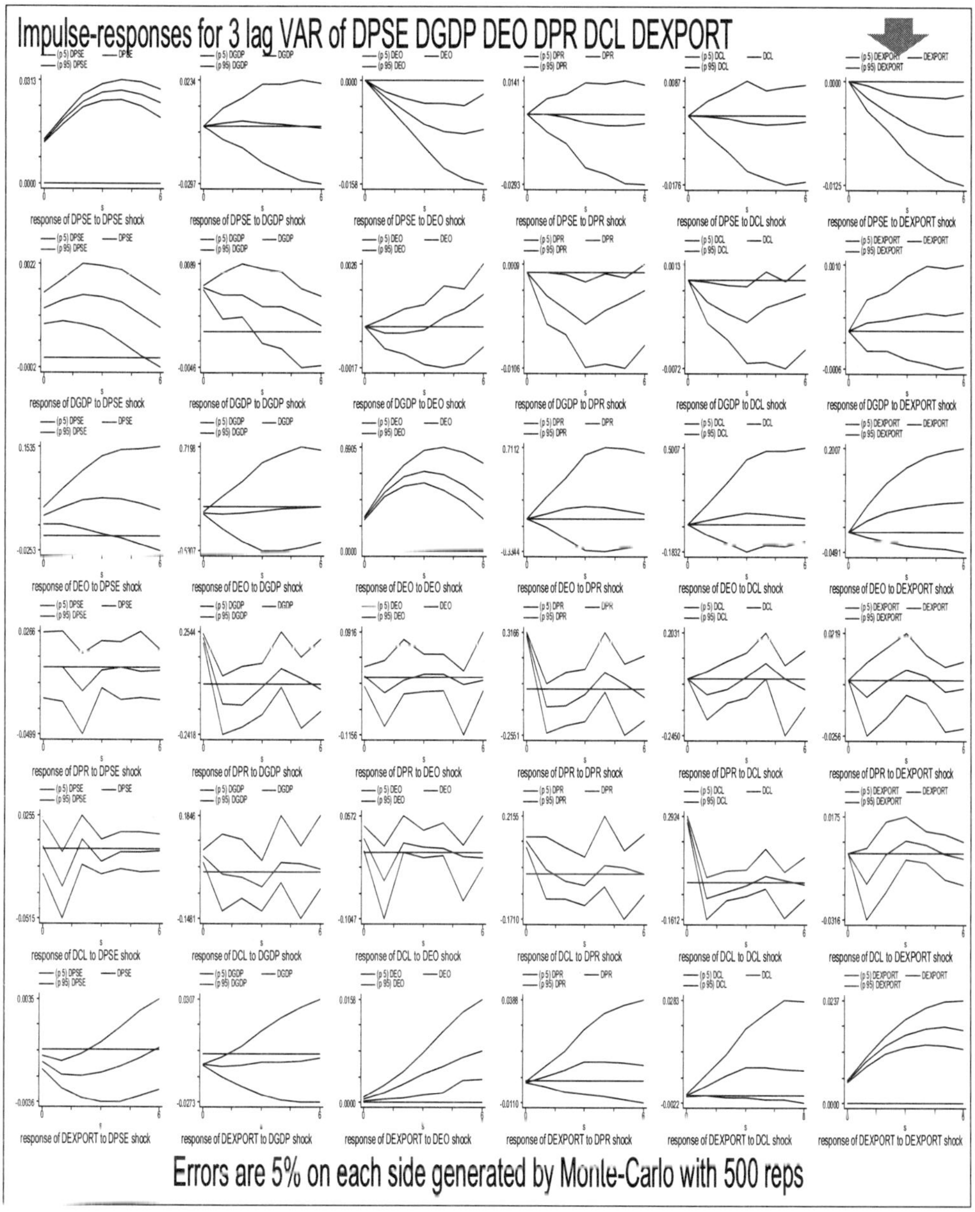

* DPSE: △Public Social Expenditure, DGDP: △GDP per Capita, DEO: △Economic Openness, DPR: △Political Rights, DCL: △Civil Liberties, DEXPORT: △Export.

<Figure 5.12> **Graphs of Panel Vector Autoregressive Model Analyses for Export**

<Table 5.18> Results of Panel Vector Autoregressive Model Analyses for Information Openness

Impulse-responses of variable in varname to the shock in column variable △Information openness								
Variables	Shock	Order	△Public social expenditure	△GDP per capita	△Economic openness	△Political rights	△Civil liberties	△Information openness
△Public social expenditure	0	1	0.0130	0.0000	0.0000	0.0000	0.0000	0.0000
	1	1	0.0194	-0.0009	-0.0025	-0.0011	-0.0011	-0.0017
	2	1	0.0250	-0.0003	-0.0046	-0.0022	-0.0017	-0.0034
	3	1	0.0274	-0.0025	-0.0069	-0.0046	-0.0027	-0.0048
	4	1	0.0279	-0.0030	-0.0081	-0.0049	-0.0025	-0.0057
	5	1	0.0265	-0.0040	-0.0086	-0.0049	-0.0023	-0.0062
	6	1	0.0237	-0.0046	-0.0081	-0.0035	-0.0014	-0.0061
△GDP per capita	0	2	0.0021	0.0069	0.0000	0.0000	0.0000	0.0000
	1	2	0.0019	0.0049	-0.0009	-0.0032	-0.0024	0.0002
	2	2	0.0019	0.0050	-0.0011	-0.0048	-0.0035	0.0002
	3	2	0.0015	0.0030	-0.0014	-0.0067	-0.0043	0.0003
	4	2	0.0015	0.0032	-0.0006	-0.0048	-0.0027	0.0003
	5	2	0.0010	0.0020	-0.0003	-0.0038	-0.0022	0.0002
	6	2	0.0006	0.0007	0.0004	-0.0025	-0.0015	0.0003
△Economic openness	0	3	0.0508	0.0742	0.2204	0.0000	0.0000	0.0000
	1	3	0.0494	0.0001	0.3730	-0.0403	-0.0342	0.0521
	2	3	0.0500	-0.0112	0.4701	-0.0491	-0.0381	0.0856
	3	3	0.0466	-0.0315	0.4939	-0.0753	-0.0409	0.1070
	4	3	0.0452	-0.0065	0.4710	-0.0441	-0.0081	0.1174
	5	3	0.0342	-0.0075	0.3888	-0.0387	-0.0072	0.1164
	6	3	0.0203	-0.0147	0.2823	-0.0358	-0.0052	0.1119
△Political rights	0	4	0.0371	0.2162	0.0474	0.2868	0.0000	0.0000
	1	4	-0.0133	-0.0909	-0.0412	-0.0825	-0.0613	-0.0150
	2	4	-0.0327	-0.1000	-0.0179	-0.0824	-0.0397	-0.0023
	3	4	-0.0029	-0.0032	0.0032	-0.0182	0.0123	0.0054
	4	4	0.0115	0.0703	0.0181	0.0822	0.0655	0.0032
	5	4	0.0032	0.0324	-0.0065	0.0297	-0.0004	-0.0072
	6	4	-0.0045	-0.0184	-0.0106	-0.0404	-0.0405	-0.0054
△Civil liberties	0	5	0.0116	0.0535	0.0372	0.1115	0.2789	0.0000
	1	5	-0.0300	-0.0241	-0.0391	0.0164	-0.0672	-0.0190
	2	5	0.0116	0.0198	0.0126	-0.0104	-0.0288	-0.0035
	3	5	-0.0190	-0.0634	-0.0036	-0.0486	-0.0182	0.0095
	4	5	0.0031	0.0375	0.0117	0.0321	0.0309	0.0052
	5	5	0.0003	0.0138	-0.0062	0.0065	0.0020	0.0000
	6	5	0.0021	0.0205	-0.0043	0.0088	0.0006	-0.0023
△Information openness	0	6	-0.0040	-0.0137	-0.0013	-0.0014	0.0003	0.0076
	1	6	-0.0051	-0.0136	0.0005	0.0050	0.0060	0.0133
	2	6	-0.0049	-0.0117	0.0025	0.0110	0.0112	0.0179
	3	6	-0.0039	-0.0074	0.0052	0.0172	0.0153	0.0210
	4	6	-0.0034	-0.0070	0.0063	0.0156	0.0132	0.0227
	5	6	-0.0023	-0.0057	0.0081	0.0127	0.0116	0.0234
	6	6	-0.0009	-0.0031	0.0094	0.0101	0.0104	0.0229

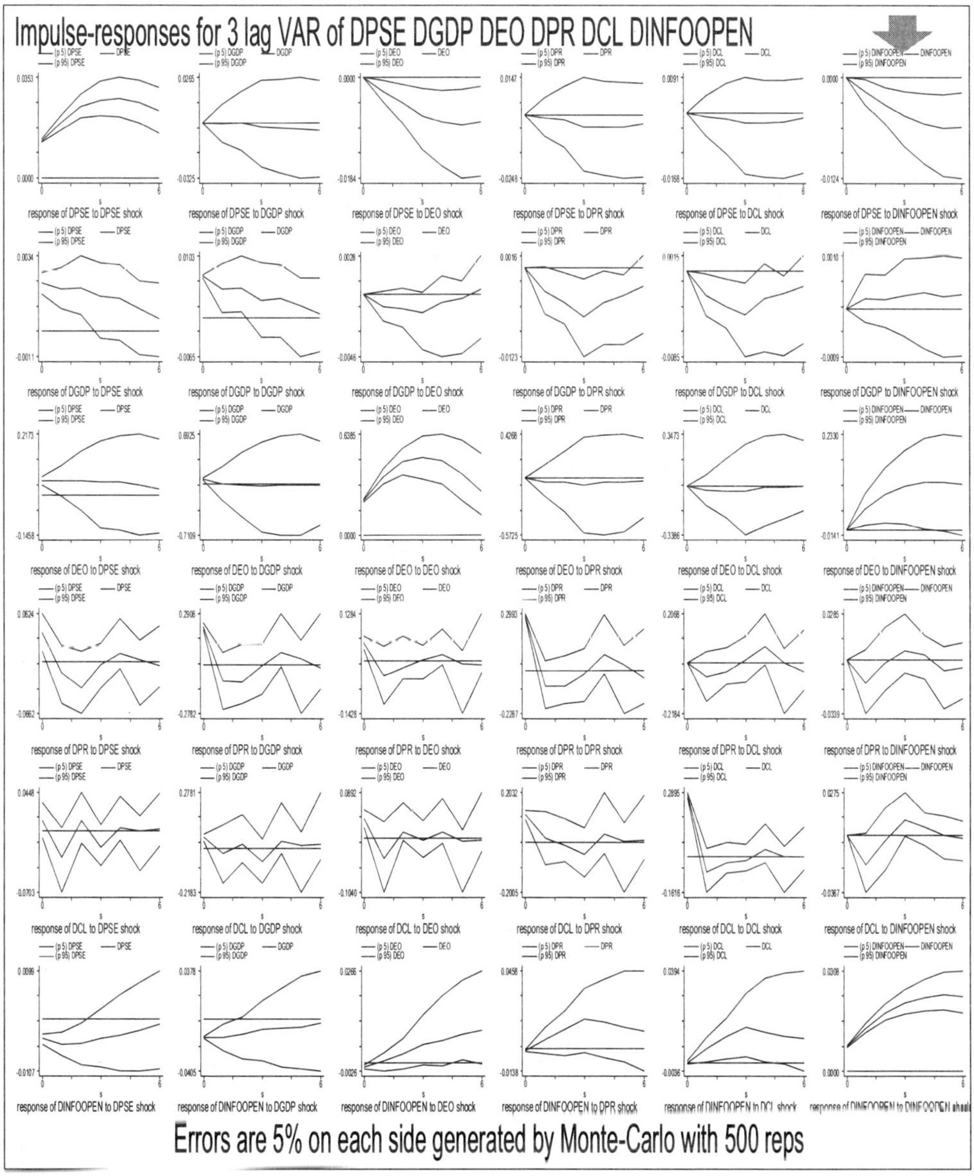

* DPSE: △Public Social Expenditure, DGDP: △GDP per Capita, DEO: △Economic Openness, DPR: △Political Rights, DCL: △Civil Liberties, DINFOOPEN: △Information Openness.

<Figure 5.13> Graphs of Panel Vector Autoregressive Model Analyses for Information Openness

3.2 Causality Analysis of ICT Industry Development and Income Inequality

In order to analyse the causal relationship between ICT industry development and income inequality, a pooled TSCS analysis is conducted with estimated household income inequality as the dependent variable, independent variables related to the ICT industry, and control variables related to welfare state development.[49]

Hypothesis
The development of the ICT industry increases income inequality.

1) Testing the Assumptions of Linear Regression and Analysis Modelling

Prior to conducting the pooled TSCS analysis, it must first be confirmed whether the pooled data meets the basic assumptions of OLS. This validation can be met via the following testing processes:

(1) The existence of multicollinearity: If the independent variables are too strongly collinear, the analysis results may be biased. Each value of the Variance Inflation Factor (hereafter VIF) is controlled below 4 in all regressions. (2) The existence of the random effect or fixed effect: The F test and Hausman test are conducted to determine the effects existing due to omitted variables. (3) The existence of autocorrelation: The Wooldridge test is conducted in order to observe whether there exists autocorrelation in residuals. (4) The existence of heteroskedasticity: Heteroskedasticity means that the residuals have constant variance in every unit and at every time. The Modified Wald test is performed to confirm heteroskedasticity.[50] The results of each test are omitted on ac-

---

[49] To achieve a more normal distribution and increase the efficacy of the analysis' performance, GDP per capita as a control variable is computed via a natural log using log transformation.

[50] The Breusch and Pagan Lagrangian multiplier test is used to observe contemporaneous correlation. However, it is impossible to conduct the test due to missing values. Contemporaneous correlation usually appears in comparative analyses across countries, so it is taken for granted that it will be utilised in studies. This assumption is understandable because the existence of contemporaneous correlation does not influ-

count of space consideration.

2) Simple Cross-sectional Regression Analyses

First, the simple cross-sectional regressions are performed, with the expectation of significant difference in the impact of the ICT industry's development between cross-sectional and over-time dimensions. The years 1996 and 2005 are chosen for analyses, as they contain relatively few missing values and can represent the 1990s and the 2000s, respectively.

$$Gini_{it} = \alpha + \beta 1X1_{it} + \beta 2X2_{it} + \cdots + e_{it}$$

(Gini: Estimated Household Income Inequality, x1, x2, ... : Variables related to the ICT industry and previously discussed relevant variables related to the development of the welfare state, i: country, t: time, e: residuals)

The following two tables (see Table 5.19 and Table 5.20) present the results of cross-sectional regressions for estimated household income inequality.[51] No significant results are found in either of the analyses. Therefore, it cannot be said with certainty that the more the ICT industry develops, the higher estimated household income inequality becomes.

---

ence the results as does the estimated coefficient and causal significance.

51 In the case of simple cross-sectional regressions in year 1996, Austria, Estonia, Poland, Switzerland and the United States are excluded due to missing values in the INVEST Model 1 and STAFF Model 1. Austria, Estonia, Luxembourg, Poland, Switzerland, and the United States are excluded due to missing values in the IMPORT Model 1. In the EXPORT Model 1 and INFO-OPENNESS Model 1, Austria, Estonia, Iceland, Luxembourg, Poland, Switzerland, and the United States are not included. In the case of simple cross-sectional regressions in year 2005, Australia, Chile, Finland, Iceland, Ireland, Israel, Mexico, the Netherlands, Norway, Slovenia, Sweden, Switzerland, the United Kingdom, and the United States are excluded due to missing values in the analysis for INVESTMENT Model 2. In the analysis of STAFF Model 2, Australia, Iceland, Ireland, Israel, Mexico, the Netherlands, Norway, Poland, Sweden, Switzerland, and the United Kingdom are not included in the analysis. Australia, Iceland, Mexico, Sweden, and Switzerland are excluded in IMPORT Model 2, EXPORT Model 2, and INFO-OPENNESS Model 2. In INVESTMENT Model 2, the simple cross-sectional regressions during year 2005 do not utilise GDP per capita as a control variable due to multicollinearity in the analysis.

<Table 5.19> Results of Simple Cross-sectional Regression Analyses for Year 1996

	Simple Cross-sectional Analysis for Estimated Household Income Inequality: 1996				
	1 INVESTMENT Model1	2 STAFF Model1	3 IMPORT Model1	4 EXPORT Model1	5 INFO-OPENNESS Model1
Dependent Variable	Estimated Household Income Inequality				
	Independent Variables				
Investment	-3.492				
	(-2.673)				
Staff		-6.993			
		(-4.232)			
Import			-6.577		
			(-5.371)		
Export				-1.147	
				(-1.34)	
Information openness					-1.388
					(-1.258)
	Control Variables				
GDP per capita	-3.223**	-1.8	-3.817**	-2.744*	-2.889*
	(-1.516)	(-1.345)	(-1.546)	(-1.43)	(-1.397)
Economic openness	-0.0211	-0.0224	-0.031	-0.0449	-0.0396
	(-0.0199)	(-0.0194)	(-0.0303)	(-0.0271)	(-0.0278)
Urban population rates	0.0739	0.0701	0.097	0.0847	0.0953
	(-0.0695)	(-0.0679)	(-0.074)	(-0.0733)	(-0.0741)
Civil liberties	1.456	1.548	1.287	1.465	1.414
	(-1.041)	(-0.994)	(-1.014)	(-1.029)	(-1.018)
Trade unemployment rates	-0.036	0.0904	0.0791	0.0968	0.105
	(-0.188)	(-0.185)	(-0.183)	(-0.199)	(-0.196)
Constant	64.46***	51.11***	68.57***	57.70***	58.60***
	(-16.5)	(-13.53)	(-15.73)	(-15.41)	(-14.94)
Observations	29	29	28	27	27
R-squared	0.515	0.535	0.554	0.532	0.543
Standard errors in parentheses					
*** p<0.01, ** p<0.05, * p<0.1					

<Table 5.20> Results of Simple Cross-sectional Regression Analyses for Year 2005

	Simple Cross-sectional Analysis for Estimated Household Income Inequality: 2005				
	1 INVESTMENT Model2	2 STAFF Model2	3 IMPORT Model2	4 EXPORT Model2	5 INFO-OPENNESS Model2
Dependent Variable	Estimated Household Income Inequality				
	Independent Variables				
Investment	-5.738				
	(-6.144)				
Staff		-13.42			
		(-8.24)			
Import			-0.939		
			(-2.439)		
Export				-0.628	
				(-0.461)	
Information openness					-0.506
					(-0.405)
	Control Variables				
GDP per capita		-0.537	-2.566*	-2.950**	-2.921**
		(-2.054)	(-1.404)	(-1.365)	(-1.376)
Economic openness	-0.0119	-0.00661	-0.00898	-0.00897	-0.0077
	(-0.0129)	(-0.0153)	(-0.016)	(-0.0127)	(-0.0131)
Urban population rates	0.00367	0.118	0.117*	0.125*	0.124*
	(-0.0796)	(-0.0781)	(-0.0632)	(-0.0609)	(-0.0613)
Civil liberties	4.136**	2.962	3.116*	3.094**	3.032**
	(-1.414)	(-1.701)	(-1.57)	(-1.443)	(-1.461)
Trade unemployment rates	0.229	0.192	0.0349	-0.0173	-0.0103
	(-0.242)	(-0.333)	(-0.251)	(-0.245)	(-0.246)
Constant	34.91***	36.63*	53.31***	57.03***	56.88***
	(-8.539)	(-19.84)	(-16)	(-15.36)	(-15.51)
Observations	20	23	29	29	29
R-squared	0.525	0.519	0.484	0.521	0.515
Standard errors in parentheses					
*** p<0.01, ** p<0.05, * p<0.1					

3) Panel-corrected Standard Errors (PCSE) Model Analyses

Similarly to the previous analyses on the relationship between public social expenditure and ICT industry variables, the basic model according to Pluemper et al's suggestion and Beck & Katz's suggestion are established. These models can be affirmed as follows:

Pluemper's model (Basic model): $Gini_{it} = \alpha + \beta 1X1_{it} + \beta 2X2_{it} + \cdots + e_{it}$

Beck & Katz's model (Comparison model):

$$Gini_{it} = \alpha + \beta 0Gini_{it-5} + \beta 1X1_{it} + \cdots + \sum \beta_i \, countrydummy_{it} + \sum \beta_{ik} \, timedummy_{kit} + e_{it}$$

(Gini: Estimated Household Income Inequality, x1, x2, ... : Variables related to the ICT industry and previously discussed relevant variables related to the development of the welfare state, i: country, t: time, e: residuals)

As shown in Table 5.21, in the INVESTMENT Model 1 and STAFF Model 1 of the Pluemper model, investment and staff show relatively strong negative relationships with estimated household income inequality. EXPORT Model 1 and INFO-OPENNESS Model 1 of the Pluemper model (see Table 5.22) show weak negative significance as well. However, in the Beck & Katz model, no significance is found in any of the models.

<Table 5.21> Results of PCSE Model Analyses 1

	Pluemper Model	Beck & Katz Model	Pluemper Model	Beck & Katz Model	Pluemper Model	Beck & Katz Model
	1	2	3	4	5	6
	INVESTMENT Model1	INVESTMENT Model2	STAFF Model1	STAFF Model2	IMPORT Model1	IMPORT Model2
Dependent Variable	Estimated Household Income Inequality					
	Independent Variables					
Estimated Household Income Inequality		0.0315		0.0116		0.00199
(5 lagged level)		(-0.0486)		(-0.0491)		(-0.046)
Investment	-1.318***	0.146				
	(-0.505)	(-0.159)				
Staff			-2.669***	0.09		
			(-0.805)	(-0.75)		
Import					-0.25	-0.0727
					(-0.251)	(-0.158)
	Control Variables					
GDP per capita	-0.999*	-0.661	-0.417	-0.790*	-0.306	-0.926**
	(-0.528)	(-0.449)	(-0.497)	(-0.454)	(-0.465)	(-0.438)
Corruption Perception Index	-0.074	0.104	0.0923	0.123	-0.129	0.0958
	(-0.162)	(-0.082)	(-0.169)	(-0.0926)	(-0.156)	(-0.0868)
Urban population rates	0.0818***	-0.0593	0.0815***	-0.069	0.0782***	-0.0551
	(-0.021)	(-0.0505)	(-0.0219)	(-0.0501)	(-0.0216)	(-0.0486)
Political rights	1.522***	0.484**	2.106***	0.562**	1.807***	0.334
	(-0.536)	(-0.196)	(-0.503)	(-0.255)	(-0.49)	(-0.223)
Civil liberties	0.828**	0.526***	0.759**	0.625***	0.749**	0.519***
	(-0.352)	(-0.149)	(-0.369)	(-0.147)	(-0.321)	(-0.147)
Trade union density	-0.0892***	0.0531**	-0.0943***	0.0576***	-0.0967***	0.0388*
	(-0.0114)	(-0.0217)	(-0.0113)	(-0.0212)	(-0.0114)	(-0.0214)
Total unemployment rates	0.0712	0.190***	0.166***	0.193***	0.126**	0.174***
	(-0.0542)	(-0.0254)	(-0.0531)	(-0.028)	(-0.0511)	(-0.0277)
Economic openness	-0.00968***	0.000512	-0.00701**	-3.50E-05	-0.00708*	-0.00469
	(-0.00353)	(-0.00659)	(-0.0032)	(-0.00676)	(-0.00378)	(-0.00716)
Constant	42.76***		35.10***	47.01***	35.30***	
	(-5.284)		(-4.769)	(-8.663)	(-4.471)	
Observations	283	237	288	241	311	263
R-squared	0.955	0.991	0.956	0.99	0.956	0.99
Number of country	32	30	32	30	32	31
Standard errors in parentheses						
*** p<0.01, ** p<0.05, * p<0.1						

<Table 5.22> Results of PCSE Model Analyses 2

	Pluemper Model	Beck & Katz Model	Pluemper Model	Beck & Katz Model
	7	8	9	10
	EXPORT Model1	EXPORT Model2	INFO-OPENNESS Model1	INFO-OPENNESS Model2
Dependent Variable	Estimated Household Income Inequality			
	Independent Variables			
Estimated Household Income Inequality		0.00422		0.00432
(5 lagged level)		(-0.0466)		(-0.0465)
Export	-0.152*	-0.0129		
	(-0.0827)	(-0.049)		
Information openness			-0.125*	-0.0139
			(-0.0684)	(-0.0416)
	Control Variables			
GDP per capita	-0.386	-0.903**	-0.37	-0.905**
	(-0.467)	(-0.442)	(-0.47)	(-0.44)
Corruption Perception Index	-0.112	0.101	-0.119	0.1
	(-0.156)	(-0.0871)	(-0.156)	(-0.0871)
Urban population rates	0.0819***	-0.0573	0.0791***	-0.0565
	(-0.0216)	(-0.0484)	(-0.0216)	(-0.0486)
Political rights	1.787***	0.332	1.793***	0.333
	(-0.483)	(-0.222)	(-0.488)	(-0.222)
Civil liberties	0.704**	0.529***	0.727**	0.526***
	(-0.319)	(-0.147)	(-0.32)	(-0.147)
Trade union density	-0.0952***	0.0397*	-0.0949***	0.0394*
	(-0.0114)	(-0.0214)	(-0.0114)	(-0.0214)
Total unemployment rates	0.133***	0.178***	0.129***	0.177***
	(-0.0496)	(-0.0268)	(-0.05)	(-0.027)
Economic openness	-0.00744**	-0.00472	-0.00657*	-0.00463
	(-0.00354)	(-0.00725)	(-0.00354)	(-0.00727)
Constant	35.75***		35.77***	
	(-4.43)		(-4.476)	
Observations	311	262	310	262
R-squared	0.956	0.989	0.957	0.99
Number of country	32	31	32	31
Standard errors in parentheses				
*** p<0.01, ** p<0.05, * p<0.1				

4) Error Correction Model (ECM) and Vector Error Correction Model (VECM) Analyses

In order to observe transitory effects and long-term permanent effects, ECM and VECM analyses are conducted according to the following models.[52] First of all, the following pre-tests are performed: Unit root tests, the Granger causality test, and a co-integration test. This is in order to avoid 'spurious regression' situations.

ECM model: $\Delta Gini_{it} = \alpha + \beta_1 \cdot Gini_{it-1} + \sum \beta^j \cdot X^j_{it-1} + \sum \beta^j_\Delta \cdot X^j_{it-1} + e_t$

VECM model:

$$\Delta Gini_{it} = \alpha + \beta_1 \cdot Gini_{it-1} + \sum \beta^j \cdot X_1{}^j_{it-1} + \sum \beta^j \cdot X_2{}^j_{it-1} \cdots + \sum \beta^j_\Delta \cdot X_1{}^j_{it-1} + \sum \beta^j_\Delta \cdot X_2 X^j_{it-1} \cdots + e_t$$

(Gini: Estimated Household Income Inequality, x1, x2, ... : Variables related to the ICT industry and previously discussed relevant variables related to the development of the welfare state, Δ: first difference, i: country, t: time, e: residuals)

First, it is evident by examining the results of the pre-tests through graphs that the pooled time-series cross-section data has trends over time.[53] This means the data can be non-stationary and have unit roots. The results of the Breitung unit-root test and Im-Pesaran-Shin unit-root test show that all series of variables have unit roots and are non-stationary. However, when they are first differenced, these variables can be stationary and do not have unit roots. Second, the results of Westerlund's error-correction-based co-integration tests show there are co-integrations between the dependent variable and independent variables.[54] This means that the relationships between the dependent variable and independent variables are linear, although all variables are

---

52 For a full interpretation of results, see the Error Correction Model (ECM) and Vector Error Correction Model (VECM) Analyses in chapter 5, section 4.

53 Please see the graphs in the figures in the appendix.

54 When performing co-integration tests, the option of lag 1 is added to each analysis because the series data are based on a series of consecutive years. The results of the Pesaran's CD tests show a strong cross-section independence. Furthermore, as shown in the aforementioned unit-root tests, the pooled time-series cross-section data has a strong serial correlation. Therefore, it is more appropriate to interpret the robust p-value via the bootstrap option. The results of the Pesaran's CD tests are omitted on account of space consideration.

non-stationary and serial correlations. Third, the results of the Granger causality test confirm the causal relationship between the dependent variable and independent variables.[55] All these results are added in the appendix on account of space consideration.[56] When conducting the tests for heteroskedasticity in each pooled regression, a panel-corrected standard error model according to Beck & Katz's suggestion is employed to perform ECM and VECM, including country dummy in the models.[57]

As the results from the ECM analyses and VECM analyses reveal (see Table 5.23 and Table 5.24), investment runs parallel with estimated household income inequality. In other words, investment has a positive transitory effect on income inequality in the short term, in addition to a positive permanent effect on income inequality in the long term. However, the other ICT industry variables show opposite results. In the ECM analysis and VECM analysis, export and information openness show negative effects in the short term and in the long term. In the case of import, the results show a negative transitory effect only in the short term. Interestingly, staff does not show any association with income inequality in the ECM analysis or the VECM analysis.[58]

---

55 For each country, the Granger causality test is conducted with first difference variables, including, the option of lag 5. The results show that two-way Granger causality exists in each relationship between the dependent variable and independent variables. However, this study's focus is not the impact of income inequality on ICT usage, but the impact of ICT usage on income inequality.

56 The results from the Granger causality test are omitted on account of space consideration.

57 Estonia, Slovakia and Slovenia are not included in the ECM and VECM analysis.

58 The long-term permanent effect of the independent variables is not calculated here. However, if verification is desired, it can be calculated by dividing the parameter for the lagged level of each variable by the negative of the lagged dependent level variable.

<Table 5.23> Results of ECM Analyses

	ECM Analysis with Country FE				
	1 INVESTMENT Model	2 STAFF Model	3 IMPORT Model	4 EXPORT Model	5 INFO-OPENNESS Model
Dependent Variable	△ Estimated Household Income Inequality				
	Independent Variables				
Estimated Household Income Inequality	-0.0334***	-0.0361***	-0.0350***	-0.0290***	-0.0301***
(Lagged level)	(-0.00533)	(-0.00617)	(-0.00608)	(-0.00569)	(-0.00582)
△Investment	0.740***				
	(-0.166)				
Investment	0.168***				
(Lagged level)	(-0.0321)				
△Staff		0.0627			
		(-0.105)			
Staff		-0.0299			
(Lagged level)		(-0.0211)			
△Import			-0.218		
			(-0.167)		
Import			-0.0458		
(Lagged level)			(-0.0321)		
△Export				-0.302***	
				(-0.0724)	
Export				-0.0425***	
(Lagged level)				(-0.0126)	
△Information openness					-0.211***
					(-0.0555)
Information openness					-0.0309***
(Lagged level)					-0.0100
Constant	1.114***	1.374***	1.320***	1.090***	-0.01
	(-0.191)	(-0.223)	(-0.218)	(-0.205)	(-0.209)
Observations	775	775	775	775	775
R-squared	0.555	0.515	0.515	0.543	0.537
Number of country	31	31	31	31	31
Standard errors in parentheses *** p<0.01, ** p<0.05, * p<0.1					

<Table 5.24> **Results of VECM Analyses**

	VECM Analysis with Country FE				
	1	2	3	4	5
	INVESTMENT Model	STAFF Model	IMPORT Model	EXPORT Model	INFO-OPENNESS Model
Dependent Variable	△ Estimated Household Income Inequality				
	Independent Variables				
Estimated Household Income Inequality (Lagged level)	-0.0461***	-0.0450***	-0.0424***	-0.0395***	-0.0392***
	(-0.00624)	(-0.00656)	(-0.00581)	(-0.0059)	(-0.00583)
△Investment	0.750***				
	(-0.151)				
Investment (Lagged level)	0.108***				
	(-0.0287)				
△Staff		0.0537			
		(-0.0984)			
Staff (Lagged level)		-0.0259			
		(-0.0198)			
△Import			-1.530***		
			(-0.215)		
Import (Lagged level)			-0.0219		
			(-0.0348)		
△Export				-0.511***	
				(-0.0666)	
Export (Lagged level)				-0.0326***	
				(-0.01)	
△Information openness					-0.457***
					(-0.0555)
Information openness (Lagged level)					-0.0210***
					(-0.0081)
	Control Variables				
△GDP per capita	-0.0301	-0.0472	-0.182	-0.0407	-0.0665
	(-0.229)	(-0.219)	(-0.221)	(-0.205)	(-0.205)
GDP per capita (Lagged level)	0.0625***	0.0523***	0.028	0.0266	0.024
	(-0.0182)	(-0.0189)	(-0.0201)	(-0.0165)	(-0.0167)
△Economic openness	0.0169***	0.0182***	0.0277***	0.0254***	0.0277***
	(-0.00379)	(-0.00414)	(-0.00378)	(-0.00348)	(-0.00346)
Economic openness (Lagged level)	-0.00143**	-0.00219***	-0.00366***	-0.00203***	-0.00256***
	(-0.000586)	(-0.000623)	(-0.000576)	(-0.000502)	(-0.0005)
△Civil Liberties	0.0311*	0.0329*	0.0374**	0.0315*	0.0327*
	(-0.0177)	(-0.0184)	(-0.0179)	(-0.0175)	(-0.0174)
Civil Liberties (Lagged level)	0.0251**	0.0342***	0.0351***	0.0255**	0.0269**
	(-0.0125)	(-0.0128)	(-0.0122)	(-0.012)	(-0.012)
△Political rights	-0.0534**	-0.0623***	-0.0636***	-0.0580***	-0.0587***
	(-0.0226)	(-0.0234)	(-0.0228)	(-0.0221)	(-0.0221)
Political rights (Lagged level)	-0.0473***	-0.0571***	-0.0694***	-0.0599***	-0.0624***
	(-0.0124)	(-0.0129)	(-0.0128)	(-0.0122)	(-0.0122)
Constant	1.066***	1.268***	1.480***	1.304***	1.352***
	(-0.241)	(-0.253)	(-0.265)	(-0.238)	(-0.242)
Observations	775	775	775	775	775
R-squared	0.598	0.576	0.61	0.621	0.625
Number of country	31	31	31	31	31
Standard errors in parentheses *** p<0.01, ** p<0.05, * p<0.1					

5) First Difference Model Analyses

The first difference model analysis can be conducted to discover the impact of short-term changes in the ICT industry on short-term changes in estimated household income inequality.[59] The equation consists of first differences between all variables.

59 Estonia, Slovakia and Slovenia are not included in the first difference model analyses. In the case of the civil liberties variable, after the first difference, 3 were added to all values in order to perform the analysis appropriately.

$$\Delta Gini_i = \beta_1 \Delta {x_1}_i + \beta_2 \Delta {x_2}_i \dots + \Delta e_i$$

(Gini: Estimated Household Income Inequality, x1, x2, ... : Variables related to the ICT industry and previously discussed relevant variables related to the development of the welfare state, Δ: first difference, i: country, e: residuals)

As shown in the following tables (see Table 5.25 and Table 5.26), investment has a positive association with estimated household income inequality during the entire period (with an estimated coefficient of +1.141 and 99% probability (*** p<0.01)), as well as the period pre-2000 (with an estimated coefficient of +1.715 and 99% probability (*** p<0.01)). Staff also shows a positive significance in the entire period (with an estimated coefficient of +0.166 and 99% probability (** *p<0.01)) and in the period post-2000 (with an estimated coefficient of +0.0858 and 95% probability (**p<0.05)). However, import shows a negative significance in the period pre-2000, with an estimated coefficient of -1.658 and 95% probability (** p<0.05). In the case of other variables, a statistical association between the development of the ICT industry and an increase in income inequality is not found in the short term.

<Table 5.25> Results of First Difference Model Analyses 1

	First Differece Model Analysis								
	1 INVESTMENT Model1	2 INVESTMENT Model2	3 INVESTMENT Model3	4 STAFF Model1	5 STAFF Model2	6 STAFF Model3	7 IMPORT Model1	8 IMPORT Model2	9 IMPORT Model3
Dependent Variables	△Estimated Household Income Inequality								
	Independent Variables								
△Investment	1.141***	1.715***	0.173						
	(-0.175)	(-0.308)	(-0.185)						
△Staff				0.166***	0.85	0.0858**			
				(-0.061)	(-0.766)	(-0.0421)			
△Import							0.109	-1.658**	-0.208
							(-0.197)	(-0.642)	(-0.175)
	Control Variables								
△GDP per capita	-0.157	-0.464	-0.32	-0.378	-0.22	-0.323	-0.465**	0.0322	0.431**
	(-0.233)	(-0.396)	(-0.236)	(-0.236)	(-0.407)	(-0.217)	(-0.235)	(-0.409)	(-0.214)
△Economic openness	0.0193***	0.0134***	0.0242***	0.0160***	0.0119**	0.0228***	0.0161***	0.0249***	0.0230***
	(-0.00341)	(-0.0049)	(-0.00385)	(-0.00347)	(-0.00508)	(-0.00376)	(-0.00357)	(-0.00698)	(-0.00378)
△Corruption Perception Index	-0.842***	-1.154***	-0.675***	-1.062***	-1.360***	-0.725***	1.027***	1.319***	-0.693***
	(-0.127)	(-0.205)	(-0.122)	(-0.127)	(-0.209)	(-0.12)	(-0.127)	(-0.208)	(-0.12)
△Urban population rates	-0.0392**	-0.0833***	0.0519**	-0.0652***	-0.118***	0.03	-0.0488**	-0.117***	0.0531**
	(-0.0192)	(-0.0287)	(-0.0214)	(-0.0205)	(-0.0293)	(-0.0237)	(-0.0197)	(-0.0289)	(-0.0215)
△Civil liberties	-0.0251	-0.0226	-0.00153	-0.0374**	-0.0465*	-0.0025	-0.0370*	-0.0403	-0.00446
	(0.0187)	(0.0255)	(-0.0243)	(-0.019)	(-0.026)	(-0.0242)	(-0.0191)	(-0.026)	(-0.0244)
Constant	0.175***	0.203**	0.0565	0.227***	0.288***	0.062	0.226***	0.286***	0.0673
	(-0.0583)	(-0.0792)	(-0.0753)	(-0.059)	(-0.0804)	(-0.0748)	(-0.0593)	(-0.0799)	(-0.0752)
Observations	775	434	341	775	434	341	775	434	341
R-squared	0.166	0.206	0.172	0.128	0.151	0.18	0.12	0.162	0.173
Number of country	31	31	31	31	31	31	31	31	31
Standard errors in parentheses									
*** p<0.01, ** p<0.05, * p<0.1									

<Table 5.26> **Results of First Difference Model Analyses 2**

	First Differece Model Analysis					
	10	11	12	13	14	15
	EXPORT Model1	EXPORT Model2	EXPORT Model3	INFO-OPENNESS Model1	INFO-OPENNESS Model2	INFO-OPENNESS Model3
Dependent Variables	△Estimated Household Income Inequality					
	Independent Variables					
△Export	0.00777	-0.137	-0.0492			
	(-0.071)	(-0.137)	(-0.0605)			
△Information openness				0.0109	-0.185	-0.0454
				(-0.0566)	(-0.124)	(-0.0476)
	Control Variables					
△GDP per capita	-0.479**	-0.205	-0.378*	-0.479**	-0.184	-0.385*
	(-0.234)	(-0.407)	(-0.218)	(-0.234)	(-0.406)	(-0.216)
△Economic openness	0.0164***	0.0149***	0.0239***	0.0163***	0.0171***	0.0237***
	(-0.00365)	(-0.00565)	(-0.0038)	(-0.00365)	(-0.00598)	(-0.00378)
△Corruption Perception Index	-1.028***	-1.347***	-0.686***	-1.029***	-1.334***	-0.686***
	(-0.128)	(-0.209)	(-0.12)	(-0.128)	(-0.209)	(-0.12)
△Urban population rates	-0.0486**	-0.114***	0.0534**	-0.0487**	-0.114***	0.0537**
	(-0.0197)	(-0.0291)	(-0.0216)	(-0.0197)	(-0.0291)	(-0.0216)
△Civil liberties	-0.0368*	-0.0478*	-0.00264	-0.0368*	-0.0467*	-0.00311
	(-0.0191)	(-0.0259)	(-0.0243)	(-0.0191)	(-0.0259)	(-0.0243)
Constant	0.226***	0.290***	0.0597	0.226***	0.290***	0.0611
	(-0.0593)	(-0.0804)	(-0.0752)	(-0.0593)	(-0.0803)	(-0.0751)
Observations	775	434	341	775	434	341
R-squared	0.12	0.151	0.172	0.12	0.153	0.172
Number of country	31	31	31	31	31	31
Standard errors in parentheses						
*** p<0.01, ** p<0.05, * p<0.1						

4. Summary

In chapter five, the relationship between the development of the ICT industry and the welfare state was analysed. For clarity and quick reference, a summation is outlined below.

First, descriptive statistics were employed in order to understand the general characteristics of the variables. Through mean value analyses, the relationship between public social expenditure and income inequality was uncovered across all OECD countries between 1985 and 2010. From this, it became apparent that countries with high levels of income inequality tend to engage in much less public social spending. Furthermore, comparisons of independent variables (total annual investment in telecommunication, total full-time staff in telecommunication, imports of telecommunication equipment, and exports of telecommunication equipment) showed at varying levels among OECD countries from 1985 to 2010.

Second, correlation analyses were conducted to uncover any statistical relationships between the variables. Public social expenditure showed positive correlations with imports of telecommunication equipment, exports of telecommunication equipment, total full-time telecommunication staff, and information openness; while the correlation between public social expenditure and total annual investments in telecommunication showed negative. Income inequality revealed negative correlations with total annual investments in telecommunication, total full-time telecommunication staff, imports of telecommunication equipment, exports of telecommunication equipment, and information openness.

Finally, simple cross-sectional regressions and a number of pooled TSCS analyses were performed in order to investigate the causal relationships between dependent variables and independent variables. The simple cross-sectional regressions revealed that public social expenditure and investment shared a strong negative significance in 2005, while import and information openness shared a positive significance during the same year.

In the PCSE model analyses, according to results of the Beck & Katz model, during pre-2000, investment in telecommunication equipment showed a positive causal relationship with social expenditure. During the same period, a significant negative relationship between public social expenditure and ICT staff was observed. Looking at import and export in ICT, export also showed a negative significance in the same period (pre-2000), while import did not reveal any significance. However, the causal relationship between pubic social expenditure and information openness was negative pre-2000 as well as post-2000.

The results of ECM analyses showed significance in all variables. Investment and import had a negative effect on public social spending in the short term, while staff had a positive effect in the short term. In the long term, staff, export, and information openness showed weak negative associations with public social expenditure. The VECM analyses yielded similar phenomena to those of the ECM analysis. Most variables showed a negative impact on public social expenditure in the short term and long term; with the exception of import, which showed positive significance in the long term. However, according to the results, import also had a negative effect in the short term.

The first difference model analyses revealed a weak negative significance between public social expenditure and investment post-2000. Export and information openness showed a weak negative relationship with public social expenditure pre-2000. Interestingly, import showed a negative significance during all periods. Conversely, only staff had a weak positive short-term impact on the change of public social expenditure for the entire period.

In case of PVAR analyses, the response of public social expenditure to investment's shock was negative, with every negative shock effect maintained strongly for up to four years, after which the effect became progressively weaker. The response of public social expenditure to staff's shock was not certain or constant, due to the negative effect and positive effect alternating every two years. However, the values of the negative effects were much higher than those of the positive effects right up until the fifth year. The response of public social expenditure to import's shock was negative. Next, export also showed negative effects, with the negative response of public social expenditure to export's shock becoming stronger with time. Similarly, in the case of information openness, the results showed negative effects with time.

In summation of the above analyses, the hypothesis 'the development of the ICT industry increases public social spending' is not proved. This is due to conflict in the causality analyses, where some results suggest a negative causal relationship between public social spending and the development of the ICT industry, while other results suggest a positive relationship between the two.

In the case of income inequality, the results of simple cross-sectional regressions showed no significant relationship in either of the analyses.

In PCSE model analyses and the Pluemper model, investment and staff showed relatively strong negative relationships with household income inequality. In the same model, export and information openness showed weak negative significances as well.

According to the results of the ECM and VECM analyses, investment had a positive transitory effect on income inequality in the short term, in addition to a positive permanent effect on income inequality in the long term. However, the other ICT industry variables showed opposite results. In the ECM analysis and VECM analysis, export and information openness showed negative effects in the short term and in the long term. In the case of import, the results showed a negative transitory effect only in the short term. Interestingly, staff did not show any association with income inequality in the ECM analysis or the VECM analysis.

Viewing the first difference model analyses, investment showed to have a positive association with income inequality during the entire period, as well as pre-2000. Staff also showed a positive significance for the entire period and post-2000. However, import showed a negative significance pre-2000. In the case of other variables, a statistical association between the development of the ICT industry and an increase in income inequality was not found in the short term.

In summation of the entire results, it can be not said with confidence that there is a positive causal relationship between income inequality and the development of the ICT industry. Therefore, the hypothesis is not proved: The development of the ICT industry does increase income inequality.

Chapter VI

ICT Usage and the Welfare State

Chapter VI ICT Usage and the Welfare State

In chapter six, the relationship between the evolution of ICT usage and the development of the welfare state is analysed using the variables presented in chapter four. The analysis adopts all 34 OECD countries as analysis objects and utilises time-series cross-section data from 1985 to 2010, spanning a total period of twenty-six years.

Descriptive statistics are employed in order to understand the general characteristics of the variables, followed by a correlation analysis to detect any statistical relationships between the variables. Next, simple cross-sectional regressions are conducted, which can show the effect of the development of ICT usage on the development of the welfare state via a cross-sectional point. Finally, several pooled TSCS analyses are carried out in order to investigate the causal relationship between dependent variables and independent variables. Control variables are employed differently, depending on what is appropriate for each analysis model. Missing values are not handled in the descriptive statistics, the correlation analyses, or simple cross-sectional regressions, but are handled in some of the pooled TSCS analyses.[60]

60 For the first difference analysis, error correction model analysis and panel vector autoregressive analysis, missing values are calculated by the moving average (with a window of five years), in order to conduct the analyses.

Hypotheses

1. *The use of ICT increases public social spending.*
2. *The use of ICT increases income inequality.*

Variables

Dependent variables:

Public Social Expenditure (PSE), Estimated Household Income Inequality (EHII)

Independent variables: Internet User Rates, Mobile Cellular Subscriptions per 100 Inhabitants, Personal Computer Numbers per 100 Inhabitants[61]

Control variables: Urban Population Rate, GDP per Capita, Total Unemployment Rate, Trade Union Density, Corruption Perception Index, Political Rights, Civil Liberties, Economic Openness

1. General Characteristics of Variables

1.1 Descriptive Statistics of the 34 OECD Countries

In descriptive statistics, original values are used without adulteration of those values. Historically, time-series cross-section data is separated into segments of two periods (before year 2000 and after year 2000), in order to observe changes over time in more detail.

The following table, informing the results of the descriptive statistics variables, reveals the growth of ICT usage and the development of the welfare state. The mean and standard deviation are calculated to the second decimal place, providing more than sufficient accuracy when looking at and explaining changes over time.

61 Henceforth, 'Mobile Cellular Subscriptions per 100 Inhabitants' will be referred to as 'mobile phones' and 'Personal Computer Numbers per 100 Inhabitants' as 'PC numbers'. Furthermore, to avoid cluttered content, 'subscriptions per 100 inhabitants' will be omitted from titles, most lists, and figures, keeping in mind that the omitted words are always implied.

<Table 6.1> **General Characteristics of Variables**

	The Entire Period			Pre-2000			Post-2000		
Variable	Obs	Mean	Std. Dev.	Obs	Mean	Std. Dev.	Obs	Mean	Std. Dev.
Public Social Expenditure	789	19.38	6.43	422	18.67	6.93	367	20.19	5.71
Estimated Household Income Inequality	651	36.97	4.92	431	36.48	5.19	220	37.93	4.21
Internet user rates	699	30.82	29.84	328	5.56	8.95	371	53.15	23.31
Mobile phones	877	42.80	46.44	503	7.22	12.35	374	90.66	29.27
PC numbers	621	23.10	20.63	387	13.25	11.19	234	39.38	22.31

* The values represent the mean and the standard deviation of each variable in the 34 OECD countries during 1985 - 2010.

As seen in the above table, the mean of Internet user rates increases dramatically, from 5.56% (standard deviation: 8.95) pre-2000, to 53.15% (standard deviation: 23.31) post-2000. Looking at the broader timeframe, the mean is 30.82% (standard deviation: 29.84) from 1985 to 2010.

Mobile phone subscriptions also increase drastically from 1985 to 2010. The mean is 7.22 (standard deviation: 12.35) pre-2000, and 90.66 (standard deviation: 29.27) post-2000. These changes confirm that mobile cellular subscriptions increase dramatically alongside Internet user rates, especially from the late 1990s to the early 2000s.

Personal computer numbers are no exception in regards to a speedy development. The mean is 13.25 (standard deviation: 11.19) in 1985-2000, and 39.38 (standard deviation: 22.31) in 2000-2010. As the mean values reveal, personal computer numbers increase rather rapidly from the late 1980s to the early 2000s.[62]

1.2 Descriptive Statistics by Country

1) Charting the Changes in Variables

Normally, before analysing data, a trend figure of each variable based on time-series data of the 34 OECD countries is analysed. However, especially considering the abundance of other data within this study, such figures are omitted on account of space consideration.

62 Please see chapter 5, section 1.1, under the heading 'Descriptive Statistics of the 34 OECD Countries.' Explanations about public social expenditure and household income inequality are omitted to avoid repetition.

2) Mean Value Analyses

The mean of each variable is analysed during the period 1985 to 2010. Here, the differences in the mean value of each independent variable are examined for each country in the format of figures as well as text, allowing for increased clarity of demonstration. Explanations regarding dependent variables and control variables are omitted to avoid repetition.[63]

(1) Comparisons of Independent Variables

❶ Internet User Rates (%)

Internet user rates are the percentage of the population using the Internet as reported by national household surveys.

Looking at Internet user rates announced by the ITU, Iceland emerges as number one, with a rate of 48.95%. Sweden (46.51%), Norway (43.61%), the Netherlands (43.15%), Denmark (42.64%), Finland (42.53%), and New Zealand (41.31%) also hold notably high positions. The United States, Switzerland, Canada, South Korea, Luxembourg, the United Kingdom, and Germany all show over 30%, which is not insignificant.

Much lower rates are observed within countries such as Poland (19.82%), Portugal (19.60%), Israel (19.10%), and Chile (16.22%), all falling below 20%. Even more surprisingly low percentages can be observed in Greece (14.83%), Turkey (11.73%) and Mexico (9.29%).

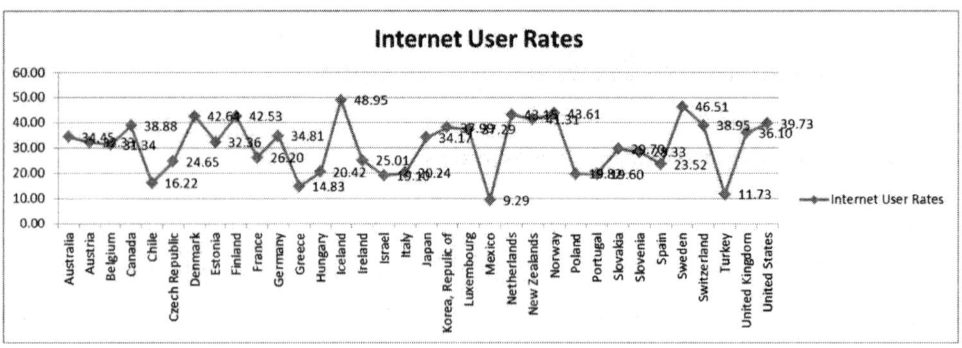

* The values represent the annual average of Internet user rates in the 34 OECD countries during 1985 -2010.

<Figure 6.1> **Internet User Rates (%)**

63 Please see chapter 5, section 2, under the heading 'Mean Value Analyses.'

❷ Mobile Cellular Subscriptions (%)

Mobile cellular subscriptions are calculated by dividing the number of mobile cellular subscriptions by the population then multiplying that number by 100.

Looking at the annual average of mobile cellular phone subscriptions in OECD countries from 1985 to 2010, Israel appears to have the most prolific subscribers, at 64.95%. They are closely followed by Italy (56.43%), Luxembourg (55.82%), Finland (55.52%), Sweden (52.30%), Norway (50.78%) and Austria (50.12%). With such high percentages, these countries can be classified as the highest group. Sliding down the scale a little are countries such as Denmark (49.77%), the United Kingdom (49.57%), Estonia (49.29%), Portugal (49.00%), and Iceland (48.72%).

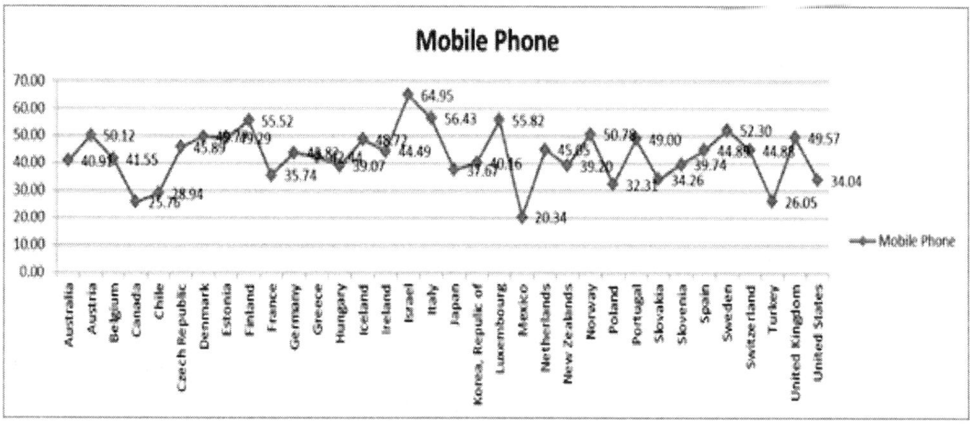

* The values represent the annual average of mobile cellular subscriptions per 100 Inhabitants in the 34 OECD countries during 1985 - 2010

<Figure 6.2> **Mobile Cellular Subscriptions (%)**

Countries showing low rates of mobile cellular subscriptions are Slovakia (34.26%), the United States (34.04%), and Poland (32.31%). Chile (28.94%), Turkey (26.05%), Canada (25.76%) and Mexico (20.34%) show the lowest rates among all OECD countries.

❶ Personal Computer Numbers (%)

Personal computer numbers are calculated by dividing the number of personal computers by the population then multiplying that number by 100.

Looking at personal computer numbers, Luxembourg shows the highest mean value (51.34%). Other countries with high mean values include Switzerland (47.69%), Norway (40.03%), Sweden (39.08%), Denmark (37.73%), the United States (37.37%), and the Netherlands (33.82%).

Countries such as the Czech Republic (9.52%), Portugal (8.89%), Hungary (7.70%), Poland (5.91%), Chile (5.89%) and Greece (5.00%) have significantly smaller mean values, meaning much fewer people enjoy the use of personal computers. Mexico (4.96%), and Turkey (2.66%), both with a mean value below 5, belong to the lowest group.

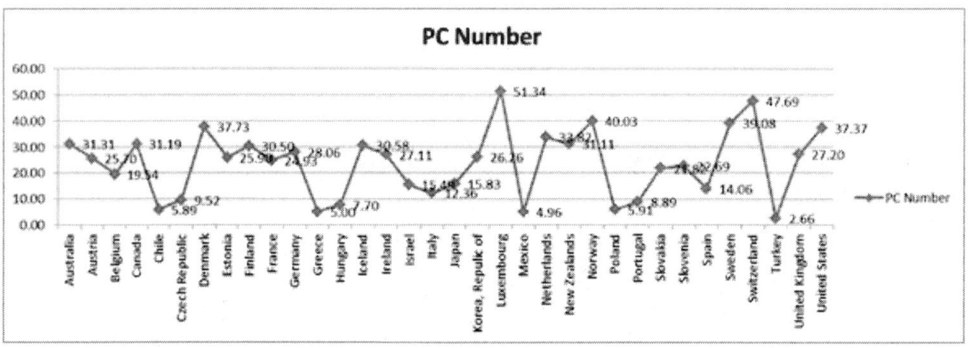

* The values represent the annual average of personal computer numbers per 100 Inhabitants in the 34 OECD countries during 1985 - 2010.

<Figure 6.3> **Personal Computer Numbers (%)**

2. Correlation Analysis

Here, the correlation analysis is performed via a pairwise deletion. An examination of the correlation analysis reveals that public social expenditure and household income inequality have a negative correlation.

<Table 6.2> **Results of Correlation Analysis**

	Public Social Expenditure	Estimated Household Income Inequality	Internet User Rates	Mobil Phones	PC Numbers
Public Social Expenditure	1				
(Sig.)	0.0000				
Estimated Household	-0.5573	1			
Income Inequality (Sig.)	0.0000	0.0000			
Internet User Rates	0.1909	-0.0619	1		
(Sig.)	0.0000	0.1683	0.0000		
Mobile Phones	0.2313	0.0608	0.8735	1	
(Sig.)	0.0000	0.1230	0.0000	0.0000	
PC Numbers	0.2380	-0.2131	0.8622	0.7240	1
(Sig.)	0.0000	0.0000	0.0000	0.0000	0.0000

Public social expenditure, when correlated with Internet user rates, mobile phones and PC numbers, show plus (+) signs. Therefore, when Internet user rates, mobile phones and PC numbers have high values, the values of public social expenditure within the given countries are also high.

Turning to income inequality, when correlated with Internet user rates, mobile phones, and PC numbers, minus signs appear. To interpret these results; when the values of Internet user rates, mobile phones, and PC numbers are high, the value of income inequality is low.

3. Causality Analysis of ICT Usage, Public Social Spending and Income Inequality

Forthwith, a causality analysis of ICT usage, public social spending, and income inequality is performed. The analysis starts on the assumption that causal relationships between dependent and independent variables or control variables are linear, i.e., the model is linear in its parameters.

3.1 Causality Analysis of ICT Usage and Public Social Spending

To begin exploring the causal relationship between ICT usage and public social spending, a pooled TSCS analysis is conducted. This is accomplished using public social expenditure as the dependent variable, independent variables related to ICT usage, and control variables related to welfare state development.[64]

Hypothesis

The use of ICT increases public social spending.

1) Testing the Assumptions of Linear Regression and Analysis Modelling

Prior to conducting the pooled TSCS analysis, it must first be confirmed whether the pooled data meet the basic assumptions of OLS. This validation can be met via the following testing processes:

(1) The existence of multicollinearity: If the independent variables are too strongly collinear, the analysis results may be biased. Therefore, each value of VIF is controlled below 4 in all regressions.

(2) The existence of the random effect or fixed effect: The F test and Hausman test are conducted to determine the effects existing due to omitted variables.

(3) The existence of autocorrelation: The Wooldridge test is conducted in order to observe whether there exists autocorrelation in residuals.

(4) The existence of heteroskedasticity: The Modified Wald test is performed to confirm heteroskedasticity.[65] The results of each test are omitted on account of space consideration.

2) Simple Cross-sectional Regression Analyses

First, the simple cross-sectional regression analyses are performed, with the expectation of a significant difference in the impact of ICT usage between the cross-sectional and over-time dimensions. The years 1996 and 2005 are chosen for analyses because they have relatively few missing values and can represent the 1990s and the 2000s respectively. The equation is as follows:

---

64 To achieve a more even distribution and increase the efficacy of the analysis' performance, GDP per capita as a control variable is computed via a natural log using log transformation.

65 Contemporaneous correlation usually appears in comparative analyses across countries, so it is widely understood that it will be utilised in studies.

$$PSE_{it} = \alpha + \beta 1X1_{it} + \beta 2X2_{it} + \cdots + e_{it}$$

(PSE: Public Social Expenditure, x1, x2, ... : Variables related to the ICT usage and previously discussed relevant variables related to the development of the welfare state, i: country, t: time, e: residuals)

The following two tables (see Table 6.3 and Table 6.4) reveal the results of the cross-sectional regression analyses for public social spendin g.[66] In 1996, there are no significant variables related to ICT usage. However, in 2005, mobile phones show a weak positive significance, with an estimated coefficient of 0.0830 and 90% probability (* $p < 0.1$).

<Table 6.3> Results of Simple Cross-sectional Regression Analyses for Year 1996

	Simple Cross-sectional Analysis for Public Social Expenditure: 1996		
	1 Internet User Rates Model 1	2 Mobile Phones Model 1	3 PC Numbers Model 1
Dependent Variable	Public Social Expenditure		
	Independent Variables		
Internet user rates	0.259		
	(-0.272)		
Mobile phones		0.0616	
		(-0.181)	
PC numbers			-0.033
			(-0.192)
	Control Variables		
GDP per capita	4.386**	4.425*	5.122**
	(-1.984)	(-2.168)	(-2.441)
Economic openness	0.031	0.0307	0.025
	(-0.0407)	(-0.044)	(-0.0403)
Urban population rates	0.0276	0.0262	
	(-0.116)	(-0.122)	
Civil liberties	-0.204	-0.675	-1.006
	(-1.787)	(-1.764)	(-1.819)
Trade unemployment rates	0.770***	0.738**	0.721**
	(-0.263)	(-0.266)	(-0.271)
Constant	-34.62	-33.18	-35.68
	(-21.49)	(-22.99)	(-22.98)
Observations	27	27	27
R-squared	0.565	0.548	0.544
Standard errors in parentheses			
*** p<0.01, ** p<0.05, * p<0.1			

66 In the case of the simple cross-sectional regressions for year 1996, Estonia, Hungary, Iceland, Israel, Luxembourg, Slovakia, and Slovenia are excluded due to missing values, so only 27 countries are utilised in the analyses. In the case of the simple cross-sectional regressions for year 2005, only 31 countries are used in the analysis for PC Numbers Model 2. Australia, Israel and Japan are omitted due to missing values, and urban population rates is excluded as a control variable due to multicollinearity.

<Table 6.4> **Results of Simple Cross-sectional Regression Analyses for Year 2005**

	Simple Cross-sectional Analysis for Public Social Expenditure: 2005		
	1 Internet User Rates Model 2	2 Mobile Phones Model 2	3 PC Numbers Model 2
Dependent Variable		Public Social Expenditure	
		Independent Variables	
Internet user rates	-0.0614		
	(-0.0551)		
Mobile phones		0.0830*	
		(-0.0465)	
PC numbers			-0.0601
			(-0.0487)
		Control Variables	
GDP per captia	7.019***	5.139***	7.207***
	(-1.675)	(-1.494)	(-1.849)
Economic openness	-0.00557	-0.0133	-0.00894
	(-0.015)	(-0.015)	(-0.0159)
Urban population rates	-0.0171	-0.0212	-0.0244
	(-0.0744)	(-0.0699)	(-0.0793)
Civil liberties	-4.226**	-3.106*	-4.610**
	(-1.84)	(-1.704)	(-2.055)
Trade unemployment rates	0.856***	0.825***	0.810***
	(-0.266)	(-0.258)	(-0.283)
Constant	-47.21**	-39.25**	-48.00**
	(-17.66)	(-15.94)	(-19.59)
Observations	34	34	31
R-squared	0.598	0.624	0.612
Standard errors in parentheses			
*** p<0.01, ** p<0.05, * p<0.1			

3) Panel-corrected Standard Errors (PCSE) Model Analyses

As shown in the tests above, the pooled TSCS data violates the basic assumptions of OLS. Therefore, in the analyses, the basic model is established using the PCSE model absent a lagged dependent variable, country dummy and time dummy according to Pluemper et al's suggestion. Next, a comparison model is established using the PCSE model, which includes a lagged dependent variable, country dummy and time dummy according to Beck & Katz's suggestion. The basic model and comparison model can be affirmed as follows:

Pluemper's model (Basic model): $PSE_{it} = \alpha + \beta 1X1_{it} + \beta 2X2_{it} + \cdots + e_{it}$

Beck & Katz's model (Comparison model):

$$PSE_{it} = \alpha + \beta 0PSE_{it-5} + \beta 1X1_{it} + \cdots + \sum \beta_i\, countrydummy_{it} + \sum \beta_{ik}\, timedummy_{kit} + e_{it}$$

(PSE: Public Social Expenditure, x1, x2, ... : Variables related to the ICT usage and previously discussed relevant variables related to the development of the welfare state, i: country, t: time, e: residuals)

When analysing the basic model and comparison model, three periods of time are represented: The entire period (from 1985 to 2010), the period before year 2000, and the period after year 2000.[67] As shown in the following tables, only Internet user rates show significant results in the Pluemper model and the Beck & Katz model. Looking at the Internet User Rates Model 1 (see Table 6.5), with an estimated coefficient of 0.0212 and 99% probability (***p<0.01), there is a positive relationship between public social expenditure and Internet user rates during the entire period. In the Beck & Katz model, Internet user rates show a weak negative significance pre-2000 (with an estimated coefficient of 0.0243 and 95% probability (**p<0.05)), and a weak positive significance post-2000 (with an estimated coefficient of 0.0268 and 99% probability (***p<0.01)). In the case of mobile phones (see Table 6.6), in the analyses of the Pluemper model, positive associations appear for the entire period (with an estimated coefficient of 0.0187 and 99% probability (***p<0.01)), as well as post-2000 (with an estimated coefficient of 0.0277 and 99% probability (***p<0.01)). In the Beck & Katz model, the association between mobile phones and public social expenditure show a weak positive significance for the entire period (with an estimated coefficient of 0.00928 and 90% probability (*p<0.1)). Looking at PC numbers (see Table 6.7), the results show a weak negative significance for the entire period (with an estimated coefficient of 0.0185 and 95% probability (**p<0.05)), as well as post-2000 (with an estimated coefficient of 0.0144 and 90% probability (*p<0.1)) in the Beck & Katz model.

[67] The reasons of these time period divisions are the same as those given in the previous analyses of chapter 4.

<Table 6.5> Results of PCSE Model Analyses for Internet User Rates

	Pluemper Model			Beck & Katz Model		
	1	2	3	4	5	6
	Internet User Rates Model1	Internet User Rates Model2	Internet User Rates Model3	Internet User Rates Model4	Internet User Rates Model5	Internet User Rates Model6
Dependent Variable	Public Social Expenditure					
	Independent Variables					
Public social expenditure				0.147***	-0.159	0.0529
(5 lagged level)				(-0.0442)	(-0.0993)	(-0.0557)
Internet user rates	0.0212***	-0.0111	0.00963	0.00147	-0.0243**	0.0268***
	(-0.00781)	(-0.0289)	(-0.0127)	(-0.00751)	(-0.0114)	(-0.00878)
	Control Variables					
GDP per capita	2.078***	1.752**	2.576***	-0.861*	-0.695	-2.062***
	(-0.403)	(-0.804)	(-0.515)	(-0.475)	(-0.878)	(-0.585)
Corruption Perception Index	0.339**	0.661**	0.348*	0.114	0.011	0.310**
	(-0.15)	(-0.313)	(-0.197)	(-0.112)	(-0.137)	(-0.144)
Urban population rates	-0.0936***	-0.0427	-0.0908***	0.137***	0.167	0.0504
	(-0.0251)	(-0.0469)	(-0.0295)	(-0.0439)	(-0.22)	(-0.0509)
Political rights	-1.777***	-3.415***	-2.878***	0.0162	-0.0928	0.108
	(-0.395)	(-0.827)	(-0.62)	(-0.3)	(-0.562)	(-0.414)
Civil liberties	0.0446	1.449**	0.0217	0.26	1.059	0.323*
	(-0.289)	(-0.737)	(-0.371)	(-0.163)	(-0.771)	(-0.173)
Trade union density	0.103***	0.0989***	0.0861***	0.0583**	0.00404	0.0828***
	(-0.0157)	(-0.0261)	(-0.017)	(-0.0231)	(-0.0554)	(-0.0244)
Total unemployment rates	0.497***	0.532***	0.562***	0.243***	0.317***	0.251***
	(-0.0441)	(-0.118)	(-0.0545)	(-0.0338)	(-0.0602)	(-0.0352)
Economic openness	-0.0109**	0.00548	-0.0102**	-0.0261***	-0.0265	-0.0302***
	(-0.00428)	(-0.00936)	(-0.0043)	(-0.0071)	(-0.0162)	(-0.00795)
Constant	-0.797	-4.933	-4.237		8.79	
	(-3.985)	(-7.588)	(-5.013)		-19.45	
Observations	455	116	339	437	112	325
R-squared	0.781	0.79	0.768	0.967	0.995	0.976
Number of country	33	32	33	33	29	32
Standard errors in parentheses						
*** p<0.01, ** p<0.05, * p<0.1						

<Table 6.6> Results of PCSE Model Analyses for Mobile Phones

	Pluemper Model			Beck & Katz Model		
	1	2	3	4	5	6
	Mobile Phones Model1	Mobile Phones Model2	Mobile Phones Model3	Mobile Phones Model4	Mobile Phones Model5	Mobile Phones Model6
Dependent Variable	Public Social Expenditure					
	Independent Variables					
Public social expenditure				0.0804*	-0.187***	0.00115
(5 lagged level)				(-0.0449)	(-0.061)	(-0.0533)
Mobile phones	0.0187***	0.00738	0.0277***	0.00928*	-0.0118	0.00724
	(-0.00389)	(-0.0117)	(-0.00641)	(-0.00505)	(-0.0122)	(-0.00603)
	Control Variables					
GDP per capita	2.087***	2.775***	2.108***	-0.614	0.139	-1.701***
	(-0.288)	(-0.409)	(-0.472)	(-0.421)	(-0.756)	(-0.597)
Urban population rates	-0.024	-0.00849	-0.0511**	0.133**	-0.158	0.116**
	(-0.0213)	(-0.0271)	(-0.026)	(-0.0576)	(-0.151)	(-0.05)
Political rights	-0.644***	-0.548**	-3.127***	-0.264	0.0015	0.128
	(-0.243)	(-0.269)	(-0.664)	(-0.197)	(-0.276)	(-0.466)
Civil liberties	-0.107	-0.146	-0.0835	0.103	-0.141	0.302*
	(-0.173)	(-0.239)	(-0.332)	(-0.136)	(-0.205)	(-0.17)
Trade union density	0.0984***	0.0871***	0.0969***	0.0250*	0.0224	0.0703***
	(-0.0115)	(-0.0145)	(-0.0167)	(-0.014)	(-0.0166)	(-0.0255)
Total unemployment rates	0.492***	0.536***	0.539***	0.276***	0.348***	0.256***
	(-0.0336)	(-0.0544)	(-0.0498)	(-0.0311)	(-0.0528)	(-0.0367)
Economic openness	-0.00419	0.0212***	-0.0122***	-0.0236***	-0.0466***	-0.0237***
	(-0.00392)	(-0.00634)	(-0.00431)	(-0.00601)	(-0.0109)	(-0.00811)
Constant	-5.516*	-14.70***	-1.538	9.775	26.53*	23.82**
	(-2.963)	(-4.157)	(-4.45)	(-7.609)	(-14.47)	(-9.425)
Observations	729	387	342	587	259	328
R-squared	0.7	0.741	0.779	0.938	0.973	0.975
Number of country	33	32	33	33	29	32
Standard errors in parentheses						
*** p<0.01, ** p<0.05, * p<0.1						

<Table 6.7> **Results of PCSE Model Analyses for PC numbers**

	Pluemper Model			Beck & Katz Model		
	1	2	3	4	5	6
	PC Numbers Model1	PC Numbers Model2	PC Numbers Model3	PC Numbers Model4	PC Numbers Model5	PC Numbers Model6
Dependent Variable	Public Social Expenditure					
	Independent Variables					
Public social expenditure				0.178***	-0.132	-0.0134
(5 lagged level)				(-0.0498)	(-0.101)	(-0.0515)
PC numbers	-0.00706	0.00765	-0.0207	-0.0185**	-0.0283	-0.0144*
	(-0.0113)	(-0.0234)	(-0.0147)	(-0.00808)	(-0.0288)	(-0.00783)
	Control Variables					
GDP per capita	2.354***	3.266***	3.114***	-0.228	-0.32	-0.659
	(-0.471)	(-0.515)	(-0.607)	(-0.554)	(-0.87)	(-0.745)
Corruption Perception Index	0.448**			-0.0692	-0.00496	0.0307
	(-0.174)			(-0.107)	(-0.141)	(-0.141)
Urban population rates	-0.0917***	-0.017	-0.0556	0.134**	0.198	0.134*
	(-0.0301)	(-0.029)	(-0.034)	(-0.0624)	(-0.227)	(-0.0692)
Political rights	-1.895***	-0.592**	-3.571***	-0.118	0.0201	0.123
	(-0.438)	(-0.278)	(-0.878)	(-0.263)	(-0.483)	(-0.478)
Civil liberties	0.0361	-0.0648	-0.245	0.322**	1.181	0.422***
	(-0.314)	(-0.239)	(-0.39)	(-0.156)	(-0.731)	(-0.151)
Trade union density	0.0924***	0.0841***	0.0839***	0.0252	0.0122	0.0434
	(-0.0161)	(-0.0161)	(-0.0191)	(-0.0258)	(-0.054)	(-0.0277)
Total unemployment rates	0.453***	0.557***	0.493***	0.169***	0.333***	0.175***
	(-0.0623)	(-0.0611)	(-0.0821)	(-0.0342)	(-0.0607)	(-0.0409)
Economic openness	-0.0014	0.0174**	-0.00436	-0.0282***	-0.0257	-0.0281***
	(-0.0045)	(-0.0084)	(-0.0046)	(-0.00742)	(-0.0177)	(-0.008)
Constant	-3.759	-18.93***	-7.74			
	(-4.729)	(-5.166)	(-6.354)			
Observations	335	331	219	320	112	208
R-squared	0.804	0.749	0.796	0.98	0.995	0.988
Number of country	33	32	33	33	29	32
Standard errors in parentheses						
*** p<0.01, ** p<0.05, * p<0.1						

4) Error Correction Model (ECM) and Vector Error Correction Model (VECM) Analyses

If non-stationary time-series data is regressed, then unit root tests, co-integration tests, and the Granger causality test are performed as pre-tests in order to avoid 'spurious regression' situations. If the series are non-stationary but co-integrated, the ECM and VECM analyses are performed. The equations of these models can be shown as follows[68]:

$$\Delta PSE_{it} = \alpha + \beta_1 \cdot PSE_{it-1} + \sum \beta^j \cdot X^j_{it-1} + \sum \beta^j_\Delta \cdot X^j_{it-1} + e_t$$

$$\Delta PSE_{it} = \alpha + \beta_1 \cdot PSE_{it-1} + \sum \beta^j \cdot X_1{}^j_{it-1} + \sum \beta^j \cdot X_2{}^j_{it-1} \dots + \sum \beta^j_\Delta \cdot X_1{}^j_{it-1} + \sum \beta^j_\Delta \cdot X_2 X^j_{it-1} \dots + e_t$$

(PSE: Public Social Expenditure, x1, x2, ... : Variables related to the ICT usage and previously discussed relevant variables related to the development of the welfare state, Δ: first difference, i: country, t: time, e: residuals)

First, the graphs reveal that the pooled time-series cross-section data

68 For a full interpretation of results, see the Error Correction Model (ECM) and Vector Error Correction Model (VECM) Analyses in chapter 5, section 4.

has trends over time.[69] The results of the Breitung unit-root test and Im-Pesaran-Shin unit-root test show that all variables have unit roots and are non-stationary. However, these variables can be stationary and do not have unit roots when they are first differenced. Second, the results of Westerlund's error-correction-based co-integration tests show there are co-integrations between the dependent variable and independent variables. Third, the results of the Granger causality test confirm the causal relationship between the dependent variable and independent variables.[70] Finally, when conducting tests for heteroskedasticity in each pooled regression, the panel-corrected standard error model according to Beck & Katz's suggestion is applied in order to carry out ECM and VECM, including country dummy in the models.[71]

As shown in Table 6.8, the results of the ECM analyses show that Internet user rates and mobile phones share a negative significance with public social expenditure, while PC numbers show no significance with public social expenditure in the long term. This can be interpreted as a negative association existing between public social spending and Internet user rates. Mobile phones also have a negative effect on increasing public social expenditure.

The results of the VECM analyses (see Table 6.9) reveal similar phenomena to those of the ECM analyses. Three variables related to ICT usage (Internet user rates, mobile phones and PC numbers) show negative effects on public social expenditure in the long term. Internet user rates show a negative relationship with public social expenditure in the short term, while mobile phones show no significant relationship in the short term. It would seem an exception, then, that PC numbers share a positive significance with public social spending in the short term.

The long-term permanent effect of Internet user rates is -0.22; that is, for each percentage point that Internet user rates grow, the long-term equilibrium level of public social spending declines by 0.22. The corresponding effect for PC numbers is -0.13. In other words, for each percent that PC numbers declines, the long-term target equilibrium for public social expenditure increases by approximately 0.13.

---

69 Please see graphs in the figures in the appendix.

70 All these results are added in the appendix on account of space consideration.

71 Estonia, Slovakia and Slovenia are not included in the ECM and VECM analysis.

<Table 6.8> Results of ECM Analyses

	ECM with Country FE		
	1 Internet User Rates Model	2 Mobile Phones Model	3 PC Numbers Model
Dependent Variable	△Public Social Expenditure		
	Independent Variables		
Public social expenditure (Lagged level)	-0.00523 (-0.00514)	-0.0067 (-0.00581)	-0.00970** (-0.00477)
△Internet user rates	-0.00391 (-0.00272)		
Internet user rates (Lagged level)	-0.000641** (-0.000277)		
△Mobile phones		0.000759 (-0.00179)	
Mobil phones (Lagged level)		-0.000409** (-0.000199)	
△PC numbers			0.00567 (-0.00504)
PC numbers (Lagged level)			-0.00068 (-0.000414)
Constant	0.292*** (-0.0761)	0.298*** (-0.0851)	0.345*** (-0.0687)
Observations	775	775	775
R-squared	0.393	0.389	0.388
Number of country	31	31	31
Standard errors in parentheses *** p<0.01, ** p<0.05, * p<0.1			

<Table 6.9> **Results of VECM Analyses**

	VECM with Country FE		
	1 Internet User Rates Model	2 Mobile Phones Model	3 PC Numbers Model
Dependent Variable	△Public Social Expenditure		
	Independent Variables		
Public social expenditure (Lagged level)	-0.0131** (-0.0055)	-0.00781 (-0.00554)	-0.0160*** (-0.00559)
△Internet user rates	-0.00713** (-0.00292)		
Internet user rates (Lagged level)	-0.00290*** (-0.000424)		
△Mobile phones		-0.000409 (-0.00213)	
Mobil phones (Lagged level)		-0.00244*** (-0.000336)	
△PC numbers			0.0114** (-0.0051)
PC numbers (Lagged level)			-0.00221*** (-0.000484)
	Control Variables		
△GDP per capita	0.446 (-0.272)	0.266 (-0.269)	0.114 (-0.273)
GDP per capita (Lagged level)	0.238*** (-0.0371)	0.266*** (-0.0394)	0.153*** (-0.0339)
△Economic openness	-0.0110** (-0.00465)	-0.0164*** (-0.00485)	-0.0147*** (-0.0047)
Economic openness (Lagged level)	-0.000298 (-0.000494)	0.000237 (-0.0005290	-0.00118** (-0.000505)
△Civil liberties	0.00173 (-0.0202)	-0.00443 (-0.0198)	0.00948 (-0.0199)
Civil liberties (Lagged level)	0.0300** (-0.015)	0.0256* (-0.0152)	0.0340** (-0.0147)
△Political rights	-0.0101 (-0.0224)	-0.00696 (-0.0212)	-0.0169 (-0.0219)
Political rights (Lagged level)	0.015 (-0.014)	0.0154 (-0.0134)	-0.00164 (-0.0135)
Constant	-1.942*** (-0.331)	-2.313*** (-0.373)	-1.027*** (-0.289)
Observations	775	775	775
R-squared	0.443	0.443	0.419
Number of country	31	31	31
Standard errors in parentheses			
*** p<0.01, ** p<0.05, * p<0.1			

5) First Difference Model Analyses

The first difference model analyses can detect the impact of short-term changes in independent variables on short-term changes in the dependent variable. This next analysis is performed to determine the impact of short-term changes in ICT usage on short-term changes in public social expenditure. The equation consists of first differences of all variables.[72]

72 Estonia, Slovakia and Slovenia are not included in the first difference model analyses.

$$\Delta PSE_i = \beta_1 \Delta x_{1_i} + \beta_2 \Delta x_{2_i} \ldots + \Delta e_i$$

(PSE: Public Social Expenditure, x1, x2, ... : Variables related to ICT usage and previously discussed relevant variables related to the development of the welfare state, Δ: first difference, i: country, e: residuals)

As shown in the following tables (see Table 6.10, Table 6.11, and Table 6.12), during pre-2000 as well as the entire period, Internet user rates share a weak negative significance with public social expenditure, with an estimated coefficient of -0.0175 (***p<0.01) and with an estimated coefficient of -0.0107 (***p<0.01). Mobile phones show positive significance post-2000, with an estimated coefficient of 0.0127 and 99% probability (***p<0.01). In the case of PC numbers, the relationship with public social expenditure shows negative significance pre-2000 (with an estimated coefficient of 0.0153 and 99% probability (***p<0.01)) and also shows a negative significance for the entire period (with an estimated coefficient of 0.0229 and 99% probability (***p<0.01)). In the short term, therefore, it can be said that PC numbers exhibit a weak negative effect on the change of public social expenditure.

In the case of the civil liberties variable, after the first difference, 3 were added to all values in order to perform the analysis appropriately.

<Table 6.10> Results of First Difference Model Analyses for Internet User Rates

	First Difference Model		
	1 Internet User Rates Model 1	2 Internet User Rates Model 2	3 Internet User Rates Model 3
Dependent Variable	△Public Social Expenditure		
	Independent Variables		
△Internet user rates	-0.0107*** (-0.003)	-0.0175*** (-0.0056)	-0.00556 (-0.00467)
	Control Variables		
△GDP per capita	0.327 (-0.268)	-0.227 (-0.459)	0.755** (-0.364)
△Economic openness	-0.0114*** (-0.00415)	-0.0152*** (-0.00558)	-0.00549 (-0.00616)
△Corruption Perception Index	0.287** (-0.146)	-0.0765 (-0.217)	0.393** (-0.191)
△Urban population rates	0.0581*** (-0.0225)	-0.016 (-0.0303)	0.206*** (-0.0341)
△Civil liberties	-0.00965 (-0.0218)	-0.00663 (-0.027)	-0.01 (-0.0385)
Constant	0.160** (-0.0681)	0.213** (-0.084)	0.0694 (-0.12)
Observations	775	434	341
R-squared	0.053	0.061	0.137
Number of country	31	31	31
Standard errors in parentheses *** p<0.01, ** p<0.05, * p<0.1			

<Table 6.11> Results of First Difference Model Analyses for Mobile Phones

	First Difference Model		
	1 Mobile Phones Model 1	2 Mobile Phones Model 2	3 Mobile Phones Model 3
Dependent Variable	△Public Social Expenditure		
	Independent Variables		
△Mobile phones	0.0016 (-0.00215)	0.00397 (-0.00375)	0.0127*** (-0.00361)
	Control Variables		
△GDP per capita	0.25 (-0.273)	0.478 (-0.447)	-0.102 (-0.388)
△Economic openness	-0.0169*** (-0.00439)	-0.0241*** (-0.00606)	-0.0158** (-0.00636)
△Corruption Perception Index	0.239 (-0.147)	-0.0273 (-0.219)	0.377** (-0.187)
△Urban population rates	0.0589*** (-0.0227)	-0.0228 (-0.0305)	0.211*** (-0.0335)
△Civil liberties	-0.00956 (-0.022)	-0.0135 (-0.0272)	0.000617 (-0.038)
Constant	0.134* (-0.0687)	0.174** (-0.0847)	-0.00742 (-0.119)
Observations	775	434	341
R-squared	0.038	0.042	0.165
Number of country	31	31	31
Standard errors in parentheses *** p<0.01, ** p<0.05, * p<0.1			

<Table 6.12> **Results of First Difference Model Analyses for PC Numbers**

	First Difference Model		
	1 PC Numbers Model 1	2 PC Numbers Model 2	3 PC Numbers Model 3
Dependent Variable	△Public social expenditure		
	Independent Variables		
△PC numbers	-0.0153*** (-0.0049)	-0.0229*** (-0.00842)	-0.00845 (-0.00571)
	Control Variables		
△GDP per capita	0.214 (-0.269)	-0.0588 (-0.448)	0.652* (-0.341)
△Economic openness	-0.0135*** (-0.00405)	-0.0175*** (-0.00543)	-0.00699 (-0.00597)
△Corruption Perception Index	0.250* (-0.146)	-0.0843 (-0.218)	0.381** (-0.19)
△Urban population rates	0.0555** (-0.0225)	-0.0209 (-0.0303)	0.202*** (-0.0339)
△Civil liberties	-0.00701 (-0.0219)	-0.00522 (-0.0271)	-0.00809 (-0.0385)
Constant	0.158** (-0.0683)	0.211** (-0.0843)	0.0657 (-0.119)
Observations	775	434	341
R-squared	0.05	0.055	0.139
Number of country	31	31	31
Standard errors in parentheses *** p<0.01, ** p<0.05, * p<0.1			

6) Panel Vector Autoregressive (PVAR) Model Analyses

Panel vector autoregressive (PVAR) model analyses can inform the response of public social expenditure to changes in ICT usage variables in the short term. The model can be affirmed by demonstration in the following equation. In order to consider the non-stationary aspects of the pool time-series cross-section data, first differences of all variables are included in the analyses.

$$\Delta PSE_{it} = \alpha + \beta_1 \Delta PSE_{it-1} + \beta_2 \Delta PSE_{it-2} + \cdots + \beta_p \Delta PSE_{it-n} + \beta_1 \Delta X_{1it-1} + \beta_2 \Delta X_{1it-2} + \cdots + \beta_p \Delta X_{1it-n} + \cdots$$
$$+ \beta_1 \Delta X_{2it-1} + \beta_2 \Delta X_{2it-2} + \cdots + \beta_p \Delta X_{2it-n} + \mu_i + e_i$$

(PSE: Public Social Expenditure, x1, x2, ... : Variables related to ICT usage and previously discussed relevant variables related to the development of the welfare state, Δ: first difference, i: country, t: time, p: lag, μ: group heterogeneity, e: residuals)

The following tables and figures show the results of the PVAR analyses. Specifically, in each of the figures, a highlighted arrow indicates three integral graph lines which shed light on the essence of this study. The pre-coded PVAR program shows the response of public social expenditure to ICT usage variables' shock from one point in time through to the sixth point in time. The figures are drawn according to the results of orthogonalized IRF (Impulse Response Function) through the Monte Carlo loop. Each figure showing the relationships between the dependent variable and independent variables consist of three graphs according to a confidence interval of 95% between the lower graph line and the upper graph line. The middle graph line can be interpreted as impulse-response function.

Examining Internet user rates, the results show a shift from a decreasing effect to an increasing effect at the fifth point in time (see the highlighted part of Table 6.13). This change can be observed in more detail under the highlighted arrow in Figure 6.4. Therefore, it can be said that public social expenditure's response to Internet user rates' shock is negative. Furthermore, the negative shock effect is constant for four years, after which the effect finally disappears. In the case of public social expenditure's response to mobile phones' shock, as shown in Table 6.14, a negative effect can be observed in the first year, only for it to switch to a positive effect in the second year. In the third year, values indicative of a positive effect become much stronger, and remain so until the sixth year. It is evident from the graph lines in Figure 6.5 that mobile phones' impact on public social expenditure ends with a positive effect. The response of public social expenditure to PC numbers' shock is negative (see the highlighted part of Table 6.15), and remains thus for six years. These results can be observed in Figure 6.6 below, under the highlighted arrow, where the middle graph line drops sharply from the first to sixth point, never rising above the zero x-line.

<Table 6.13> Results of Panel Vector Autoregressive Model Analyses for Internet User Rates

Impulse-responses of variable in varname to the shock in column variable	△Internet user rates							
Variables	Shock	Order	△Public social expenditure	△GDP per capita	△Economic openness	△Political rights	△Civil liberties	△Internet user rates
△Public social expenditure	0	1	0.0220	0.0000	0.0000	0.0000	0.0000	0.0000
	1	1	0.0226	-0.0072	-0.0038	-0.0088	-0.0064	-0.0017
	2	1	0.0262	-0.0107	-0.0057	-0.0152	-0.0104	-0.0014
	3	1	0.0230	-0.0157	-0.0086	-0.0235	-0.0141	-0.0016
	4	1	0.0247	-0.0155	-0.0089	-0.0212	-0.0111	-0.0012
	5	1	0.0221	-0.0160	-0.0102	-0.0198	-0.0101	0.0001
	6	1	0.0179	-0.0159	-0.0100	-0.0168	-0.0086	0.0010
△GDP per capita	0	2	0.0069	0.0049	0.0000	0.0000	0.0000	0.0000
	1	2	0.0051	0.0038	-0.0008	-0.0038	-0.0027	-0.0006
	2	2	0.0048	0.0037	-0.0008	-0.0061	-0.0043	-0.0005
	3	2	0.0026	0.0023	-0.0009	-0.0086	-0.0054	-0.0006
	4	2	0.0029	0.0024	-0.0001	-0.0066	-0.0036	-0.0004
	5	2	0.0019	0.0015	0.0001	-0.0052	-0.0029	0.0003
	6	2	0.0006	0.0004	0.0006	-0.0035	-0.0020	0.0007
△Economic openness	0	3	0.0056	-0.0297	0.2140	0.0000	0.0000	0.0000
	1	3	0.0060	-0.0391	0.3799	0.0271	0.0049	-0.0366
	2	3	0.0349	-0.0284	0.4857	0.0335	0.0079	-0.0377
	3	3	0.0289	-0.0275	0.5149	0.0138	-0.0023	-0.0395
	4	3	0.0399	-0.0096	0.4904	-0.0068	-0.0123	-0.0271
	5	3	0.0386	0.0052	0.4173	-0.0324	-0.0243	-0.0139
	6	3	0.0430	0.0251	0.3172	-0.044	-0.0279	0.0022
△Political rights	0	4	0.1946	0.1173	0.0301	0.2822	0.0000	0.0000
	1	4	-0.0711	-0.0561	-0.0415	-0.0896	-0.0584	0.0293
	2	4	-0.1197	-0.0655	-0.0170	-0.0786	-0.0375	-0.0102
	3	4	0.0173	0.0159	0.0099	-0.0025	0.0211	0.0024
	4	4	0.0552	0.0365	0.0099	0.0825	0.0627	-0.0047
	5	4	0.0266	0.0191	-0.0106	0.0302	0.0008	0.0135
	6	4	-0.0334	-0.0165	-0.0160	-0.0480	-0.0436	0.0018
△Civil liberties	0	5	0.0277	0.0084	0.0340	0.1045	0.2789	0.0000
	1	5	-0.0415	-0.0094	-0.0391	0.0277	-0.0548	0.0270
	2	5	0.0320	0.0189	0.0085	0.0141	-0.0127	0.0011
	3	5	-0.0402	-0.0202	0.0013	-0.0270	-0.0089	-0.0100
	4	5	0.0226	0.0195	0.0108	0.0240	0.0203	-0.0043
	5	5	0.0009	0.0053	-0.0063	-0.0077	-0.0073	-0.0025
	6	5	0.0125	0.0116	-0.0029	0.0025	0.0003	-0.0037
△Internet user rates	0	6	0.1016	0.0452	0.0261	-0.0187	-0.0089	0.1592
	1	6	0.0369	0.0013	0.0045	-0.0569	-0.0418	0.2310
	2	6	0.0565	0.0083	0.0127	-0.0484	-0.0385	0.3242
	3	6	0.0139	-0.0185	0.0065	-0.0429	-0.0344	0.3734
	4	6	0.0278	-0.0088	0.0186	0.0234	0.0068	0.4096
	5	6	0.0005	-0.0211	0.0153	0.0507	0.0155	0.4181
	6	6	-0.0056	-0.0183	0.0227	0.0871	0.0347	0.3997

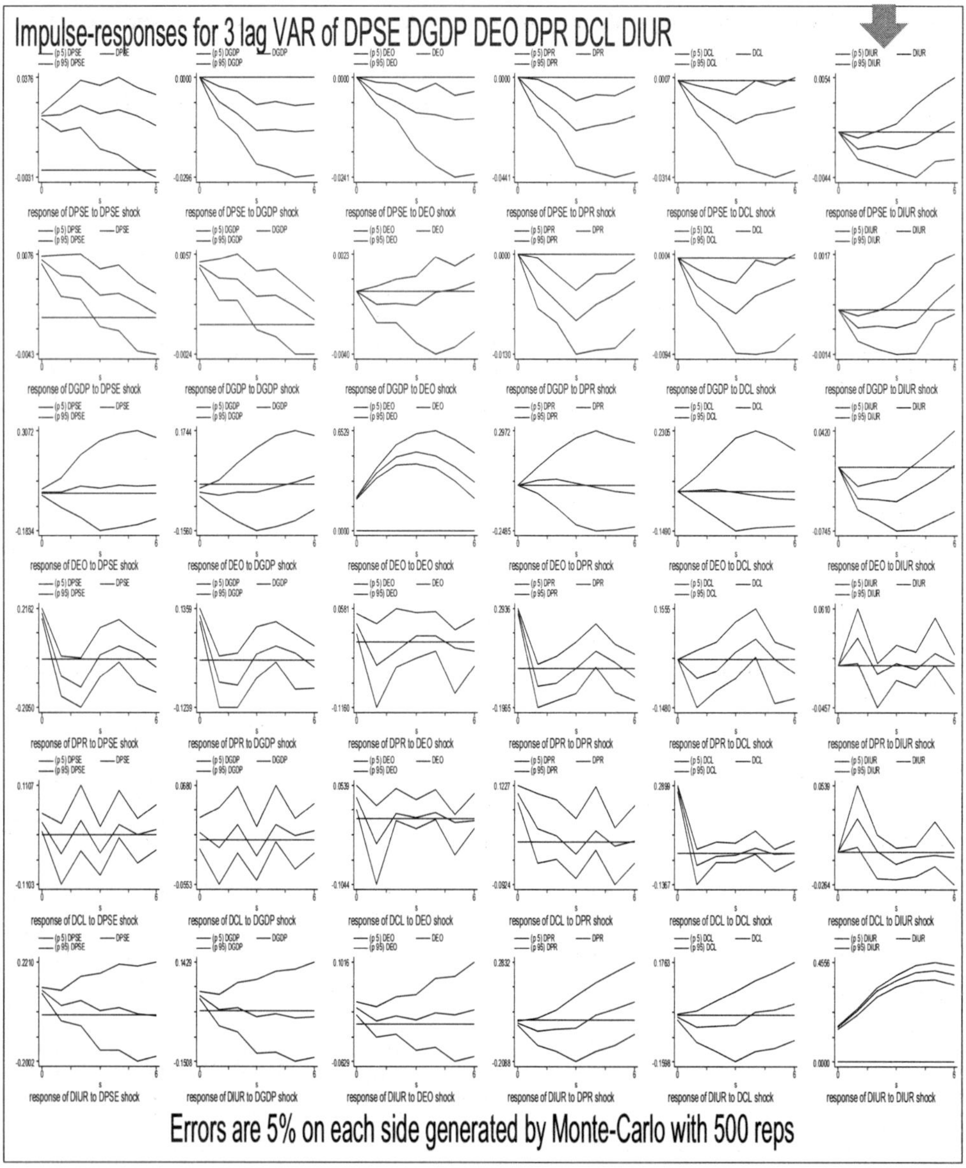

* DPSE: △Public Social Expenditure, DGDP: △GDP per Capita, DEO: △Economic Openness, DPR: △Political rights, DCL: △Civil Liberties, DIUR: △Internet User Rates.

<Figure 6.4> Graphs of Panel Vector Autoregressive Model Analyses for Internet User Rates

<Table 6.14> Results of Panel Vector Autoregressive Model Analyses for Mobile Phones

Impulse-responses of variable in varname to the shock in column variable

△Mobile phone

Variables	Shock	Order	△Public social expenditure	△GDP per capita	△Economic openness	△Political rights	△Civil liberties	△Mobile phones
△Public social expenditure	0	1	0.0192	0.0000	0.0000	0.0000	0.0000	0.0000
	1	1	0.0212	-0.0066	-0.0036	-0.0073	-0.0050	-0.0002
	2	1	0.0260	-0.0092	-0.0058	-0.0124	-0.0081	0.0004
	3	1 .	0.0246	-0.0137	-0.0087	-0.0197	-0.0114	0.0010
	4	1	0.0258	-0.0136	-0.0095	-0.0186	-0.0094	0.0017
	5	1	0.0238	-0.0138	-0.0109	-0.0178	-0.009	0.0033
	6	1	0.0199	-0.0137	-0.0109	-0.0155	-0.0078	0.0043
△GDP per capita	0	2	0.0068	0.0057	0.0000	0.0000	0.0000	0.0000
	1	2	0.0049	0.0041	-0.0009	-0.0041	-0.0029	-0.0003
	2	2	0.0048	0.0042	-0.0009	-0.0064	-0.0044	-0.0003
	3	2	0.0028	0.0025	-0.0011	-0.0092	-0.0057	-0.0002
	4	2	0.0029	0.0025	-0.0003	-0.0071	-0.0039	0.0000
	5	2	0.0021	0.0018	-0.0002	-0.0056	-0.0031	0.0008
	6	2	0.0008	0.0006	0.0002	-0.0038	-0.0023	0.0012
△Economic openness	0	3	-0.0363	-0.0676	0.2180	0.0000	0.0000	0.0000
	1	3	-0.0491	-0.0879	0.3897	0.0530	0.0264	-0.0281
	2	3	-0.0033	-0.0596	0.4996	0.0959	0.0561	-0.0258
	3	3	0.0170	-0.0405	0.5323	0.1045	0.0622	-0.0216
	4	3	0.0400	-0.0121	0.5056	0.0766	0.0408	-0.0066
	5	3	0.0448	0.0063	0.4316	0.0226	0.0077	0.0069
	6	3	0.0588	0.0343	0.3310	-0.0145	-0.0108	0.0222
△Political rights	0	4	0.1565	0.1268	0.0235	0.2772	0.0000	0.0000
	1	4	-0.0346	-0.0397	-0.0376	-0.0728	-0.0463	0.0303
	2	4	-0.1155	-0.0828	-0.0180	-0.0851	-0.0415	-0.0118
	3	4	0.0127	0.0154	0.0119	-0.0021	0.0182	-0.0027
	4	4	0.0381	0.0338	0.0081	0.0680	0.0529	-0.0038
	5	4	0.0355	0.0319	-0.0074	0.0388	0.0102	0.0115
	6	4	-0.0241	-0.0157	-0.0163	-0.0456	-0.0425	0.0029
△Civil liberties	0	5	0.0213	0.0102	0.0339	0.1039	0.2767	0.0000
	1	5	-0.0177	0.0069	-0.0385	0.0332	-0.0536	0.0345
	2	5	0.0139	0.0092	0.0028	0.0046	-0.0214	-0.0050
	3	5	-0.0399	-0.0261	0.0025	-0.0260	-0.0091	-0.0075
	4	5	0.0136	0.0174	0.0091	0.0200	0.0192	-0.0076
	5	5	0.0082	0.0115	-0.0031	0.0032	0.0020	-0.0036
	6	5	0.0104	0.0125	-0.0039	0.0034	-0.0003	-0.0053
△Mobile phones	0	6	0.2563	0.1624	0.0673	-0.0041	-0.0076	0.2216
	1	6	0.1743	0.0732	0.0692	-0.1148	-0.0979	0.3223
	2	6	0.2251	0.0943	0.1308	-0.1373	-0.1290	0.4354
	3	6	0.1726	0.0409	0.1654	-0.1915	-0.1679	0.4971
	4	6	0.2147	0.0725	0.2211	-0.1030	-0.1077	0.5338
	5	6	0.1996	0.0687	0.2264	-0.0820	-0.1099	0.5510
	6	6	0.1839	0.0734	0.2227	-0.0554	-0.0999	0.5268

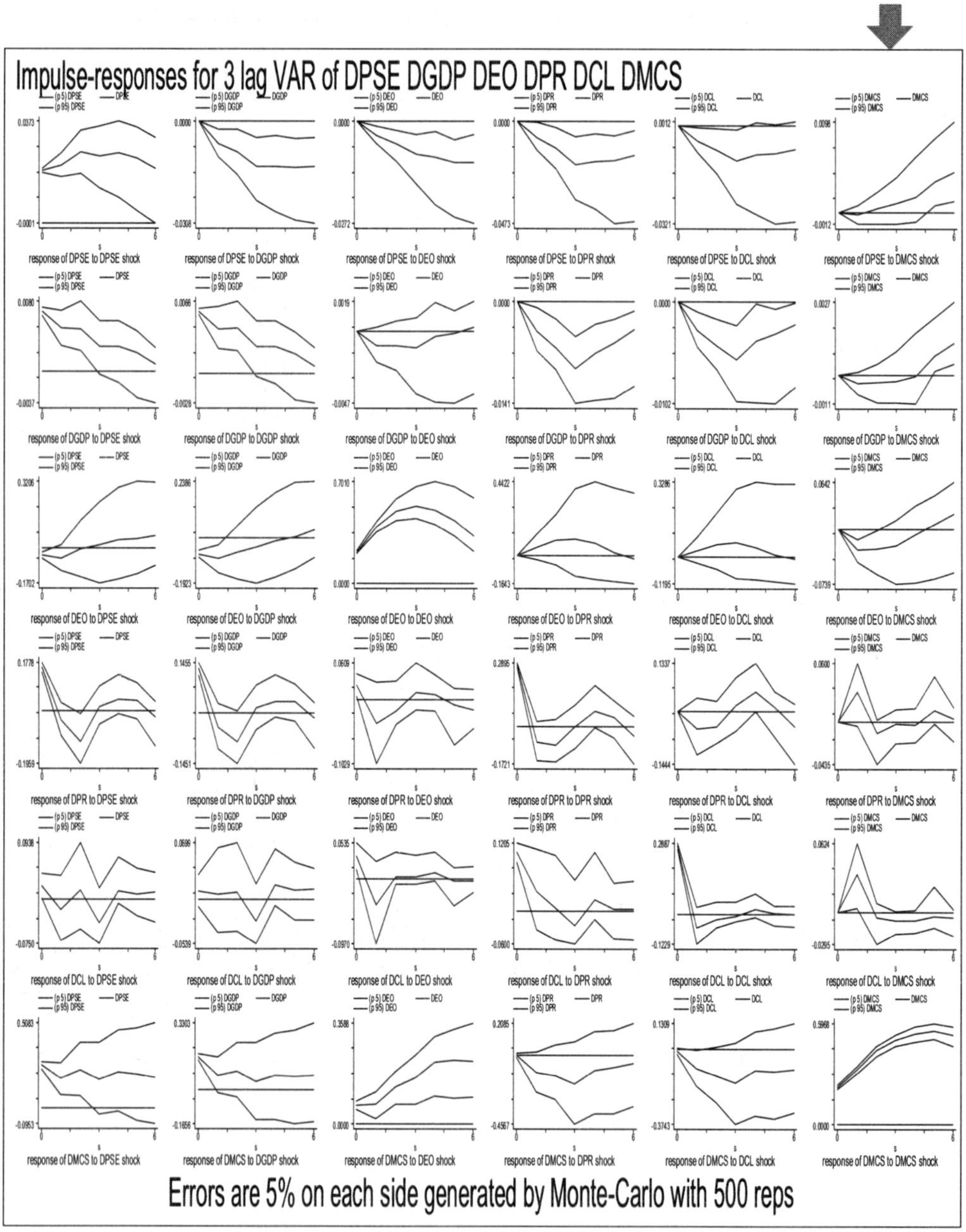

* DPSE: △Public Social Expenditure, DGDP: △GDP per Capita, DEO: △Economic Openness, DPR: △Political Rights, DCL: △Civil Liberties, DMCS: △Mobile Phones.

<Figure 6.5> Graphs of Panel Vector Autoregressive Model Analyses for Mobile Phones

<Table 6.15> Results of Panel Vector Autoregressive Model Analyses for PC Numbers

Impulse-responses of variable in varname to the shock in column variable

△PC number								
Variables	Shock	Order	△Public social expenditure	△GDP per capita	△Economic openness	△Political rights	△Civil liberties	△PC numbers
△Public social expenditure	0	1	0.0166	0.0000	0.0000	0.0000	0.0000	0.0000
	1	1	0.0207	-0.0045	-0.0026	-0.0050	-0.0039	-0.0032
	2	1	0.0239	-0.0091	-0.0035	-0.0100	-0.0066	-0.0024
	3	1	0.0242	-0.0122	-0.0055	-0.0143	-0.0082	-0.0044
	4	1	0.0260	-0.0116	-0.0057	-0.0131	-0.0062	-0.0035
	5	1	0.0245	-0.0114	-0.0066	-0.0117	-0.0055	-0.0038
	6	1	0.0201	-0.0129	-0.0058	-0.0113	-0.0055	-0.0027
△GDP per capita	0	2	0.0048	0.0055	0.0000	0.0000	0.0000	0.0000
	1	2	0.0033	0.0039	-0.0003	-0.0034	-0.0024	-0.0008
	2	2	0.0029	0.0035	0.0001	-0.0051	-0.0035	-0.0007
	3	2	0.0016	0.0020	0.0002	-0.0067	-0.0041	-0.0011
	4	2	0.0026	0.0030	0.0007	-0.0043	-0.0022	-0.0008
	5	2	0.0014	0.0016	0.0009	-0.0035	-0.0020	-0.0004
	6	2	0.0003	0.0003	0.0014	-0.0024	-0.0015	-0.0001
△Economic openness	0	3	-0.0587	-0.1143	0.2265	0.0000	0.0000	0.0000
	1	3	-0.0103	-0.0624	0.3918	0.1061	0.0481	-0.0407
	2	3	0.0018	-0.0692	0.5003	0.1318	0.0626	-0.0236
	3	3	0.0315	-0.0229	0.5278	0.1694	0.0760	-0.0410
	4	3	0.0021	-0.0541	0.5121	0.0980	0.0323	-0.0144
	5	3	0.0324	0.0053	0.4468	0.0928	0.0363	-0.0272
	6	3	0.0327	0.0145	0.3580	0.0418	0.0152	0.0024
△Political rights	0	4	0.2241	0.2636	-0.0197	0.3174	0.0000	0.0000
	1	4	-0.1595	-0.2092	-0.0204	-0.1809	-0.1095	0.0346
	2	4	-0.0716	-0.0490	-0.0087	-0.0477	-0.0156	-0.0359
	3	4	-0.0036	-0.0129	0.0158	-0.0288	0.0208	0.0295
	4	4	0.1364	0.1719	-0.0138	0.1815	0.1147	-0.027
	5	4	-0.0547	-0.0755	-0.0145	-0.0607	-0.0656	0.0481
	6	4	-0.0317	-0.0145	-0.011	-0.0379	-0.0386	-0.0368
△Civil liberties	0	5	0.0748	0.0781	0.0139	0.1244	0.2784	0.0000
	1	5	-0.0782	-0.0707	-0.04	-0.0273	-0.0865	0.0369
	2	5	0.0145	0.0205	0.0069	0.0089	-0.0161	-0.0147
	3	5	-0.0430	-0.0481	0.012	-0.0476	-0.0106	0.0045
	4	5	0.0590	0.0789	0.0005	0.0748	0.0515	-0.0106
	5	5	-0.0193	-0.0239	-0.0091	-0.0289	-0.0251	0.0165
	6	5	0.0086	0.0213	-0.0104	0.0058	-0.0033	-0.0146
△PC numbers	0	6	0.0112	-0.0190	0.0195	-0.0214	-0.0055	0.0757
	1	6	0.0261	-0.0040	0.0112	-0.0106	-0.0017	0.0813
	2	6	0.0227	-0.0313	0.0246	-0.0290	-0.0074	0.1386
	3	6	0.0349	-0.0159	0.0201	-0.0112	0.0010	0.1392
	4	6	0.0246	-0.0419	0.0322	-0.0277	-0.0057	0.1746
	5	6	0.0393	-0.0188	0.0324	-0.0020	0.0077	0.1623
	6	6	0.0272	-0.0386	0.0433	-0.0161	-0.0002	0.1764

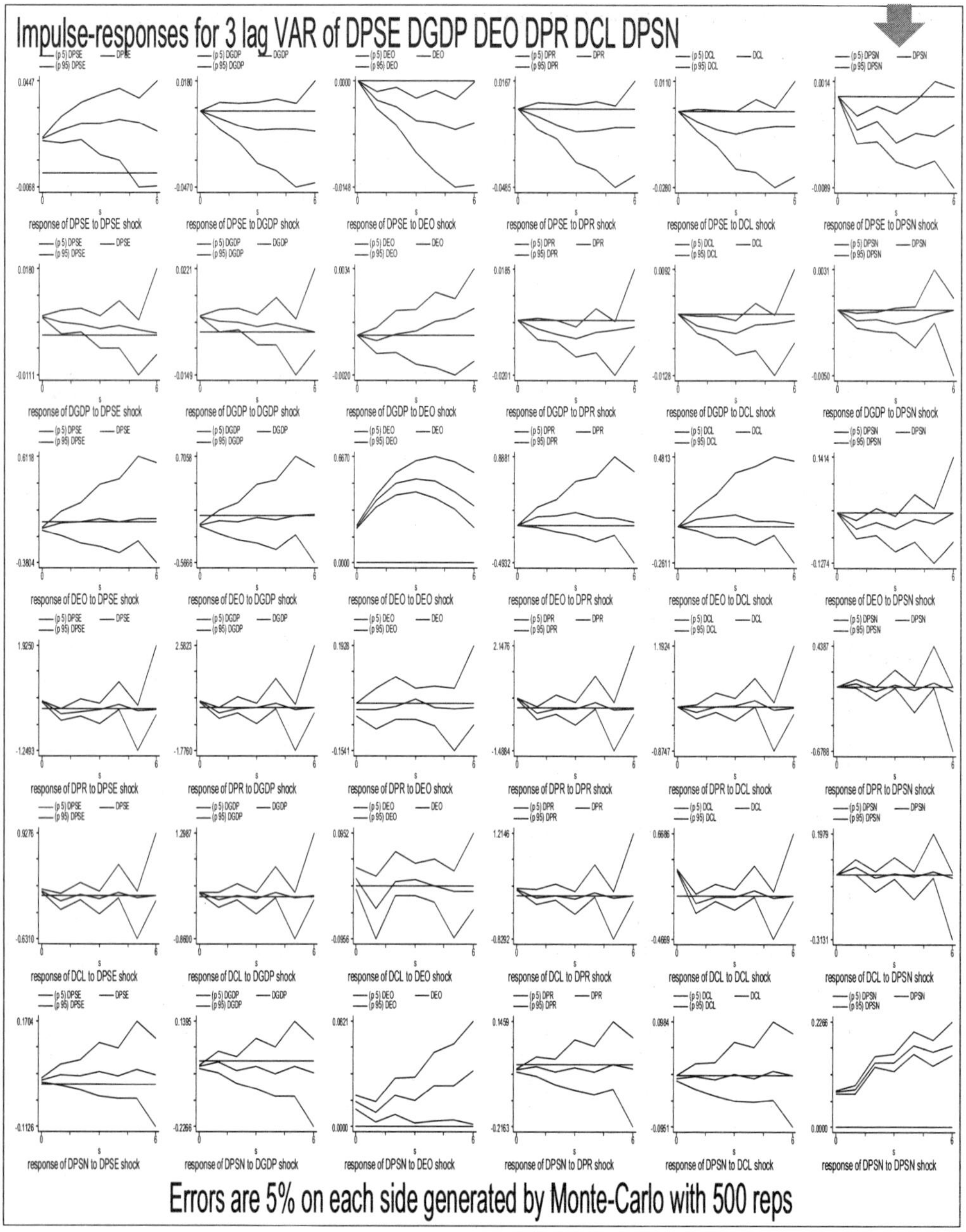

* DPSE: △Public Social Expenditure, DGDP: △GDP per Capita, DEO: △Economic Openness, DPR: △Political Rights, DCL: △Civil Liberties, DPSN: △PC Numbers.

<Figure 6.6> **Graphs of Panel Vector Autoregressive Model Analyses for PC numbers**

3.2 Causality Analysis of ICT Usage and Income Inequality

In order to analyse the causal relationship between ICT usage and income inequality, a pooled TSCS analysis is conducted using estimated household income inequality as the dependent variable, independent variables related to ICT usage, and the following control variables related to welfare state development.[73]

Hypothesis
The use of ICT increases income inequality.

1) Testing the Assumptions of Linear Regression and Analysis Modelling

Prior to conducting the pooled TSCS analysis, it must first be confirmed whether the pooled data meet the basic assumptions of OLS. This validation can be met via the following testing processes:

(1) The existence of multicollinearity: If the independent variables are too strongly collinear, the analysis results may be biased. Therefore, each value of VIF is controlled below 4 in all regressions.
(2) The existence of the random effect or fixed effect: The F test and Hausman test are conducted to determine the effects existing due to omitted variables.
(3) The existence of autocorrelation: The Wooldridge test is conducted in order to observe whether there exists autocorrelation in residuals.
(4) The existence of heteroskedasticity: The Modified Wald test is performed to confirm heteroskedasticity.[74] The results of each test are omitted on account of space consideration.

[73] To achieve a more even distribution and increase the efficacy of the analysis' performance, GDP per capita as a control variable is computed via a natural log using log transformation.

[74] Contemporaneous correlation usually appears in comparative analyses across countries, so it is widely accepted that it will be utilised in studies.

2) Simple Cross-sectional Regression Analyses

The simple cross-sectional regression analyses are conducted with the expectation of a significant difference in the impact of ICT usage's increase between the cross-sectional and over-time dimensions. The years for analyses chosen are 1996 and 2005, which have relatively few missing values and can represent the 1990s and the 2000s respectively.

$$Gini_{it} = \alpha + \beta 1X1_{it} + \beta 2X2_{it} + \cdots + e_{it}$$

(Gini: Estimated Household Income Inequality, x1, x2, ... : Variables related to ICT usage and previously discussed relevant variables related to the development of the welfare state, i: country, t: time, e: residuals)

The following two tables (see Table 6.16 and 6.17) present the results of cross-sectional regressions for household income inequality.[75] In the simple cross-sectional regression analysis for year 1996, only PC numbers have a weak negative significance, with an estimated coefficient of -0.224 and 90% probability (*p<0.1). However, no significant results are found in the analyses of year 2005. Therefore, it cannot be said with certainty that household income inequality increases alongside ICT usage.

[75] In all three models within the simple cross-sectional regressions for 1996 (Internet User Rates 1, Mobile Phones Model 1, and PC Numbers Model 1), Austria, Estonia, Poland, Switzerland and the United State are excluded due to missing values. Internet User Rates Model 2 and Mobile Phones Model 2 simple cross-sectional regressions for 2005 exclude the same aforementioned countries due to missing values. In PC Numbers Model 2 simple cross-sectional regressions for 2005, Austria, Estonia, Israel, Japan, Poland, Switzerland and the United State are excluded due to missing values. In PC Numbers Model 1 for 1996, GDP per capita is not utilised via simple cross-sectional regressions as a control variable due to multicollinearity in the analysis.

<Table 6.16> Results of Simple Cross-sectional Regression Analyses for Year 1996

	Simple Cross-sectional Analysis for Estimated Household Income Inequality: 1996		
	1 Internet User Rates Model 1	2 Mobile Phones Model 1	3 PC Numbers Model 1
Dependent Variable	Estimated Household Income Inequality		
	Independent Variables		
Internet user rates	-0.211		
	(-0.193)		
Mobile phones		-0.126	
		(-0.122)	
PC numbers			-0.224*
			(-0.119)
	Control Variables		
GDP per capita	-1.949	-1.618	
	(-1.39)	(-1.509)	
Economic openness	-0.0258	-0.0331	-0.0139
	(-0.02)	(-0.0217)	(-0.0207)
Urban population rates	0.0722	0.0857	0.0968
	(-0.0702)	(-0.0723)	(-0.0749)
Civil liberties	1.429	1.585	1.573
	(-1.077)	(-1.043)	(-1.056)
Trade unemployment rates	-0.00876	0.0103	-0.0502
	(-0.187)	(-0.186)	(-0.183)
Constant	51.06***	47.33***	32.30***
	(-14.01)	(-14.9)	(-6.547)
Observations	29	29	29
R-squared	0.505	0.502	0.491
Standard errors in parentheses			
*** p<0.01, ** p<0.05, * p<0.1			

<Table 6.17> **Results of Simple Cross-sectional Regression Analyses for Year 2005**

	Simple Cross-sectional Analysis for Estimated Household Income Inequality: 2005		
	6	7	8
	Internet User Rates Model 2	Mobile Phones Model 2	PC Numbers Model 2
Dependent Variable	Estimated Household Income Inequality		
	Independent Variables		
Internet user rates	-0.0789		
	(-0.0464)		
Mobile phones		-0.0695	
		(-0.0407)	
PC numbers			-0.065
			(-0.0447)
	Control Variables		
GDP per capita	-1.47	-1.953	-1.263
	(-1.404)	(-1.314)	(-1.604)
Economic openness	-0.0116	-0.00686	-0.0135
	(-0.0121)	(-0.0126)	(-0.013)
Urban population rates	0.139**	0.0959	0.122*
	(-0.0609)	(-0.0601)	(-0.0678)
Civil liberties	2.534	3.018**	2.467
	(-1.477)	(-1.414)	(-1.696)
Trade unemployment rates	-0.00739	0.0184	-0.0419
	(-0.237)	(-0.236)	(-0.259)
Constant	45.49***	54.58***	43.83**
	(-14.98)	(-14.63)	(-17.04)
Observations	29	29	27
R-squared	0.541	0.541	0.47
Standard errors in parentheses			
*** p<0.01, ** p<0.05, * p<0.1			

3) Panel-corrected Standard Errors (PCSE) Model Analyses

Similarly to the previous analyses on the relationship between household income inequality and ICT usage variables, the basic model according to Pluemper et al's and Beck & Katz's suggestion are constructed. These models can be affirmed as follows:

Pluemper's model (Basic model): $Gini_{it} = \alpha + \beta 1X1_{it} + \beta 2X2_{it} + \cdots + e_{it}$

Beck & Katz's model (Comparison model):

$$Gini_{it} = \alpha + \beta 0Gini_{it-5} + \beta 1X1_{it} + \cdots + \sum \beta_i\, countrydummy_{it} + \sum \beta_{ik}\, timedummy_{kit} + e_{it}$$

(Gini: Estimated Household Income Inequality, x1, x2, ... : Variables related to ICT usage and previously discussed relevant variables related to the development of the welfare state, i: country, t: time, e: residuals)

As shown in Table 6.18 as follows, in the Internet User Rates Model 1 of the Pluemper model and the Beck & Katz Model, Internet user rates show a weak positive relationship with household income inequality.

The Mobile Phones Model 1 of the Pluemper model shows a weak positive significance as well, with an estimated coefficient of 0.0143 and 99% probability (***p<0.01). In the case of PC numbers, no models yield a notable significance.

<Table 6.18> Results of PCSE Model Analyses

	Pluemper Model	Beck & Katz Model	Pluemper Model	Beck & Katz Model	Pluemper Model	Beck & Katz Model
	1	2	3	4	5	6
	Internet User Rates Model1	Interent User Rates Model2	Mobile Phonex Model1	Mobile Phones Model2	PC Numbers Model1	PC Numbers Model2
Dependent Variable	Estimated Household Income Inequality					
	Independent Variables					
EHII(5 lagged level)		-0.00556		0.00113		0.0344
		(-0.0451)		(-0.0462)		(-0.046)
Internet user rates	0.0176***	0.0125**				
	(-0.00662)	(-0.00588)				
Mobile phones			0.0143***	0.0047		
			(-0.00475)	(-0.00474)		
PC numbers					-0.0157	-0.00446
					(-0.0108)	(-0.00604)
	Control Variables					
GDP per capita	-0.554	-0.764*	-0.672	-0.856**	-0.132	-0.69
	(-0.468)	(-0.415)	(-0.461)	(-0.426)	(-0.524)	(-0.472)
Corruption Perception Index	-0.118	0.0837	-0.0578	0.0978	-0.06	0.152*
	(-0.155)	(-0.086)	(-0.153)	(-0.087)	(-0.169)	(-0.0848)
Urban population rates	0.0760***	-0.05	0.0860***	-0.0442	0.0774***	0.0551
	(-0.0219)	(-0.0468)	(-0.0214)	(-0.0485)	(-0.0222)	(-0.0525)
Political rights	1.790***	0.275	1.779***	0.317	2.006***	0.333
	(-0.485)	(-0.222)	(-0.472)	(-0.228)	(-0.523)	(-0.204)
Civil liberties	0.839***	0.464***	0.859***	0.577***	0.626*	0.522***
	(-0.324)	(-0.146)	(-0.31)	(-0.149)	(-0.357)	(-0.143)
Trade union density	-0.0914***	0.0417**	-0.0919***	0.0482**	-0.101***	0.0530**
	(-0.0114)	(-0.0203)	(-0.0113)	(-0.0204)	(-0.0116)	(-0.0214)
Total unemployment rates	0.145***	0.181***	0.159***	0.184***	0.119**	0.184***
	(-0.05)	(-0.026)	(-0.051)	(-0.0265)	(-0.0526)	(-0.0259)
Economic openness	-0.00993***	-0.00275	-0.0116***	-0.00303	-0.00795**	0.000764
	(-0.00335)	(-0.00565)	(-0.00344)	(-0.00601)	(-0.0034)	(-0.00596)
Constant	36.98***	46.07***	36.76***		34.06***	44.13***
	(-4.406)	(-7.822)	(-4.294)		(-4.854)	(-8.028)
Observations	314	265	314	265	289	243
R-squared	0.957	0.989	0.959	0.99	0.951	0.991
Number of country	32	31	32	31	32	30
Standard errors in parentheses						
*** p<0.01, ** p<0.05, * p<0.1						

4) Error Correction Model (ECM) and Vector Error Correction Model (VECM) Analyses

In order to observe transitory effects and long-term permanent effects, ECM and VECM analyses are carried out according to the following models.[76] First of all, unit root tests, the Granger causality test, and a co-integration test are performed in order to avoid 'spurious regression' situations.

ECM model: $\Delta Gini_{it} = \alpha + \beta_1 \cdot Gini_{it-1} + \sum \beta^j \cdot X^j_{it-1} + \sum \beta^j_\Delta \cdot X^j_{it-1} + e_t$

76 For a full interpretation of results, see the Error Correction Model (ECM) and Vector Error Correction Model (VECM) Analyses in chapter 5, section 4.

VECM model:

$$\Delta Gini_{it} = \alpha + \beta_1 \cdot Gini_{it-1} + \sum \beta^j \cdot X_{1it-1}^j + \sum \beta^j \cdot X_{2it-1}^j \dots + \sum \beta_\Delta^j \cdot X_{1it-1}^j + \sum \beta_\Delta^j \cdot X_2 X_{it-1}^j \dots + e_t$$

(Gini: Estimated Household Income Inequality, x1, x2, ... : Variables related to ICT usage and previously discussed relevant variables related to the development of the welfare state, Δ: first difference, i: country, t: time, e: residuals)

Through the results of pre-tests, it can first be observed via the graphs that the pooled time-series cross-section data has trends over time.[77] This means the data can be non-stationary and have unit roots. The result of the Breitung unit-root test and Im-Pesaran-Shin unit-root test show that all variables have unit roots and are non-stationary. However, when they are first differenced, these variables can be stationary and absent unit roots. Second, the results of Westerlund's error-correction-based co-integration tests show there are co-integrations between the dependent variable and independent variables.[78] This means that the relationship between the dependent variable and independent variables is linear, although all variables are serial correlations and non-stationary. Third, the results of the Granger causality test confirm the causal relationship between the dependent variable and independent variables.[79] All these results are added in the appendix on account of space consideration.[80] When conducting the tests for heteroskedasticity in each pooled regression, a panel-corrected standard error model according to Beck & Katz's suggestion is employed to perform ECM and VECM, in-

77 Please see graphs in the figures in the appendix.

78 When performing co-integration tests, the option of lag 1 is added in each analysis, because the series data are based on a series of consecutive years. The results of the Pesaran's CD tests show a strong cross-section independence. Furthermore, as shown in the aforementioned unit-root tests, the pooled time-series cross-section data has a strong serial correlation. Therefore, it is more appropriate to interpret the robust p-value via the bootstrap option. The results of the Pesaran's CD tests are omitted on account of space consideration.

79 For each country, the Granger causality test is conducted with first difference variables including lag 5. The results show that two-way Granger causality exists in each relationship between the dependent variable and independent variables. However, this study's focus is not the impact of income inequality on ICT usage, but the impact of ICT usage on income inequality.

80 The results from the Granger causality test are omitted on account of space consideration.

cluding country dummy in the models.[81]

The results yielded from the ECM analyses (see Table 6.19) reveal that all variables remain synchronised with household income inequality in the short term. In other words, they have a positive transitory effect on household income inequality. PC numbers in particular have a positive permanent effect on household income inequality in the long term. The long-term effect of PC numbers is approximately 0.02. This means that, for each percent PC numbers increase, the long-term target equilibrium for household income inequality also increases by approximately 0.02. However, PC numbers stand alone in this effect, because the other ICT usage variables show no significance with household income inequality in the long term.

In the VECM analyses (see Table 6. 20), Internet user rates and PC numbers show positive effects in the short term. In the long term, all three variables show a weak positive significance. Therefore, it is safe to state that the association between household income inequality and ICT usage is positive. The long-term effects of Internet user rates, mobile phones, and PC numbers are about 0.04, 0.02, and 0.06, respectively.

<Table 6.19> Results of ECM Analyses

	ECM Analysis with Country FE		
	1 Internet User Rates Model	2 Mobile Phones Model	3 PC Numbers Model
Dependent Variable	△ Estimated Household Income Inequality		
	Independent Variables		
Estimated Household Income Inequality (Lagged level)	-0.0433*** (-0.00722)	-0.0398*** (-0.00699)	-0.0430*** (-0.00669)
△Internet user rates	0.00752*** (-0.00163)		
Internet user rates (Lagged level)	0.000184 (-0.000198)		
△Mobile phones		0.00301** (-0.00132)	
Mobile phones (Lagged level)		-6.05E-06 (-0.000134)	
△PC numbers			0.0153*** (0.00252)
PC numbers (Lagged level)			0.000810*** (-0.000237)
Constant	1.578*** -0.256	1.466*** -0.248	1.535*** -0.235
Observations	775	775	775
R-squared	0.522	0.515	0.528
Number of country	31	31	31
Standard errors in parentheses *** p<0.01, ** p<0.05, * p<0.1			

81 Estonia, Slovakia and Slovenia are not included in the ECM and VECM analyses.

<Table 6.20> **Results of VECM Analyses**

	VECM Analysis with Country FE		
	1 Internet User Rates Model	2 Mobile Phones Model	3 PC Numbers Model
Dependent Variable	△ Estimated Household Income Inequality		
	Independent Variables		
Estimated Household Income Inequality (Lagged level)	-0.0540*** (-0.00628)	-0.0494*** (-0.00625)	-0.0483*** (-0.006)
△Internet user rates	0.00936*** (-0.00195)		
Internet user rates (Lagged level)	0.00225*** (-0.000341)		
△Mobile phones		-0.000266 (-0.00155)	
Mobile phones (Lagged level)		0.00137*** (-0.000265)	
△PC number			0.00977*** (-0.00292)
PC number (Lagged level)			0.00266*** (-0.000376)
	Control Variables		
△GDP per capita	-0.308 (-0.221)	-0.036 (-0.22)	-0.269 (-0.218)
GDP per capita (Lagged level)	-0.0713*** (-0.0266)	-0.0539* (-0.0309)	-0.0377 (-0.0232)
△Economic openness	0.0164*** (-0.00438)	0.0212*** (-0.00469)	0.0155*** (-0.00444)
Economic openness (Lagged level)	-0.00293*** (-0.00064)	-0.00296*** (-0.000663)	-0.00248*** (-0.000642)
△Civil Liberties	0.0404** (-0.0172)	0.0407** (-0.0179)	0.0330* (-0.017)
Civil Liberties (Lagged level)	0.0364*** (-0.012)	0.0392*** (-0.0125)	0.0296** (-0.0118)
△Political rights	-0.0687*** (-0.0215)	-0.0672*** (-0.0224)	-0.0639*** (-0.0211)
Political rights (Lagged level)	-0.0839*** (-0.0131)	-0.0746*** (-0.0133)	-0.0722*** (-0.0125)
Constant	2.776*** (-0.349)	2.449*** (-0.371)	2.188*** (-0.293)
Observations	775	775	775
R-squared	0.608	0.59	0.604
Number of country	31	31	31
Standard errors in parentheses *** p<0.01, ** p<0.05, * p<0.1			

5) First Difference Model Analyses

The first difference model analyses are performed to uncover the impact of short-term changes in ICT usage on short-term changes in household income inequality. The equation consists of the first differences between all variables.[82]

$$\Delta Gini_i = \beta_1 \Delta x_{1_i} + \beta_2 \Delta x_{2_i} \dots + \Delta e_i$$

(Gini: Estimated Household Income Inequality, x1, x2, ... : Variables related to the ICT

82 Estonia, Slovakia and Slovenia are not included in the first difference model analyses. In the case of the civil liberties variable, after the first difference, 3 were added to all values in order to perform the analysis appropriately.

industry and previously discussed relevant variables related to the development of the welfare state, Δ: first difference, i: country, e: residuals)

As shown in Table 6.21, Internet user rates show a weak negative significance pre-2000, with an estimated coefficient of -0.0152 and 99% probability (***p<0.01). However, post-2000, results show a weak positive relationship with household income inequality. Mobile phones (see Table 6.22) show a negative significance pre-2000, and during the entire period. However, mobile phones reveal a positive significance post-2000, with an estimated coefficient of 0.0105 and 99% probability (***p<0.01). PC numbers (see Table 6.23) show a negative significance for the entire period as well as pre-2000. Conversely, it appears a positive significance exists post-2000, with an estimated coefficient of 0.0133 and 99% probability (***p<0.01). Interestingly, therefore, it can be interpreted that Internet user rates, mobile phones, and PC numbers have positive short-term effects on household income inequality during the period post-2000. However, all three variables share a negative association with household income inequality during the period pre-2000.

<Table 6.21> **Results of First Difference Model Analyses 1: Internet User Rates**

	First Differece Model Analysis		
	1 Internet User Rates Model 1	2 Internet User Rates Model 2	3 Internet User Rates Model 3
Dependent Variables	△Estimated Household Income Inequality		
	Independent Variables		
△Internet user rates	-0.00354	-0.0152***	0.0231***
	(-0.00262)	(-0.00535)	(-0.00267)
	Control Variables		
△GDP per capita	-0.462**	-0.689	-1.073***
	(-0.234)	(-0.439)	(-0.208)
△Economic openness	0.0179***	0.0175***	0.0160***
	(-0.00363)	(-0.00533)	(-0.00352)
△Corruption Perception Index	1.012***	1.103***	-0.707***
	(-0.127)	(-0.207)	(-0.109)
△Urban population rates	0.0484**	-0.109***	0.0373*
	(-0.0196)	(-0.029)	(-0.0195)
△Civil liberties	-0.0367*	-0.0438*	0.000679
	(-0.0191)	(-0.0258)	(-0.022)
Constant	0.233***	0.315***	0.00821
	(-0.0595)	(-0.0803)	(-0.0683)
Observations	775	434	341
R-squared	0.122	0.165	0.322
Number of country	31	31	31
Standard errors in parentheses			
*** p<0.01, ** p<0.05, * p<0.1			

<Table 6.22> **Results of First Difference Model Analyses 2: Mobile Phones**

	First Differece Model Analysis		
	4 Mobile Phones Model1	5 Mobile Phones Model 2	6 Mobile Phones Model 3
Dependent Variables	△Estimated Household Income Inequality		
	Independent Variables		
△Mobile phones	-0.00789*** (-0.00184)	-0.0152*** (-0.0035)	0.0105*** (-0.00225)
	Control Variables		
△GDP per capita	-0.333 (-0.234)	-0.741* (-0.418)	-0.990*** (-0.242)
△Economic openness	0.0230*** (-0.00376)	0.0243*** (-0.00567)	0.0164*** (-0.00395)
△Corruption Perception Index	-0.996*** (-0.126)	-1.383*** (-0.204)	-0.692*** (-0.116)
△Urban population rates	-0.0551*** (-0.0195)	-0.112*** (-0.0285)	0.0584*** (-0.0208)
△Civil liberties	-0.0376** (-0.0189)	-0.0416 (-0.0255)	0.0059 (-0.0236)
Constant	0.250*** (-0.0589)	0.324*** (-0.0792)	0.00886 (-0.0738)
Observations	775	434	341
R-squared	0.14	0.185	0.221
Number of country	31	31	31
Standard errors in parentheses			
*** p<0.01, ** p<0.05, * p<0.1			

<Table 6.23> **Results of First Difference Model Analyses 3: PC numbers**

	First Differece Model Analysis		
	7 PC Numbers Model 1	8 PC Numbers Model 2	9 PC Numbers Model 3
Dependent Variables	△Estimated Household Income Inequality		
	Independent Variables		
△PC numbers	-0.0105** (-0.00426)	-0.0371*** (-0.0079)	0.0133*** (-0.00354)
	Control Variables		
△GDP per capita	-0.523** (-0.234)	-0.839** (-0.42)	-0.501** (-0.211)
△Economic openness	0.0180*** (-0.00352)	0.0181*** (-0.00509)	0.0230*** (-0.0037)
△Corruption Perception Index	-1.024*** (-0.127)	-1.449*** (-0.205)	-0.712*** (-0.118)
△Urban population rates	-0.0500** (-0.0196)	-0.113*** (-0.0284)	0.0521** (-0.021)
△Civil liberties	-0.0349* (-0.019)	-0.0376 (-0.0254)	-0.00417 (-0.0238)
Constant	0.239*** (-0.0593)	0.334*** (-0.0791)	0.0472 (-0.0738)
Observations	775	434	341
R-squared	0.126	0.191	0.204
Number of country	31	31	31
Standard errors in parentheses			
*** p<0.01, ** p<0.05, * p<0.1			

4. Summary

In chapter six, the relationship between the increase of ICT usage and the welfare state was analysed. For clarity and quick reference, a summation is outlined below.

First, descriptive statistics were employed in order to understand the general characteristics of the variables. The mean value analyses allowed the relationship between public social expenditure and income inequality to be observed across all OECD countries from 1985 to 2010. It remains likely that countries ranked at the highest end of public social spending have the lowest levels of income inequality. Furthermore, comparisons of Internet user rates, mobile cellular subscriptions, and personal computer numbers as independent variables revealed themselves at significantly different levels across countries during that time.

Second, correlation analyses were conducted to uncover any statistical relationships between the variables. Public social expenditure, when correlated with Internet user rates, mobile phones and PC numbers, showed positive significances. In the case of income inequality, when correlated with Internet user rates, mobile phones, and PC numbers, the signs appeared negatively.

Finally, simple cross-sectional regressions and a number of pooled TSCS analyses were performed in order to investigate the causal relationship between dependent variables and independent variables. In case of public social spending, the results of simple cross-sectional regressions showed that in 1996, there were no significant variables related to ICT usage. However, in 2005, mobile phones showed a weak positive significance.

In PCSE model analyses, according to results of the Pluemper model, the causal relationship between public social expenditure and Internet user rates showed a positive significance during the entire period. In the Beck & Katz model, Internet user rates showed a weak negative significance pre-2000, as well as a weak positive significance post-2000. In the case of mobile phones, in the analyses of the Pluemper model, the positive associations appeared for the entire period as well as post-2000.

In the Beck & Katz model, the association between mobile phones and public social expenditure showed a weak positive significance for the entire period. Looking at PC numbers through the Beck & Katz model, the results showed a weak negative significance for the entire period, as well as post-2000.

According to the results of the ECM analyses, Internet user rates and mobile phones shared a negative significance with public social expenditure, while PC numbers showed no significance with public social expenditure in the long term. The results of the VECM analyses revealed similar phenomena to those of the ECM analyses. Three variables related to ICT usage (Internet user rates, mobile phones and PC numbers) showed negative effects on public social expenditure in the long term. Internet user rates showed a negative relationship with public social expenditure in the short term, while mobile phones showed no significant relationship with public social expenditure in the short term. It would seem an exception, then, that PC numbers shared a positive significance with public social spending in the short term.

According to first difference model analyses, during entire period as well as pre-2000, Internet user rates shared a weak negative significance with public social expenditure. Mobile phones showed a positive significance post-2000. In the case of PC numbers, the relationship with public social expenditure showed negative significance pre-2000 and during the entire period. In the short term, therefore, it can be said that PC numbers exhibited a weak negative effect on the change of public social expenditure.

In case of PVAR analyses, the results showed that public social expenditure's response to Internet user rates' shock was negative. In the case of public social expenditure's response to mobile phones' shock, no consistency or certainty exists. However, the graph lines of the analysis results are enough to reveal that mobile phones' impact on public social expenditure ended with a positive effect. The response of public social expenditure to PC numbers' shock was negative.

In summation, it could not be said that there is a definite positive causal relationship between public social spending and the usage of ICT. Therefore, the hypothesis 'the use of ICT does increase public social spending' is not proved. In fact, it can be observed that, overall, the results of causality analyses suggest that there is a negative causal relationship between public social spending and the increase of ICT usage. A significant point to make here, however, is that the increase of mobile phones did lead to the increase of public social spending according to most analysis results, with the exception of the results of the ECM analyses.

In case of income inequality, the results of simple cross-sectional regressions showed that for year 1996, only PC numbers had a weak negative significance. No significant results were found in the analyses for year 2005. Therefore, according to these results, it cannot be said with certainty that household income inequality increased alongside ICT usage. In the case of the PCSE model analyses, looking at the Pluemper model and the Beck & Katz model, Internet user rates showed a weak positive relationship with household income inequality. In the pluemper model, mobile phones showed a positive significance with income inequality, while PC numbers yielded no notable significance with income inequality. The results yielded from the ECM analyses revealed that all variables had a positive transitory effect on household income inequality. PC numbers in particular had a positive permanent effect on household income inequality in the long term. However, PC numbers stand alone in this effect, because the other ICT usage variables showed no significance with household income inequality in the long term.

In the VECM analyses, Internet user rates and PC numbers showed positive effects in the short term. In the long term, all three variables show a weak positive significance. According to first difference model analyses, Internet user rates showed a weak negative significance pre-2000. However, results showed a weak positive relationship with household income inequality post-2000. Mobile phones showed negative significance pre 2000 and during the entire period. However, post-2000, mobile phones revealed a positive significance. PC numbers showed a negative significance for the entire period as well as pre-2000. Conversely, it appears a positive significance showed post-2000.

Examining the results collectively, it does appear that the increase of internet usage led to the increase of income inequality post-2000.

Therefore, it can tentatively be said that there is a positive causal relationship between income inequality and ICT usage since 2000, but not pre-2000. That is, the analysis results suggest that the hypothesis 'the use of ICT does increase income inequality' is only partially proved.

Chapter VII

The Development of the E-government and Welfare State:

Human Capital, Infrastructure, E-Participation, and Web-Measure

Chapter VII The Development of the E-government and Welfare State: Human Capital, Infrastructure, E-Participation, and Web-Measure

Chapter seven analyses the relationship between the e-government and the welfare state using variables as presented in chapter four. In this analysis, public social spending is the only dependent variable.[83] The analysis is performed with all 34 OECD countries as analysis objects. These objects are used to create time-series cross-section data, drawing on sources from the following years: 2003, 2004, 2005, 2008, and 2010.[84] This analysis therefore investigates changes over the period 2003-2010.

Only raw data are used in the analyses of this chapter, excluding all missing values for the sake of reliability and validity.[85] Descriptive statistics are employed in order to understand the general characteristics of the variables, followed by a correlation analysis to uncover any statistical relationships between the variables. Finally, utilising the pooled TSCS data, several regressions are performed according to the appropriate models. The aim of this is to investigate the causal relationship between the dependent variable and independent variables. Control variables are applied differently in the analyses.

83 Income inequality is excluded as a dependent variable due to missing values in the analysis

84 The years from which data are drawn are neither annual nor biennial, resulting in irregular data. Therefore, they are handled statistically for the convenience of conducting this analysis: 2003→1, 2004→2, 2005→3, 2008→4, and 2010→5.

85 Fortunately, this pooled time-series cross-section data has few missing values.

Hypothesis

1. The development of the e-government increases public social spending.

Variables

Dependent variables: Public Social Expenditure

Independent variables: E-Government Index, E-Participation Index, Human Capital Index, Infrastructure Index, Web Measure Index

Control variables: Urban Population Rate, GDP per Capita, Total Unemployment Rates, Trade Union Density, Corruption Perception Index, Political Rights, Civil Liberties, Economic Openness

1. General Characteristics of Variables

1.1 Descriptive Statistics of the 34 OECD Countries

The following table shows the results of descriptive statistics variables, elucidating the relationship between the e-government and the development of the welfare state. Here, the mean and standard deviation are calculated to the second decimal place, providing more than sufficient accuracy when looking at and explaining changes over time.

<Table 7.1> **General Characteristics of Variables**

Variables	Observation	Mean	Std. Dev.	Mi	Max
Public Expenditure	167	20.51	5.76	5.37	32.39
E-Participation	170	0.47	0.26	0.03	1.00
E-Government	170	0.71	0.11	0.48	0.93
Human Capital Index	170	0.95	0.04	0.77	0.99
Infrastructure	170	0.55	0.17	0.13	0.86
Web Measure Index	170	0.64	0.18	0.29	1.00

* The values represent the mean and the standard deviation of each variable in the 34 OECD countries during 2003-2010.

The above table reveals that, between years 2003 and 2010, the mean value of public social spending is 20.51% and the standard deviation is 5.76.

Looking at the table in more detail, the e-participation index shows a mean of 0.47 and a standard deviation of 0.26, the e-government index shows a mean of 0.71 and a standard deviation of 0.11, the human capital index shows a mean of 0.95 and a standard deviation of 0.04, and the infrastructure index shows a mean of 0.55 and a standard deviation of 0.17. In the case of the web measure index, the mean value is 0.64 and the standard deviation is 0.18.

1.2 Descriptive Statistics by Country

1) Charting the Changes in Variables

Before analysing the data, in order to delineate the changes in variables, a trend graph of each variable based on the time-series cross-section data of the 34 OECD countries must be analysed. The graphs are omitted on account of space consideration.

2) Mean Value Analyses

The mean of each variable is analysed during the period 2003 to 2010. For clarity of results, the differences between the mean values of the dependent variable for each country are examined, as are the differences between the mean values of the independent variables for each country. The data is presented via figures and tables among explanatory text.[86] Explanations on control variables are omitted on account of space consideration.

(1) Comparisons of Dependent Variables

❶ Public Social Expenditure

The mean value of public social expenditure is compared between countries from year 2003 to 2010. As seen in the figure below, with a mean value of 29.82% in public social expenditure, France is the country to record the highest value. Sweden and Denmark follow closely with

86 Please see chapter 4, section 1.2, under the heading 'Descriptive Statistics by Country.'

28.91% and 28.03% respectively. Austria shows 27.72% and Belgium shows 27.20%. These five countries rank in the highest positions. Germany (26.88%), Finland (26.53%), and Italy (25.52%) can also be considered to yield high rates of public social spending.

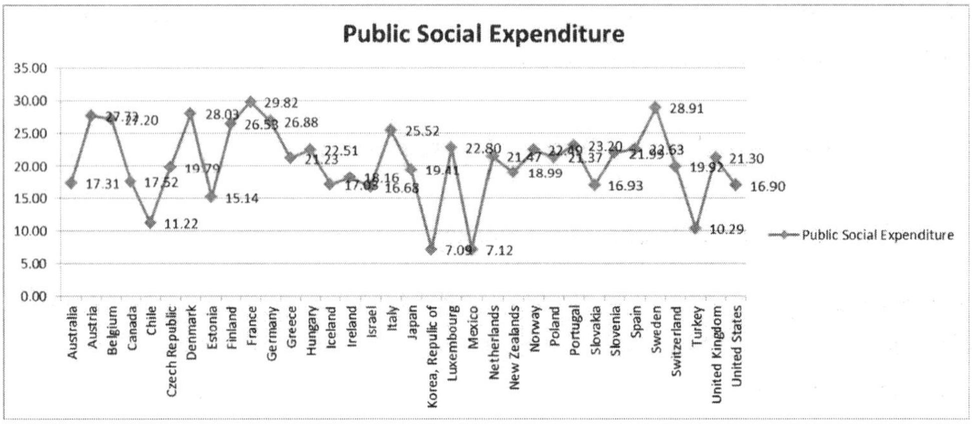

* The values represent the average of public social expenditure in the 34 OECD countries during 2003-2010.

<Figure 7.1> Public Social Expenditure from 2003 to 2010

Descending slightly to smaller mean values are countries yielding percentages between 20% and 25%. These include Portugal (23.20%), Luxembourg (22.80%), Spain (22.63%), Hungary (22.51%), Norway (22.49%), Slovenia (21.99%), the Netherlands (21.47%), Poland (21.37%), the United Kingdom (21.30%), and Greece (21.23%).

Sitting low on the graph line are Chile (11.22%), Turkey (10.29%), Mexico (7.12%), and South Korea (7.09%). These four countries are shown to commit the least to public social spending among OECD countries.

(2) Comparisons of Main Independent Variables

The following is a comparison of indices used in the analysis as independent variables, representing the e-government's development in different countries.

❶ E-Participation Index

Looking at the e-participation index in OECD countries from 2003 to 2010, the United States sits at number one with a ranking of 0.91. The United Kingdom and South Korea follow, with rankings of 0.84 and 0.82 respectively. Not much further down the scale is Canada (0.79), New Zealand (0.76), Australia (0.76), Denmark (0.70), Estonia (0.69), the Netherlands (0.65) and Mexico (0.65). All of these countries belong to the highest group on the e-participation index.

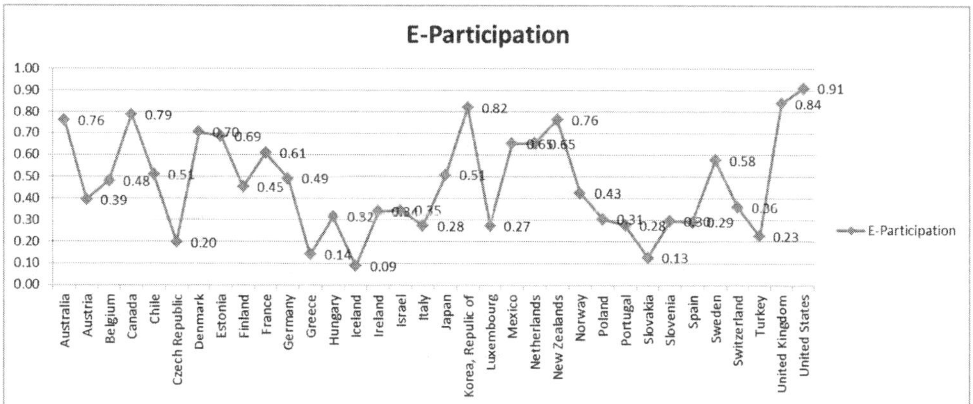

* The numbers represent the average values of the e-participation index in the 34 OECD countries during 2003-2010.

<Figure 7.2> E-Participation Index

Among the lowest performers in the arena of e-participation are Spain (0.29), Portugal (0.28), Italy (0.28), Luxembourg (0.27), Turkey (0.23), and the Czech Republic (0.20). Positions for the lowest e-participation values are occupied by Greece (0.14), Slovakia (0.13), and Iceland (0.09).

❷ E-Government Index

Observing the e-government index, the United States, Denmark and Sweden rank at 0.89, 0.87 and 0.86 respectively; the highest values among OECD countries. South Korea and the United Kingdom's values are both 0.84, while Canada and Australia recorded 0.83. Countries with slightly lesser rankings are the Netherlands (0.80), Finland (0.77), Germany (0.76), New Zealand (0.75), and Switzerland (0.75).

Lower performers in this sphere are Italy, Slovenia, Spain, and Chile, all with a ranking of 0.65. The Czech Republic (0.62), Portugal (0.62), Hungary (0.61), Poland (0.59), Mexico (0.58), Greece (0.57), Slovakia (0.57) and Turkey (0.49) show the lowest e-government values among OECD countries.

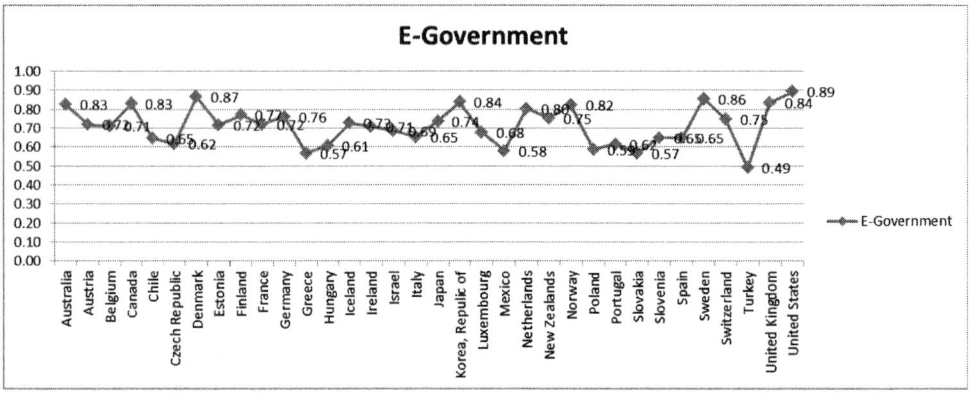

* The numbers represent the average values of the e-government in the 34 OECD countries during 2003-2010.

<Figure 7.3> **E-Government Index**

❸ Human Capital Index

Looking at the human capital index, Australia, Finland, New Zealand, the Netherlands, Norway, and Denmark are recorded at 0.99, taking the highest positions for the human capital index among OECD countries. Belgium, Sweden, the United Kingdom, Canada, and Spain all show 0.98; only marginally lower-ranking than those at the top.

In contrast, the Czech Republic (0.92), Slovakia (0.91), Luxembourg (0.91), Chile (0.91), Mexico (0.86), and Turkey (0.80) belong to the group of countries yielding the lowest rankings in the human capital index.

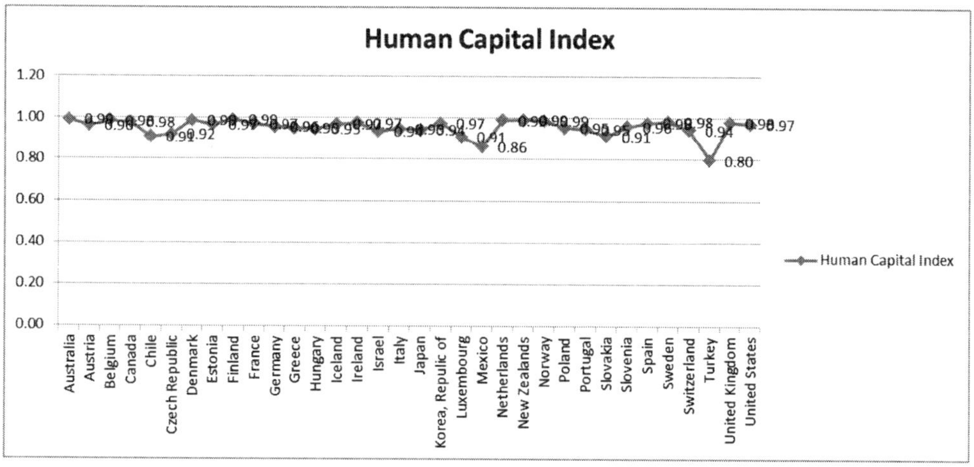

* The numbers represent the average value of the human capital index in the 34 OECD countries during 2003-2010.

<Figure 7.4> **Human Capital Index**

④ Infrastructure Index

Moving on to the infrastructure index, the highest ranking is Sweden (0.82). Next in line are Denmark (0.76), Iceland (0.74), Switzerland (0.73), the Netherlands (0.73), Norway (0.73), and the United States (0.73), all with high levels of functionality in regards to infrastructure.

Countries with a low degree of establishment regarding infrastructure are Israel (0.46), Spain (0.44), Portugal (0.44), the Czech Republic (0.41), Greece (0.35), Hungary (0.34), Slovakia (0.34) and Poland (0.30). Countries with an infrastructure index below 0.30 are Chile (0.27), Turkey (0.20), and Mexico (0.17), indicating a probable level of inadequacy in this area.

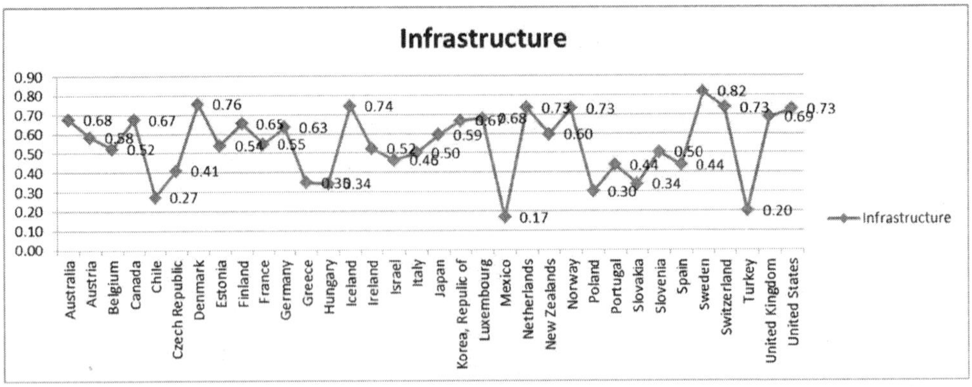

* The numbers represent the average values of the infrastructure index in the 34 OECD countries during 2003-2010.

<Figure 7.5> **Infrastructure Index**

⑤ Web Measure Index

For the web measure index in OECD countries from 2003 to 2010, the United States sits at number one with a ranking of 0.98. South Korea and Denmark follow with rankings of 0.87 and 0.85. Not much further down the scale is the United Kingdom (0.84), Canada (0.84), Australia (0.81), Sweden (0.77), Chile (0.76), Norway (0.75), and Mexico (0.71). All of these countries belong to the highest group on the web measure index.

Among the lowest achievers in this arena are Slovenia (0.49), Turkey (0.48), Iceland (0.47), and Portugal (0.46). Positions for the lowest web measure index values are occupied by Slovakia (0.45), Luxembourg (0.45), and Greece (0.40).

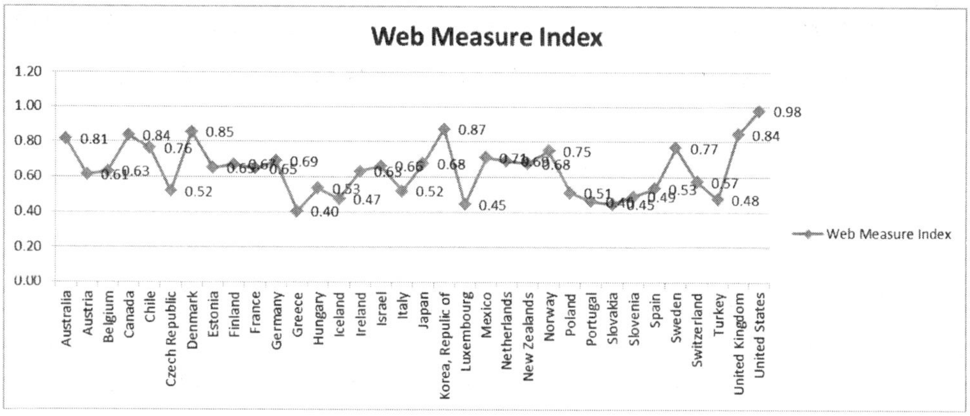

* The numbers represent the average values of the web measure index in the 34 OECD countries during 2003-2010.

<Figure 7.6> **Web Measure Index**

2. Correlation Analysis

Here, the correlation analysis is performed via a pairwise deletion.

<Table 7.2> **Results of Correlation Analysis**

	Public Social Expenditure	E-Participation	E-Government	Human Capital	Infrastructure	Web Measure
Public Social Expenditure	1					
(Sig.)	0.0000					
E-Participation	-0.1285	1				
(Sig.)	0.0980	0.0000				
E-Government	0.1405	0.6862	1			
(Sig.)	0.0701	0.0000	0.0000			
Human Capital	0.4542	0.3372	0.6665	1		
(Sig.)	0.0000	0.0000	0.0000	0.0000		
Infrastructure	0.3409	0.3776	0.8104	0.6748	1	
(Sig.)	0.0000	0.0000	0.0000	0.0000	0.0000	
Web Measure	-0.1706	0.7880	0.8086	0.3032	0.3873	1
(Sig.)	0.0275	0.0000	0.0000	0.0001	0.0000	0.0000

Investigating the results of the correlation analysis, public social expenditure and the e-participation index are revealed to share a negative correlation. Public social expenditure and the web measure index also share a negative correlation. However, public social expenditure correlated with the e-government index, the human capital index, and the infrastructure index, all show plus signs.

3. Causality Analysis of the E-Government and Development of Public Social Spending

In this section, several causality analyses of the development of the e-government and public social spending are conducted. This is accomplished using public social expenditure as the dependent variable, independent variables related to ICT usage, and control variables related to welfare state development.[87] The analyses start with the assumption that causal relationships between dependent and independent variables and /or control variables are linear, i.e., the model is linear in its parameters.

1) Testing the Assumptions of Linear Regression and Analysis Modelling

Prior to performing the pooled TSCS analysis, it must first be confirmed whether the pooled data meets the basic assumptions of OLS. This is accomplished through the following testing processes.

(1) The existence of multicollinearity: If the independent variables are too strongly collinear, the analysis results may be biased. Therefore, each value of VIF is controlled below 4 in all regressions. (2) The existence of the random effect or fixed effect: The F test and Hausman test are conducted to determine the effects existing due to omitted variables. (3) The existence of autocorrelation: The Wooldridge test is conducted in order to observe whether there exists autocorrelation in residuals. (4) The existence of heteroskedasticity: The Modified Wald test is performed to confirm heteroskedasticity.[88] The results of each test are omitted on account of space consideration.

---

[87] To achieve a more even distribution and increase the efficacy of the analysis' performance, GDP per capita as a control variable is computed via a natural log using log transformation.

[88] Contemporaneous correlation usually appears in comparative analyses across countries, so it is taken for granted that it will be utilised in studies.

2) Simple Cross-sectional Regression Analyses

First, simple cross-sectional regressions are performed, with the expectation of a significant difference in the impact of ICT usage between the cross-sectional and over-time dimensions. 2003 and 2010 are chosen as the years for analyses. The equation is as follows:

$$PSE_{it} = \alpha + \beta 1X1_{it} + \beta 2X2_{it} + \cdots + e_{it}$$

(PSE: Public Social Expenditure, x1, x2, ... : Variables related to the e-government and previously discussed relevant variables related to the development of the welfare state, i: country, t: time, e: residuals)

The following two tables (see Table 7.3 and Table 7.4) present the results of cross-sectional regression analyses for public social spending, examining a separate year within each table. No significant variables related to the e-government can be found in either year, as shown in the results.[89]

[89] In the case of the simple cross-sectional regressions of year 2003, Israel and Turkey are excluded due to missing values, so only 32 countries are utilised in the analyses. In the case of the simple cross-sectional regressions for year 2010, Hungary, Iceland, Israel, Luxembourg, the Czech Republic, and Turkey are excluded due to missing values, so only 28 countries are used in the analyses.

<Table 7.3> Results of Simple Cross-sectional Regression Analyses for Year 2003

	Simple Cross-sectional Analysis for Public Social Expenditure: 2003				
	1	2	3	4	5
	E-Participation Model1	E-Government Model1	Human Capital Model1	Web Measure Model1	Infrastructure Model1
Dependent Variable			Public Social Expenditure		
			Independent Variables		
E-Participation	-1.245				
	(-3.275)				
E-Government		-3.588			
		(-9.852)			
Human Capital			8.644		
			(-24.93)		
Web Measure				0.768	
				(-5.071)	
Infrastructure					-1.951
					(-4.281)
			Control Variables		
GDP per capita	0.501	0.733	0.148	0.287	
	(-1.239)	(-1.57)	(-1.321)	(-1.263)	
Political rights	-6.028	-5.893	-5.328	-5.655	-5.793
	(-3.571)	(-3.509)	(-3.649)	(-3.503)	(-3.412)
Economic openness	0.00233	0.00124	0.00614	0.00537	0.00258
	(-0.0153)	(-0.0166)	(-0.0156)	(-0.0165)	(-0.0145)
Trade union	0.0699*	0.0755**	0.0748**	0.0772**	0.0888**
	(-0.0383)	(-0.0351)	(-0.0352)	(-0.0363)	(-0.0354)
Elderly population	0.923***	0.929***	0.971***	0.990***	1.013***
	(-0.301)	(-0.297)	(-0.276)	(-0.308)	(-0.259)
Constant	6.799	6.075	-0.408	6.051	10.13
	(-12.37)	(-12.33)	(-22.98)	(-12.47)	(-7.199)
Observations	32	32	32	32	32
R-squared	0.689	0.689	0.688	0.687	0.688
Standard errors in parentheses					
*** p<0.01, ** p<0.05, * p<0.1					

<Table 7.4> Results of Simple Cross-sectional Regression Analyses for Year 2010

	Simple Cross-sectional Analysis for Public Social Expenditure: 2010				
	1	2	3	4	5
	E-Participation Model1	E-Government Model1	Human Capital Model1	Web Measure Model1	Infrastructure Model1
Dependent Variable			Public Social Expenditure		
			Independent Variables		
E-Participation	-2.33				
	(-3.561)				
E-Government		-11.18			
		(-10.93)			
Human Capital			31.53		
			(-41.26)		
Web Measure				-5.467	
				(-5.352)	
Infrastructure					-0.403
					(-6.166)
GDP per capita	1.799	2.951	0.931	2.396	
	(-1.929)	(-2.364)	(-1.9)	(-2.052)	
Political rights	-1.073	-1.649	0.218	-1.646	-1.655
	(-2.542)	(-2.595)	(-2.928)	(-2.595)	(-2.506)
Economic openness	0.0149	0.015	0.0175	0.00977	0.0145
	(-0.0194)	(-0.0189)	(-0.0189)	(-0.0202)	(-0.0186)
Trade union	0.0853	0.0813	0.0851	0.0803	0.113**
	(-0.0505)	(-0.0497)	(-0.05)	(-0.0499)	(-0.0438)
Elderly population	0.952***	0.867***	1.031***	0.820**	1.019***
	(-0.262)	(-0.278)	(-0.264)	(-0.299)	(-0.256)
Constant	-12.02	-15.29	-37.56	-13	4.506
	(-20.09)	(-20.25)	(-41.2)	(-19.79)	(-7.099)
Observations	28	28	28	28	28
R-squared	0.686	0.695	0.688	0.695	0.671
Standard errors in parentheses					
*** p<0.01, ** p<0.05, * p<0.1					

3) Panel-corrected Standard Errors (PCSE) Model Analyses

In the case that the pooled TSCS data violates the basic assumptions of OLS, as it does here, students tend to suggest using the PCSE model (in case of existing heteroscedasticity and contemporaneous correlation), including a lagged dependent variable (in case of existing autocorrelation), and including country dummy and time dummy (in case of an existing fix effect in unobserved variables).

In this analysis, as in the previous analyses of chapter five and six, the basic model is established using the PCSE model without a lagged dependent variable, country dummy, and time dummy. For the comparison model, however, a five-year lagged dependent variable is not included because the time-series cross-section data is too short to include a five-year lagged dependent variable in the equation. Therefore, in the analyses, the basic model is established using the PCSE model absent a lagged dependent variable, country dummy, and time dummy, according to Pluemper et al's suggestion. Next, the comparison model is established using the PCSE model without a lagged dependent variable, but including country dummy and time dummy, according to Beck & Katz's suggestion (1995).[90] The basic model and comparison model can be reaffirmed as follows:

Pluemper's model (Basic model): $PSE_{it} = \alpha + \beta 1X1_{it} + \beta 2X2_{it} + \cdots + e_{it}$

Beck & Katz's model (Comparison model):

$$PSE_{it} = \alpha + + \beta 1X1_{it} + \cdots + \sum \beta_i\, countrydummy_{it} + \sum \beta_{ik}\, timedummy_{kit} + e_{it}$$

(PSE: Public Social Expenditure, x1, x2, ... : Variables related to the e-government and previously discussed relevant variables related to the development of the welfare state, i: country, t: time, e: residuals)

As shown in Table 7.5, in the case of the e-government index as ana-

90 As aforementioned, the time-series data are observed neither annually nor biennially, resulting in irregular data. Therefore, theoretically, it can be assumed that a lagged dependent variable is included in the model. Nonetheless, this model could be seen as imperfect due to existing autocorrelation, given that the time intervals of the observed time-series data are shorter than five years.

lysed via the Pluemper model, a negative association appears with public social expenditure, with an estimated coefficient of -8.306 and 95% probability (**p<0.5). The association between the human capital and public social expenditure in the Beck & Katz model show a positive significance, with an estimated coefficient of 18.73 and 99% probability (***p<0.01). Interestingly, the infrastructure index shows converse results in the Pluemper model as compared to the Beck & Katz model. That is, in the Beck & Katz model, the infrastructure index shows positive significance (with an estimated coefficient of 6.004 and 99% probability (***p<0.01)), while it shows a negative significance (with an estimated coefficient of -6.664 and 95% probability (**p<0.5)) in the Pluemper model. These converse results can be understood in light of differences in the idiosyncrasies and internal political economic environment of each country, as well as the various effects of time. Where the web measure index is concerned, the result of the pluemper model shows a negative significance, with an estimated coefficient of -2.771 and 90% probability (*p<0.1).

<Table 7.5> **Results of PCSE Model Analyses for E-government 1**

	Pluemper Model	Beck & Katz Model	Pluemper Model	Beck & Katz Model	Pluemper Model	Beck & Katz Model
	1	2	3	4	5	6
	E-Participation Model1	E-Participation Model2	E-Government Model1	E-Government Model2	Human Capital Model1	Human Capital Model2
Dependent Variable	Public Social Expenditure					
	Independent Variables					
E-Participation	0.24	0.522				
	(-1.184)	(-0.444)				
E-Government			-8.306**	2.248		
			(-3.797)	(-1.769)		
Human Capital					10.74	18.73***
					(-11.04)	(-5.538)
	Control Variables					
GDP per capita	-0.386	-7.476***	0.142	-7.593***	-0.461	-7.772***
	(-0.765)	(-0.922)	(-0.802)	(-0.894)	(-0.8)	(-0.903)
Corruption Perception	0.377	1.249***	0.566**	1.217***	0.338	1.147***
	(-0.235)	(-0.256)	(-0.222)	(-0.257)	(-0.234)	(-0.242)
Political rights	0.231	-1.004***	-0.437	-1.042***	0.661	-1.421***
	(-0.844)	(-0.329)	(-0.804)	(-0.312)	(-0.976)	(-0.372)
Economic openness	0.00813	-0.0302**	0.00371	-0.0303**	0.0093	-0.0333**
	(-0.00645)	(-0.0138)	(-0.00643)	(-0.0137)	(-0.00668)	(-0.013)
Trade union	0.0722***	0.178***	0.0680***	0.173***	0.0701***	0.171***
	(-0.0181)	(-0.0288)	(-0.0194)	(-0.0289)	(-0.0184)	(-0.0256)
Elderly population	1.234***	-0.649***	1.159***	-0.609***	1.218***	-0.659***
	(-0.137)	(-0.194)	(-0.136)	(-0.199)	(-0.134)	(-0.181)
Constant	0.643	88.31***	2.328	88.02***	-8.731	74.97***
	(-5.481)	(-9.619)	(-5.275)	(-9.5)	(-9.893)	(-10.11)
Observations	156	156	156	156	156	156
R-squared	0.765	0.983	0.778	0.982	0.756	0.984
Number of country	33	33	33	33	33	33
Standard errors in parentheses						
*** p<0.01, ** p<0.05, * p<0.1						

<Table 7.6> **Results of PCSE Model Analyses for E-government 2**

	Pluemper Model	Beck & Katz Model	Pluemper Model	Beck & Katz Model
	7	8	9	10
	Infrastructure Model1	Infrastructure Model2	Web Measure Model1	Web Measure Model2
Dependent Variable	Public Social Expenditure			
	Independent Variables			
Infrastructure	-6.664**	6.004***		
	(-3.096)	(-2.23)		
Web measure			-2.771*	-0.0948
			(-1.544)	(-0.721)
	Control Variables			
GDP per capita	0.362	-7.833***	-0.142	-7.565***
	(-0.876)	(-0.866)	(-0.758)	(-0.909)
Corruption Perception	0.631***	1.128***	0.450**	1.263***
	(-0.237)	(-0.24)	(-0.217)	(-0.256)
Political rights	-0.0491	-1.429***	-0.198	-1.234***
	(-0.734)	(-0.359)	(-0.835)	(-0.332)
Economic openness	0.00672	-0.0360***	0.0047	-0.0300**
	(-0.00589)	(-0.0137)	(-0.00636)	(-0.0133)
Trade union	0.0745***	0.155***	0.0660***	0.179***
	(-0.0184)	(-0.0269)	(-0.0191)	(-0.0295)
Elderly population	1.227***	-0.507**	1.154***	-0.663***
	(-0.125)	(-0.221)	(-0.142)	(-0.196)
Constant	-4.505	88.69***	1.636	89.94***
	(-6.466)	(-8.939)	(-5.354)	(-9.512)
Observations	156	156	156	156
R-squared	0.77	0.983	0.765	0.983
Number of country	33	33	33	33
Standard errors in parentheses				
*** p<0.01, ** p<0.05, * p<0.1				

4) First Difference Model Analyses

The first difference model analyses can detect the impact of short-term changes in independent variables on short-term changes in the dependent variable.[91] Therefore, these analyses are performed to observe the impact of short-term changes in the e-government's development on short-term changes in public social expenditure. The equation consists of first differences of all variables.

$$\Delta PSE_i = \beta_1 \Delta x_{1_i} + \beta_2 \Delta x_{2_i} \ldots + \Delta e_i$$

(PSE: Public Social Expenditure, x1, x2, ... : Variables related to the e-government and previously discussed relevant variables related to the development of the welfare state, Δ: first difference, i: country, e: residuals)

As shown in Table 7.7, the e-government index shows negative significance, with an estimated coefficient of -4.220 and 90% probability (*p<0.1). The web measure index also shows negative significance, with an estimated coefficient of -2.384 and 99% probability (***p<0.01).

91 Israel is not included in the first difference model analyses, due to the missing values of Israel's trade union variable.

Therefore, it can be interpreted that the increases in the e-government index and the web measure index negatively influence the increase of public social spending in the short term. Conversely, the infrastructure index has a positive short-term impact on the change of public social expenditure, with an estimated coefficient of 7.867 and 99% probability (***p<0.01). However, the e-participation index and the human capital index show no significance in the results.

<Table 7.7> Results of First Difference Model Analyses: E-government

	First Difference Model				
	1	2	3	4	5
	E-Particiaption Modell	E-Government Modell	Human Capital Modell	Infrastructure Modell	Web Measure Modell
Dependent Variable			△Public Social Expenditure		
			Independent Variables		
△E-Participation	0.798				
	(-0.571)				
△E-Government		-4.220*			
		(-2.265)			
△Human capital			6.953		
			(-9.164)		
△Infrastructure				7.867***	
				(-2.564)	
△Web measure					-2.384***
					(-0.775)
			Control Variables		
△GDP per capita	-4.671***	-4.325***	-4.811***	-5.209***	-4.154***
	(-0.706)	(-0.736)	(-0.711)	(-0.702)	(-0.702)
△Corruption Perception Index	0.279	0.323	0.287	0.422	0.417
	(-0.278)	(-0.276)	(-0.28)	(-0.262)	(-0.262)
△Political rights	-0.0578	-0.683	-0.399	-0.47	-0.973
	(-0.797)	(-0.791)	(-0.783)	(-0.752)	(-0.781)
△Economic openness	-0.0266**	-0.0268**	-0.0281**	-0.0353***	-0.0294**
	(-0.0133)	(-0.0132)	(-0.0134)	(-0.0131)	(-0.0129)
△Trade union	0.0559	0.0676	0.0561	0.0398	0.0681
	(-0.0505)	(-0.0505)	(-0.0508)	(-0.0492)	(-0.0492)
△Elderly population	1.048***	0.778**	1.012***	1.053***	0.626*
	(-0.321)	(-0.342)	(-0.322)	(-0.311)	(-0.335)
Constant	0.867***	0.932***	0.885***	0.946***	0.972***
	(-0.157)	(-0.156)	(-0.157)	(-0.152)	(-0.153)
Observations	121	121	121	122	122
R-squared	0.446	0.454	0.44	0.473	0.474
Number of country	33	33	33	33	33
Standard errors in parentheses					
*** p<0.01, ** p<0.05, * p<0.1					

4. Summary

In chapter seven, the relationship between the increase of the development of the e-government and the welfare state was analysed. For clarity and quick reference, a summation is outlined below.

First, descriptive statistics were employed in order to understand the general characteristics of the variables. Through mean value analyses, public social expenditure was observed across OECD countries from 2003 to 2010. Furthermore, independent variables such as the e-government index, the e-participation index, the human capital index, the infrastructure index, and the web measure index showed at different relative levels across the countries during the given timeframe.

Second, a correlation analysis was conducted to uncover any statistical relationships between the variables. Looking at the results of the correlation analysis, public social expenditure and the e-participation index were revealed to share a negative correlation. Public social expenditure and the web measure index also shared a negative correlation. However, public social expenditure correlated with the e-government index, the human capital index, and the infrastructure index, all showed a positive significance.

Finally, simple cross-sectional regressions and a number of pooled TSCS analyses were performed in order to investigate the causal relationship between public social spending and the development of the e-government. The results of simple cross-sectional regressions showed that no significant variables related to the e-government can be found in 2003 and 2010.

In the PCSE model analyses, in the case of the e-government index as analysed via the Pluemper model, a negative association appeared with public social expenditure. The association between human capital and public social expenditure in the Beck & Katz model showed a positive significance. Interestingly, the infrastructure index showed converse results in the Pluemper model as compared to the Beck & Katz model. That is, in the Beck & Katz model, the infrastructure index showed positive, while it showed a negative significance in the Pluemper model. In case of the web measure index, the results revealed through the pluemper model showed a negative significance.

According to first difference model analyses, the e-government index and the web measure index showed negative significances. However, the infrastructure index had a positive short-term impact on the change of public social expenditure. Interestingly, the e-participation index and the human capital index showed no significances in the results.

Summarising the analysis results, there is no certainty of a positive causal relationship between public social spending and the e-government's development. Therefore, the hypothesis 'the development of the e-government increases public social spending' is not proved. However, it appeared that the increase of the e-government index did lead to the decrease of public social spending.

Chapter VIII

Conclusion : Informatisation and the Welfare State

Chapter VIII

Conclusion : Informatisation and the Welfare State

In order to identify the causal relationship between informatisation and the development of the welfare state (i.e., public social spending and income inequality), this study explores and attempts to prove hypotheses. This is achieved through the analyses of multifarious data drawn from studies on the welfare state performed by scholars, institutions, and international organisations.

The purpose of this chapter is to reaffirm the mechanism of the relationship between informatisation and the development of the welfare state; and to further demonstrate whether the hypotheses presented in previous chapters are proved. Thereafter, the implications of the results from a theoretical perspective are considered. Finally, what manner of studies could be constructed in order to build upon the present aggregation of information and knowledge is explored at length.

1. The Mechanism of the Relationship between Informatisation and the Welfare State

Historically, informatisation in the second-half of the twentieth century can be considered as a new era, divergent from the previous era because of the numerous changes in economy, politics, and social culture caused by informatisation. First of all, many economies were drastically altered due to the development of the ICT industry and ICT-related industries, the increase in employment of skilled ICT workers, and flexibility of the relationship between labour and capital. Moreover, during the informatisation process, information was realised as a new production factor. Alongside human capital and social capital, information itself is now a major contributor to economic growth. In the political sphere, informatisation introduced electronic media as political instruments to be utilised for political strategies and campaigns. Besides, informatisation brought about vastly extended social network movements and network politics, allowing citizen participation in the formation of political agendas and political decision-making processes, absent the constraints of time and space. The development of the e-government, e-governance, and e-democracy led to heightened transparency and efficiency in administration and political decision-making processes via a much wider scale of intercommunication.

Informatisation was a major game-changer in social culture too, contributing to the formation of new work-family relationships, increasing the demand for information and technology labour, reducing time and space constraints in household and community-related economic activities, and changing the traditional role division between men and women. In view of the above factors, it is easy to envisage how informatisation also affected the building of social relationships and the activities played out in people's day-to-day lives through more active and widespread intercommunication.

However, a side effect of informatisation was the deepening of inequalities due to the rapid change in how people access and utilise information. Many who were unable to adapt found themselves excluded from social and political participation; especially the socio-economically underprivileged. In addition, the development of ICT brought with it changes in industrial structure and occupational structure, leading to segmentation in the labour market, job insecurity and unemployment. Ultimately, it seemed obvious that the aforementioned social problems led to the income gap, and finally the polarisation of wealth.

Many labels characterise the changes in the internal and international political economic environment, i.e., neo-liberalism, globalisation, global economic crises, and financial crises. The welfare state made numerous efforts to combat these uncharted types of inequalities caused by informatisation. Ironically, devices which arose from informatisation, such as informatisation of welfare, e-welfare, and u-welfare, aided the welfare state in addressing the very inequality problems that arose from the information process in the first place. The aim of the welfare state was to acclimate to the ever-changing environment created by the development of ICT and, in doing so, found three areas in which to utilise informatisation. One was management of public social services, increasing welfare efficacy. Another was the delivery of public social services and more efficient welfare, also allowing for transparency. Third was the demand for public social services, securing people's right to select the services specific to their needs. None of the above would have been possible without computerisation and automation; integral elements of informatisation.

2. Summary and Demonstration of the Analysis Results

2.1 Summary of the Analysis Results

1) The Development of the ICT Industry and Public Social spending

First of all, when the data was explicated by the causality analyses, the relationship between the development of the ICT industry and public social spending was revealed as follows:

According to the results of the simple cross-sectional regressions, during 2005, public social expenditure had a negative relationship with investment, but shared positive relationships with both import and information openness.

In the PCSE model analyses, the results as revealed by the Pluemper model analyses showed no relationship between the development of ICT industry and public social spending. However, when data from before and after year 2000 were analysed separately via the Beck & Katz model, they yielded slightly different results. Investment showed a positive causal relationship with public social expenditure pre-2000, while staff and export had negative effects on public social spending during the same period. Interestingly, the causal relationship between pubic social expenditure and information openness was negative during pre-2000 as well as post-2000.

According to the results of the ECM analyses, in the short term, investment and import affected public social spending negatively, and staff affected public social spending positively. In the long term, public social expenditure shared weak negative associations with staff, export, and information openness. Along the same vein, the VECM analyses revealed that, in the short term, investment and import had a negative impact on public social expenditure, while staff had a positive impact. Also similarly to the ECM analyses, the VECM analyses showed that public social spending had a negative relationship with staff, export, and information openness in the long term.

The first difference model analyses uncovered slightly different results when data from before and after year 2000 were analysed separately. Post-2000, investment had a negative relationship with public social expenditure. Pre-2000, export and information openness had a weak negative relationship with public social expenditure. Notably, import showed a negative impact on public social spending during all periods. Only staff had a weak positive short-term impact on public social expenditure for the entire period.

In the PVAR analyses, the response of public social expenditure to investment's shock and import's shock were both negative, while its response to staff's shock was uncertain and inconsistent. The negative response of public social expenditure to export's shock became stronger with time. Similarly, in the case of information openness, the results showed increasingly negative effects with time.

To sum up the above results, the hypothesis 'the development of the ICT industry increases public welfare spending' was not proved. Some factors had a negative impact and some factors had a positive impact depending on the time period and analysis model. However, it would seem apparent from these causality analyses that there exists a relatively negative causal relationship between public welfare spending and the development of the ICT industry.

2) The Development of the ICT Industry and Income Inequality

Through the causality analyses, the relationship between the development of the ICT industry and income inequality can be viewed as follows:

According to the results of simple cross-sectional regression analyses, no significant relationship between the development of the ICT industry and income inequality can be found during 1996 or 2005.

In the PCSE model analyses, the Pluemper model showed household income inequality to share relatively strong negative relationships with investment and staff, and showed household income inequality to share weak negative relationships with export and information openness. Similarly to the cross-sectional regression analyses, results of the Pluemper model also did not yield any significant relationship between the development of the ICT industry and income inequality.

In the ECM analyses, investment had a positive transitory effect on income inequality in the short term and a positive permanent effect on income inequality in the long term. However, export and information openness showed negative effects on income inequality in the short term as well as the long term. Similarly to the ECM analyses, the VECM analyses revealed that investment had positive effects on income inequality in the short term and in the long term. Again revealing parallel results, VECM showed export and information openness to have negative effects on income inequality in the short and long term. The short-term results showed that import had a negative transitory effect on income inequality. Staff displayed no association with income inequality in both the ECM analyses and the VECM analyses.

Looking at the first difference model analyses, when data from before and after year 2000 were analysed separately, they again yielded slightly different results. Investment had a positive association with both income inequality and staff for the entire period. Investment also showed a positive association pre-2000, while staff showed a positive association post-2000. However, import revealed a negative significance with income inequality pre-2000. In the case of other variables, a statistical association between the development of the ICT industry and an increase in income inequality did not show in the short term.

In summation of these results, the hypothesis 'the development of the ICT industry does increase income inequality' was not proved. Some factors had a negative impact and some had a positive impact, depending on the time period and analysis model. Nevertheless, the results of the causality analyses do suggest that there is more of a positive causal relationship between income inequality and the development of the ICT industry than a negative causal relationship.

3) ICT Usage and Public Social spending

The results of the causality analyses bring to light the relationship between ICT usage and public social spending as follows:

In the results of the simple cross-sectional regression analyses, in 1996, there was no significant relationship between ICT usage and public social spending. However, in 2005, mobile phones had a positive association with public social spending.

In the PCSE model analyses, through the results of the Pluemper model, the causal relationship between public social expenditure and Internet user rates were revealed to share a positive relationship during the entire period. In the Beck & Katz model, Internet user rates had a weak negative relationship with public social spending pre-2000, but a weak positive relationship post-2000. In the case of mobile phones, in the analyses of the Pluemper model, positive associations appeared for the entire period as well as post-2000. In the Beck & Katz model, the association between mobile phones and public social expenditure showed a weak positive relationship for the entire period. The Beck & Katz model also showed that PC numbers had a weak negative effect on the increase of public social expenditure for the entire period and post-2000.

Investigating the results of the ECM analyses showed that Internet user rates and mobile phones shared a negative association with public social expenditure in the long term, while PC numbers showed no causal relationship with public social expenditure in the long term. The results of the VECM analyses revealed similar phenomena to those of the ECM analyses. That is, Internet user rates and mobile phones had negative effects on public social expenditure in the long term. In the VECM analyses, however, PC numbers had a negative effect on public social expenditure in the long term. In the short term, Internet user rates had a negative relationship with public social expenditure, while mobile phones showed no significant relationship for the same time period. It is rather conspicuous to note, at this point, that PC numbers had a positive effect on the increase of public social spending in the short term.

In the first difference model analyses, during the entire period as well as pre-2000, Internet user rates had a weak negative effect on the public social expenditure. Mobile phones, on the other hand, showed a positive association with public social spending post-2000. In the case of PC numbers, the causal relationship with public social expenditure was negative for the entire period, as well as pre-2000.

The results of the PVAR analyses revealed that public social expenditure's response to Internet user rates' shock was negative. In the case of public social expenditure's response to mobile phones' shock, the graph lines of the analysis results were enough to reveal that mobile phones' impact on public social expenditure ends with a positive effect. The response of public social expenditure to PC numbers' shock was negative.

In summation, it cannot be said that there was a definite positive causal relationship between public social spending and the usage of ICT. Therefore, the hypothesis 'the use of ICT does increase public welfare spending' was not proved. Overall, the results of the causality analyses do unmask what would seem a rather negative causal relationship between public social spending and the increase of ICT usage as opposed to a positive relationship.

4) ICT Usage and Income Inequality

The results of the causality analysis on the relationship between ICT usage and income inequality as follows:

The results of the simple cross-sectional regressions show that, for year 1996, only PC numbers had a weak negative relationship with income inequality, while no significant results were found in the analyses for year 2005.

In PCSE model analyses, through the Pluemper model and the Beck & Katz Model, Internet user rates revealed weak positive effects on the increase of income inequality. In the Pluemper model, mobile phones showed a weak positive association with income inequality as well.

According to the results yielded from the ECM analyses, Internet user rates, mobile phones, and PC numbers revealed a positive transitory effect on household income inequality. PC numbers in particular showed a positive permanent effect on household income inequality in the long term. The other ICT usage variables, however, showed no causal relationship with household income inequality in the long term. In the VECM analyses, the results showed that Internet user rates and PC numbers had positive effects on the increase of income inequality in the short term. In the long term, all three variables related to ICT usage had weak positive effects on the increase of income inequality.

The first difference model analyses showed that, pre-2000, the effect of internet user rates on income inequality was negative, while it showed positive post-2000. Mobile phones had a negative association with income inequality during the entire period and pre-2000. However, post-2000, the effect of mobile phones on the increase of income inequality became positive. PC numbers had a negative association with income inequality during the entire period, as well as pre-2000. Conversely, the effects appeared positively post-2000.

In summation of the above results, it can be tentatively asserted that there was a positive causal relationship between income inequality and ICT usage after year 2000, but not before. That is, the analysis results suggest that the hypothesis 'the use of ICT does increase income inequality' was only partially proved.

5) E-government and Public Social spending

The results of the causality analysis elucidated the relationship between the development of the e-government and public social spending as follows:

Looking at the results of the simple cross-sectional regression analyses, none of the variables related to the e-government had a causal relationship with the welfare state during years 2003 or 2010.

In PCSE model analyses, in the case of the e-government index, the analysis of the Pluemper model showed a negative association with public social expenditure. In the Beck & Katz model, the association between human capital and public social spending was positive. It is noteworthy the results for the infrastructure index in the Pluemper model and in the Beck & Katz model was converse. That is, in the Beck & Katz model, the infrastructure index had a positive effect on the increase of public social spending, while it had a negative effect on public social spending in the Pluemper model. The web measure index's association with public social spending was negative in the results of the Pluemper model.

As revealed by the first difference model analyses, the e-government index and the web measure index had a negative effect on the increase of public social spending. However, the infrastructure index had a positive short-term impact on the change of public social expenditure. Interestingly, the e-participation index and the human capital index showed no causal relationship with public social spending in the analysis results.

Summarising the analyses, there were no certain results showing a positive causal relationship between public welfare spending and the e-government's development. Therefore, the hypothesis 'the development of the e-government increases public welfare spending' is not proved.

2.2 Consolidation and Demonstration of Analysis Results

The analysis results relating to the causal relationship between informatisation and the welfare state are consolidated and demonstrated through the table below.[92]

According to analysis results on the relationship between the development of the ICT industry and the welfare state, driving factors for public social spending included staff in the short term and import in the long term. In contrast, hindering factors for public social spending included investment, import, export, and information in the short term. In the long term, staff, export, and information openness were included as hindering factors.

Driving factors for income inequality included investment and staff in the short term. In the long term, investment was included as a driving factor for income inequality. On the contrary, hindering factors included import, export and information openness in the short term. In the long term, export and information openness acted as hindering factors for income inequality.

<Table 8.1> **Deveolpment of the ICT Industry and the Welfare State: Driving Factors and Hindering Factors 1**

Hypothesis	Variable	Analysis Period	Time Term	Public Social Spending		Income Inequality	
				Driving Factor	Hindering Factor	Driving Factor	Hindering Factor
1. The development of the ICT industry increases public social spending	Investment	1985-2010	Short		○★,■(**),△	○★,■(*,***)	
			Long			○★	
	Staff		Short	○★,■(***)		■(**,***)	
			Long		○★		
	Import		Short		○, ★,■(*,**,***),△		★,■(*)
			Long	★			
2. The development of the ICT industry increases income inequality	Export		Short		■(*),△		○★
			Long		○★		○★
	Information Openness		Short		■(*),△		○★
			Long		○★		○★

92 The results of the simple cross-sectional regression analyses are excluded in this section because the analysis method is not time dimensional. The results of the PCSE analyses are also excluded because the analysis method using level variables can be criticized. This is due to the utilisation of each country's individual characteristics, as well as the monotonically increasing or monotonically decreasing phenomena over time.

1) ○: Results of ECM Analyses, ★: Results of VECM Analyses, ■: Results of First Difference Model Analyses, △: Results of PVAR Analyses.

2) * Before Year 2000, ** After Year 2000, ***Entire Period.

3) Investment: Total Annual Investments in Telecommunication, Import: Imports of Telecommunication Equipment, Export: Exports of Telecommunication Equipment, Staff: Total Full-time Telecommunication Staff.

According to analysis results on the relationship between the increase of ICT usage and the welfare state, driving factors for public social spending included mobile phones and PC numbers in the short term. In the long term, no driving factors were found in the results. In contrast, hindering factors for public social spending included Internet user rates and PC numbers in the short term. In the long term, all three variables (Internet user rates, mobile phones, and PC numbers) acted as hindering factors for public social spending.

Driving factors for income inequality comprised Internet user rates, mobile phones, and PC numbers in the short term. In the long term, Internet user rates, mobile phones, and PC numbers also acted as driving factors for income inequality. In contrast, in the short term, hindering factors for income inequality included Internet user rates, mobile phones, and PC numbers.

<Table 8.2> ICT Usage and the Welfare State: Driving Factors and Hindering Factors 2

Hypothesis	Variable	Analysis Period	Time Term	Public Social Spending		Income Inequality	
				Driving Factor	Hindering Factor	Driving Factor	Hindering Factor
1. The use of ICT increases public social spending. 2. The use of ICT increases income inequality	Internet User Rates	1985-2010	Short		★,■(*,***),△	○★,■(**)	■(*)
			Long		○★	★	
	Mobile Phones		Short	■(**),△		○,■(**)	■(*, ***)
			Long		○★	★	
	PC Numbers		Short	★	△	○,★,■(**)	■(*, ***)
			Long		★,■(*,***)	○★	

1) ○: Results of ECM Analyses, ★: Results of VECM Analyses, ■: Results of First Difference Model Analyses, △: Results of PVAR Analyses.

2) * Before Year 2000, ** After Year 2000, ***Entire Period.

3) Internet User Rates: Rate of Internet Users for the Past One Year vs Total Population, Mobile Phones: Mobile Cellular Subscriptions per 100 Inhabitants, PC Numbers: Personal Computer Numbers per 100 Inhabitants.

According to the analysis results on the relationship between the development of the e-government and the welfare state, driving factors for public social spending included infrastructure in the short term. In contrast, hindering factors for public social spending included the e-government index and web measure index in the short term.

<Table 8.3> E-government and the Welfare State: Driving Factors and Hindering Factors 3

Hypothesis	Variable	Analysis Period	Time Term	Public Social Spending	
				Driving Factor	Hindering Factor
1. The development of the e-government increases public social spending.	E-government Index	2003-2010	Short		■
			Long		
	Infrastructure Index		Short	■	
			Long		
	Human Capital Index		Short		
			Long		
	Web Measure Index		Short		■
			Long		
	E-Participation Index		Short		
			Long		

1) ■: Results of First Difference Model Analyses

Given the types of transformations that have taken place in society, as well as the rate at which such transformations and developments have accelerated, special attention should be afforded the period after the year 2000. That special attention should be given to this timeframe is supported by the results shown in studies regarding informatisation; a terrain which has widened in scope and grown at an unprecedented rate in both public and private sectors since the year 2000.

3. Theoretical Implications and Suggestions for Continuous Studies

The main purpose of this study is to find out the influence informatisation has on the development of the welfare state. The role, function and importance of ICT is not only growing, but moving forward with impressive velocity. The social and economic implications of these rapid changes are deeply compelling, and must be observed with a macroscopic eye in order to discover whether informatisation has a positive or negative impact on the development of the welfare state in this modern global society.

Unfortunately, despite its blatantly obvious importance, issues surrounding informatisation have not recently attracted a great amount of attention in comparative social policy studies and comparative welfare state studies. In fact, there is a conspicuous lack of studies dealing with the relationship between informatisation and the development of the welfare state from the theoretical perspective.

This study is built upon the idea that the welfare state's basic purpose is the pursuit of 'guaranteeing basic life quality' and 'solving inequalities,' hence delving so deeply into the impact of informatisation on income inequality and public social spending.

To achieve the study goal, two major questions were presented at the beginning:

I. Does informatisation hinder increasing public social spending?
II. Does informatisation deepen income inequality in the society?

With these two questions under scrutiny, several hypotheses were established and proved. It was via an extensive and meticulous process that these questions were finally answered.

3.1 Theoretical Implications of the Welfare State Theory

Here, the question of whether informatisation has a positive or negative impact on the development of the welfare state in this rapidly changing modern society is comprehensively answered. While interpreting the results discovered through this study, the following answers surfaced:

The first answer is that the development of the ICT industry contributed to the decrease of public social spending in the gross. Except for staff and import, most variables related to the ICT industry's development (investment, export, and information openness) indicated that they had a negative impact on the increase of public social spending. The interpretation of these results can be explained from three angles.

From the first angle, the nature of the ICT industry has been characterised by flexibility, creativity, and rapidity. In the globalisation process, these characteristics put a heavy emphasis on competitiveness and efficiency in the domestic and the global environment. To achieve a greater amount of export, more countries invested aggressively in the ICT sector. In the labour market, those with higher ICT skills and/or ICT education are respected and in increasing demand. For the government and entrepreneurs, it was more important to survive on the battlefield of the ICT sectors and to increase the national wealth through gaining higher profits, especially considering the process of globalisation. Therefore, in order to create business-friendly environments, 'friendly' corporate policies took priority over providing satisfactory welfare needs and protecting labourers from social risks. That is, during the rapid information process, the underprivileged (such as people pushed aside by competition, maladjusted persons, and latecomers in the labour market) received less attention and often became victims of the struggle for survival. As a result, pre-welfare political measures such as social security programs became weaker in the labour market.

From the second angle, staff showed a positive effect on public social spending in the short term but a negative effect in the long term. ICT workers, especially those with low skill levels, were easily confronted with job insecurity and unemployment in the new flexible labour market. During the aforementioned rapid information process, numerous ICT workers faced such difficulties. In the process, mutual confidence in existing labour-management relations was drastically diminished. Moreover, when most people attempted to search for new job openings, they were required to participate in education and training in the new field of ICT. Until they found jobs and met the cost of living, the welfare state had to support them financially. It is reasonable to suggest that it were these phenomena that led to the increase of public social spending in the short term and the decrease of public social spending in the long term.

The third angle is what the increase in imports of telecommunication equipment meant to the improvement of active and wide intercommunication. In reality, the beginnings of most discussions on important social issues, especially welfare issues, began in cyberspace. The expansion of global social networking prompted an awakening of human and social rights. In other words, advanced welfare states went through a learning process via continuously and rapidly expanding social network services, which ultimately led to the increase of public social spending.

Consequently, according to the results of this study, the summation of the aforementioned viewpoints suggest that the development of the ICT industry contributed somewhat to the reduction of the welfare state through the decrease of public social spending, rather than an expansion of the welfare state through the increase of public social spending.

The second answer is that the increase of ICT usage contributed to the decrease of public social spending in the gross. The variables related to ICT usage, such as Internet user rates, mobile phones, and PC numbers, ultimately showed negative effects on the increase of public social spending, with the exception of the short term positive effects of mobile phones and PC numbers. The interpretation of these results can be seen from two viewpoints.

On one hand, ICT usage improved the efficiency and transparency of welfare administration through computerisation, automatisation, and standardisation. The management and delivery of public social welfare were restructured systematically and effectively, so that governments could save on welfare administrative costs. Moreover, the timely and appropriate response to urgent welfare needs prevented public social spending on the government's part, in turn preventing the snowball effect of additional expenses caused by the secondary social risks. However, through ICT integration in the public welfare sector, an emphasis was placed on individual responsibilities and the tests for the eligibility of welfare benefits became stricter. Most welfare recipients had to experience poorly formed and potentially humiliating processes strictly managed and controlled by newly emerging digital welfare systems in order to become welfare service recipients.

On the other hand, mobile phone usage and PC numbers increased public social spending. Through free and active intercommunication between citizens and the government, the response of the government to citizen's welfare needs became more rapid and effective. This was especially the case for the underprivileged, who were often previously unable to obtain information on public welfare services. Now, through governmental social network services, help was not just on the horizon but potentially ready and waiting. However, although intensive utilisation of ICT could sometimes help overcome life crises in the short term, this method did not guarantee the improvement of life quality for needy people in the long term.

Consequently, according to the results of this study, the summation of the aforementioned viewpoints suggest that the increase of ICT usage contributed somewhat to the reduction of the welfare state through the decrease of public social spending, rather than helping expand of the welfare state through the increase of public social spending.

The third answer is that the development of the ICT industry contributed to the increase of income inequality in the gross. Excepting import, export, and information openness; investment and staff strongly indicated a positive impact on the increase of income inequality. The interpretation of these results can be seen from two viewpoints.

On one hand, as informatisation rapidly progressed, aggressive investments in the ICT sector and a selective high regard for skilled ICT workers led to less respect for maladjusted workers, who were often lesser-educated, low income earners, a member of a disadvantaged group such as the elderly or disabled, and so on. Therefore unfamiliar phenomena proliferated, such as social exclusion caused by the digital divide, the segmentation of the labour market caused by industrial and occupational structure, the decline of confidence and loyalty that previously existed in labour-manager relations, and increases in job insecurity, unemployment, and poverty. Over time, such unfortunate circumstances further widened the income gap, and ultimately, aggravated the polarisation of wealth.

On the other hand, the negative impact of import, export, and information openness on the decrease of income inequality can be explained by the increase of general national wealth and the expansion of social networks. It is a natural train of thought that higher exports could lead to higher economic profits, and higher economic profits could contribute to an increase in national wealth. Venturing one step further, the increase of national wealth allowed the government to introduce and implement social welfare programs to combat income inequality. Finally, portions of the financial pie could be distributed towards higher numbers of needy people. In addition, it is necessary to remember that the expansion of social networks began with the import of telecommunication equipment. Through the increase of Internet usage, internal cyber communities formed and grew to become global community networks. Namely, inequality issues became global social issues. Everywhere that inequality existed, appropriate political responses were researched, introduced, and discussed.

Consequently, according to the results of this study, the summation of the aforementioned viewpoints suggest that the increase of ICT usage contributed somewhat to the reduction of the welfare state through the increase of income inequality, rather than the expansion of the welfare state through the decrease of income inequality.

The fourth answer is that the increase of ICT usage contributed to the increase of income inequality in the gross. Internet user rates, mobile phones, and PC numbers showed indubitably their positive effects on the increase of income inequality since year 2000. During the rapid informatisation process, people less skilled and/or educated in ICT (primarily the underprivileged) started off at a disadvantage in regards to finding jobs, keeping jobs, and receiving promotions. In contrast, people highly knowledgeable or educated in ICT (primarily falling inside the high economic bracket) had the upper hand. With weakening social security measures in the flexible labour market, such converse situations were aggregated and accelerated. Ultimately, the information gap led to differences in income, social status, empowerment, and finally resulted in social stratification and unequal social structure. This cyclic phenomena heightened income inequality.

According to the results of this study, the summation of the aforementioned viewpoints suggest that the increase of ICT usage contributed somewhat to the reduction of the welfare state through the increase of income inequality, rather than the expansion of the welfare state through the decrease of income inequality.

The fifth answer is that it cannot necessarily be confirmed that the adoption of ICT in the public sector has a positive impact on the development of the welfare state. In particular, the analysis results on the short-term negative effects of the e-government index and web measure index on the increase of public social spending confirmed the problems caused by informatisation since year 2000. Only the infrastructure index indicated a positive effect on the increase of public social spending in the short term. These analysis results can be understood thus: The adoption of web services in public sectors alone is not sufficient for the development of the welfare state. However, active and frequent usage of web services alongside equally active and frequent feedback from the government regarding welfare needs could provide the catalyst to jump-start the necessary positive developments into action.

According to the results of this study, assuming that citizens and governments did not use ICT for welfare, it cannot be said with credence that the development of the e-government led to the growth of the welfare state through the increase of public social spending.

In conclusion, considering the results of this study on the causal relationship between informatisation and the development of the welfare state among OECD countries, focusing on public social spending and income inequality, it can be said that informatisation influenced the development of the welfare state negatively rather than positively.

At this point, when looking back on the suicide of the mother and two daughters as mentioned at the beginning of this study, the contents herein contain several meaningful conclusions. If this family had had the chance to utilise telecommunication and to inform authorities or professionals of their real situation; if they could have gained information helpful for overcoming crises; if they had access to new welfare services online so that they could alert people to their situation; if others had noticed via the online services their lack of aid and empathised; if the government had provided appropriate welfare services for them rapidly, then that family might still be living in Seoul, South Korea. The essential and basic point is that, although the potential to be helped by urgent financial support in the short term existed, they were unable to escape their life crisis without continued follow-ups through the public social service system. This is the reason the welfare state must play a significant role in the acceleration of informatisation.

3.2 Suggestions for Continuous Studies on the Welfare State

This study analysed and discussed informatisation and the welfare state as they exist within all OECD countries using a quantitative comparative approach, and therefore holds a high level of significance in regards to the relationship between informatisation and the welfare state. In the analysis results of this study, meanings and roles of informatisation as driving factors and hindering factors for the development of the welfare state were discovered towards the purpose that these results can contribute to an understanding of the development of the welfare state. Moreover, the results can provide a sort of orientation for the future of the welfare state.

For all that, this study had several limitations. First, it focused solely on public social spending and income inequality to observe the development of the welfare state. However, it should not be ignored that several countries, rather than concentrating on the government's provisions of welfare or the market, have instead focused on family, NGO, and religious organisations. These countries are quite different to those who pay more attention to the government's role for supply of public welfare services and income distribution through taxation. Therefore, what was not dealt with in this study is the relationship between informatisation and the development of the welfare state in the non-mandatory sector; an area that deserves observation and attempts towards an increased understanding from now into the future. In addition, continuous studies must be conducted on the relationship between the development of the e-government and the welfare state; especially in regards to income inequality issues which were not dealt with in this study due to missing values. Furthermore, many indices related to informatisation must be utilised in order that studies can explain the development of the welfare state, allowing verification and proof of causal relationships.

If the above mentioned limits can be overcome, and the analysis results of this study remain unchanged and adhere to the truth of the current era, the 'informatisation theory' will maintain significant meaning as one of the several influential perspectives on the development of the welfare state today.

Bibliography

Korean

Bae, Deuk Jong et al. (2008). The Search for an Appropriate Level of Korean Public Social Expenditures in Comparison with OECD Countries, *Korean Public Management Review*, 22(2), pp. 199~224.

Baek, Seungho. (2003). The Study on the Determinants of Information Inequality, *Korean Journal of Social Welfare Studies*, vol. 22, pp. 81-106.

Baek, Ukin. (2013). *History of the Computer*, Seoul: Hangilsa.

Could the Songpagu One Mother and Two Daughters be Alive? The Fact the President does not Know. (2014, March 05). Moneytoday, p. A2.

Cho, Joo Eun. (2001). Information Inequality and the Disabled, *Korean Institute of Information Scientists and Engineers*, 2001(2), pp. 534-538.

Cho, Youngjun (2010.12). Convergence Technology and Methods for the Development of the Convergence Industry, *CEo Report 2010*. No. 41.

Choi, Jeongeun. (2014). The Background of Income Inequality's Aggravation in OECD countries and their Response, *Foreign Economic Focus*, 2014(40), Seoul: Bank of Korea.

Go, Samseog. (2012). Digital Divide and Digital Information Welfare Policy in Digital Governance Age- Focusing on E-Inclusion Policy, *Digital Media Trend*, vol. 72, pp. 5-35.

Go, Kyounghwan et al. (2009). 2007 Social Spending Trends in Korea and Income Security Systems for Retired Persons in OECD countries, *Policy Paper*. Seoul: Korea Institute for Health and Social Affairs.

Han, Yeongbin. (2005). Informatisation and the Development Strategy of Sweden, *Zeitschrift der Koreanisch-Deutschen Gesellschaft fuer Sozialwissenschaft*, 15(1), pp. 59-80.

Internet and Smart Phone Addition among Adolescents get Increasingly Worse. (2014, March 24). Hankyoreh, Retrieved from http://www.hani.co.kr/arti/society/society general/629546.html

Homepage of Korea Health and Welfare Information Service. Retrieved from http://edu.khwis.or.kr/index.jsp

Hwang, Geun & Kim, Yongsu. (2005). A Study on the Use of Mass Media and Political Socialization, *Journal of Political Communication*, Vol. 3. pp. 117-151.

Illegal Pay-outs and Numbers of False Unemployment Benefit Recipients on the Decrease. (2014, January 14). Policy News

Jang, Shijun. (2006). *The Concept of Social Capital and Educational Implications*, Seoul: Korea Education Research Information and Service.

Jeong, Gukhwan et al. (1996). *The Information Society: Concept, Meaning and Approaches*. Seoul: The National Information Society Agency.

Jeong, Jangho. (2005). The Status and Challenges of the ICT industry, *Journal of The Korean Institute of Communication Sciences*, 22(1), pp. 101-110.

Jeong, Hyunjun and Park, Hyunshin. (2010). The Status and Implications of the ICT Industry Viewed through Economic Indicators, *Broadcasting and Communication Policy*, 22(23), pp. 59-83.

Jeong, Youngcheol, (2008). The Definition and Model of e-Welfare and u-Welfare in a Ubiquitous Society, *Health and Welfare Policy Forum*, pp. 48-66.

Jeong, Yunsu and Kim, Miwon. (2004). Paradigm of Informatization in Social Welfare: Preliminary Discussion and Application. *Journal of Social Science*, Vol. 21, pp. 63~79.

Jin, Sanggi and Jo, Jeongmun. (2012). An Analysis of the Impact of National ICT Development on Economic Growth, Informatisation policy, 19(3), pp. 64-93.

Jin, Sanggi. (2013). Time-series Analysis of Changes in the Information Gap in Korea: Focusing on the Information Gap Index, *Journal of Korean Association for Regional Information Society*, 16(3), pp. 161-188.

Jo, Hwasun. (2012). Political Participation and the Future of Democracy in the Age of Social Networking, *Korean Journal of Political Science,*19(3), pp. 23-48.

Jung, Sunyoung. (2011). International Comparison of Total Factor Productivity in ICT Industries: A Stochastic Frontier Approach, *Economics Study*, 59(1). pp. 25-53.

Kang, Hongyoul., Cha, Namkyoung., Kang, Sanghyun., and Kim, Eunmi. (2002). The Socio-economic Implications of the Digital Divide, *Working Paper*, Seoul: Korea Information Society Development Institute.

Kang, Hongyoul. (2004). Reading IT Innovations in "Ubiquity", *KISDI Issue Report*, 2004(26), Seoul: KISDI.

Killing Each Other to Live One Day More than Children. (2014, March 14). Pressian. Retrieved from http://www.pressian.com/news/article.html?no=115415.

Kim, Gu. (2014). An Exploratory Analysis on the Relationship between the Digital Divide and Social Exclusion in Korea, *Journal of Korean Association for Regional Information Society*, 17(2), pp.61-88.

Kim, Jongkil. (2012). Development of ICT and the Conditions of 'Smart Welfare', *Society and Theory*, No. 21, pp. 645-696.

Kim, Munjo. (1998). Informationization Relevant to the Transformation of Women's Social Status, *Journal of Asian Women*, pp. 46-65.

Kim, Munjo. (1998). Potential Diagnosis of the Mature Information Society, *Journal of Social Research*, Vol. 1. pp. 51-80.

Kim, Munjo and Kim, Jongkil. (2002). The Digital Divide: Conceptual and Practical Implications, *Korean Journal of Sociology*, 36(4), pp. 123-155.

Kim, Seongguk et al. (1996). *Progress in Informatisation and Social Change*.Pusan: The Labor Research Institute of Pusan National University.

Kim, Seungtae. (2013). Information Policy of the Smart Society and E-government. Seoul: Beumunsa.

Konno, Haruki. (2013) The Black Company: The Monster Consuming Japan. In Yongtag Lee (Ed. & Trans.), Seoul: Readysetgo. (Original work published 2012).

Korea Institute for Health and Social Affairs (KIHSA) and Ministry of Health and Welfare (MHW). (2001). Study on Knowledge and Information of Health and Welfare, Seoul: Author.

Lee, Changsun. (1993). Information Society and Change of Labor, *Journal of Social Science*, Vol. 11, pp. 217-248.

Lee, Jaehyuck. (2008). Human Capital and Social Capital: Reinterpretation of Korean Economic Growth, *Discourse 201*, pp. 5-34.

Lee, Kyoungnam. (2013). Focus: The Current State of the Female Workforce in the ICT Sector and its Implications, *Information and Communications Policy*, 25(14), Seoul: Korea Information Society Development Institute.

Lee, Kyoungtae. (2011). *A Study on the Relationships among Social Security, Social Polarization, Social Capital and the Administrative Corruption; Focusing on the OECD Member States* (Doctoral Dissertation, University of Seoul, South Korea). Retrieved from http://libproxy.knu.ac.kr/90a6552/_Lib_Proxy_Url/www.riss.kr/search/detail/DetailView.do?p_mat_type=be54d9b8bc7cdb09&control_no=68f0dac216819009ffe0bdc3ef48d419

Lee, Myoungjin and Park, Kitae. (2009). The Issue Change of Digital Divide Studies and Its Implication, *Information Policy*, 16(3), pp. 3~17.

Lee, Jaesung, (2009). Welfare Informatisation in the Ubiquitous Age, *Journal of Korean Association for Regional Information Society*, 12(4), pp. 171～196.

Lee, Sohee. (2003). *Understanding Internet Addiction*. Seoul: Hakjisa.

Lee, Soobum and Kim, Dongwoo. (2012). The Impact of Using Social Media with Political Purposes on the Intention of Political Participation of Social Media Users, *Journal of Public Relations*, 16(1), pp. 78-111.

Lee, Younghwan. (2000). A Study on the Information Welfare Standard, *Condition and Welfare*, No. 7, pp. 228-268.

LG Communicatopia Institute. (1999). *The Information Revolution, Life Revolution and Consciousness Revolution*. Seoul: Baesanseodang.

Min, Insik and Choi, Pilseon. (2009). *STATA Panel Data Analysis*. Seoul: Jiphil Media.

Min, Insik and Choi, Pilseon. (2014). *STATA Time Series Data Analysis*, Seoul: Jiphil Media.

Min, Young. (2011), The Digital Divide among Internet Users: An Analysis of Digital Access, Literacy, and Participation, *Journal of Communication Research*, 48(1), pp. 150-187.

National Information Society Agency (NIA). (2010). *2010 UN E-Government Evaluation, Global Informatisation Policy Resources*. Seoul: Author.

National Information Society Agency (NIA). (2014). 2013 A New Digital Divide Analysis and Recommendations in the Smart Age, *Research Paper*, Seoul: National Information Society Agency.

National Intelligence Agency Staff Members Ordered to Post Comments under News Items while Moving between Cafes. (2015, February 10). Kyunghyang Shinmun.

Nearly 20 pct. of Koreans Classified as `Impoverished': Report. (2012, December 21). Dong-A Ilbo.

Not Qualified to Say 'Happy People' without Solving Poverty. (2015, January 07). Seoul Shinmun.

Older Generation's Suicide Epidemic. (2011, May 10). Hankyoreh.

Park, Eunmi. (2000). A Study on the Welfare Paradigm of the Information Society: Focusing on Informatisation of Welfare, *Korean Human Relations Review*, 5(1), pp. 194~214.

Park, Gukheum. (2007). The Effect of Informatisation on Unemployment: Focusing on Analysing the Informatisation Index, *Journal of Korean Association for Regional Information Society*, 10(3), pp. 95-119.

Park, Hyoungjun. (1995). Informatisation and Communication in the E-space of South Korea: An Application of Habermas's Public Sphere Theory, Paper Published in Symposium of Korea Sociological Association, pp. 153-177.

Park, Hee. (1999). Labor Flexibility of the Information Society and Industrial Welfare Strategy, Paper Published in Symposium of Korea Sociological Association, pp.73-82.

Park, Jun, Choi, Hong, and Park, Seongmin. (2011). The New Policy Environment Introducing Social Media, *SERI CEO Information*.vol. 808. Seoul: Samsung Economic Research Institute.

Park, Suyong. (2012). Policies of the ICT Industry in the Convergence Age, *Journal of Korean Institute of Communication Science*, 30(1), pp. 17-19.

Park, Youngmi. (2004). The Equity of Access to Information Welfare, *The Journal of Korean Social Welfare Administration*, 6(1), pp. 120-122.

Seo, Ijong. (2000). The Structured Digital Information Gap: Social Problems, *Information and Society*, vol. 2, pp. 68-87.

Seo, Ijong. (2001). The Information Gap and Information Inequality, *National IT Industry Promotion*, 3(1), pp. 17-30.

Seo, Ijong. (2008, December). The Digital Divide and Human Rights of Older People, In a Book (Sociology during the 60 Years since the Establishment of South Korea: Looking at the next 60 Years.) Published as the Result of a Biannual Social Competition Run by *The Korean Sociological Association*, pp. 566-580.

Seo, Jin-Wan and Park, Hee-Bong. (2003). The Possibility of Formulating the Social Capital in Virtual Community: Use of Internet and Social Capital, *The Korea Association for Policy Studies*, 12(1). pp. 27-49.

Shin, Seungchoon. (2013). The Dysfunction of Information in the Smart Society: A Focus on the Information Divide of the Information Poor, *Journal of Regional Development*, 13(1), pp. 104-135.

Smart Phone Addiction; 1 of 4 Youths in Danger...Middle School Students- The Conditions for Double Income families are Worsening for Children. (2014, March 25). Dongailbo, p. A15.

Son, Sangyoung, Kim, Byoungjun, and O, Taewon. (2000). *The Maintenance Plan of the Legal System for Welfare Information Telecommunication*. Gyeonggi-do: Korea Information Society Development Institute.

Song, Taesu. (2010). Study on the Disputation of Flexible Labor Market and the Theory on 'New Relation between Labor and Management', *Working Paper of the Federation of Korean Trade Unions Research Center*. Seoul: Federation of Korean Trade Unions Research Center.

Tattered Welfare Standards, Only Citizens are Distressed. (2012. October 14). Korea Economic Daily.

The Evolution of Video Conferencing Systems: The Expansion to Remote Medical Treatment and Remote Education. (2014, December 17). Edaily.

The First Televised Trial in the History of Judicature, with 20,000 Pages of Documented Evidence (20 Times that of the Average Criminal Trial). (2014, November 12). Chosun Ilbo.

The Ministry of Information and Communication, Leaders of Road Safety for Children. (2007, January 15). Asia Economy.

The National Health Insurance Corporation: The Reason for the Enforcement of the Medical Carer Management System. (2011, October 11). Week Kyunghyang, No. 945.

The Travel of Visually Impaired People Becomes More Comfortable. (2013, April 18). Digital Times.

U, Jongmo. (2003). Information Inequalities and the Social Welfare Approach, *The Journal of Humanities and Social Science Research*, vol. 9, pp. 361-384.

Wemakeprice Creates a Stir, Taking Advantage of Probationary Employees and Firing Regular Workers. (2015, January 16). Hankyoreh.

Yang, Seungmok and Kim, Suah. (2002). Electronic Democracy and Information Democracy, *The Journal of Communication Research 39*, pp. 137-183.

Yang, Seungmok and Kim, Sooah. (2002). Electronic Democracy and Information Democracy, *Journal of Communication Research*, vol. 39, pp. 137-183.

Yang, Seungmock, Song, Hoguen and Jo, Gwonjung. (2002). Information Democracy and Information Welfare Policy in the Knowledge-based Society: A Solution for the Digital Divide, *Korean Social Science Review*, 24(1), pp. 79-112.

Yun, Sangjin. (2012). *What is a platform?*, Seoul: Hanbitbiz, p. 45, 49.

Yun, Youngmin. (2000). *The Politics of Cyberspace*, Seoul: Hanyang University Press.

German

Alber, Jens. (1982). *Vom Armenhaus zum Wohlfahrtsstaat: Analysen zur Entwicklung der Sozialversicherung in Westeuropa.* Frankfurt; New York: Campus.

Castles, Francis G., Obinger, Herbert, and Leibfried, Stephan.(2005). Bremst der Föderalismus den Leviathan? Bundesstaat und Sozialstaat im internationalen Vergleich, 1880-2005, *Politische Vierteljahresschrift*, 46(2), pp. 215-237.

Nohlen, Dieter. (2001). *Kleines Lexikon der Politik*. München: C. H. Beck Verlag.

Jahn, Detlef. (2006). *Einführung in die Vergleichende Politikwissenschaft*. Wiesbaden: VS Verlag für Sozialwissenschaften.

Jahn, Detlef. (2009). Globalisierung als Galtonproblem: Reginonale und temporale Diffusionsschuebe, In Susanne Pickeletl al (Hrsg.), *Methoden der Vergleichenden Politik- und Sozialwissenschaft: Neue Entwicklungen und Anwendungen*, Wiesbaden: VS Verlag für Sozialwissenschaften; GWV Fachverlag GmbH, pp. 87 112.

Lessenich, Stephan. (2000). Soziologische Erklaerungsansätze zu Entstehung und Funktion des Sozialstaats, In Jutta Allmendinger und Wolfgang Ludwig- Mayerhofer (Hrsg.), *Soziologie des Sozialstaats.Gesellschaftliche Grundlagen, historische Zusammenhänge und aktuelle Entwicklungstendenzen*. Weinheim/München: Juventa, pp. 39-78.

Obinger, Herbert. (2002). Föderalismus und Wohlfahrtsstaatliche Entwicklung. Österreich und die Schweiz imVergleich, *Politische Vierteljahresschrift*, 43(2), pp. 235-271.

Rauland, Jan & Bauer, Oliver. (2011). Statistische Analyse des Einflusses von Informationsund Kommunikationstechnologien auf die Produktivität von Unternehmen, *Auszug aus Wirtschaft und Statistik*, Wiesbaden: Statistisches Bundesamt, pp.1066-1082.

Rieger, Elmar and Leibfried, Stephan. (2001). *Grundlagen der Globalisierung: Perspektiven des Wohlfahrtsstaates*. Frankfurt am Main: SuhrkampVerlag.

Schmidt, Manfred G. (2004). *Wörterbuch zur Politik* (2nd ed.). Stuttgart: Alfred Körner.

Wagschal, Uwe and Obinger, Herbert. (2000). Der Einfluss der Direktdemokratie auf die Sozialpolitik, *Politische Vierteljahresschrift*, 41(3), pp. 466-497.

English

Achen, C. H. (2000, July). Why Lagged Dependent Variables can Suppress the Explanatory Power of Other Independent Variables, *Proceeding of the annual meeting of Political Methodology*. Los Angeles: CA.

Adema, Willem, Fron, Pauline and Ladaique, Maxime. (2011). Is the European Welfare State Really More Expensive? Indicators on Social Spending, 1980-2012; and a Manual to the OECD Social Expenditure Database (SOCX), *OECD Social, Employment and Migration Working Papers*, No. 124. Paris: OECD.

Ahn, Sanghoon. (2004). Explanations about Economic Openness, In the *Codebook for Korean Welfare State Data Set*. Seoul: Seoul National University. Retrieved from http://www.unc.edu/~jdsteph/common/data-common.html.

Amenda, Willem and Whiteford, Peter. (2010). Public and Private Social Welfare, In Francis G. Castles et al (Eds.), *The Oxford Handbook of the Welfare State* (pp. 121-138). Oxford; New York: Oxford University Press.

Alber, Jens & Gilbert, Neil. (2009). *United in Diversity?; Comparing Social Models in Europe and America*, New York: Oxford University Press.

Alshomrani, Saleh. (2012). A Comparative Study on United Nations E-Government Indicators between Saudi Arabia and USA, *Journal of Emerging Trends in Computing and Information Sciences*, 3(3), pp. 411-420.

Arts, Wil A. and Gelissen, John. (2010). Models of the Welfare State, In Francis G. Castles et al (Eds.), *The Oxford Handbook of the Welfare State* (pp. 569-583). Oxford; New York: Oxford University Press.

Beck, Nathaniel and Katz, Jonathan N. (1995). What to Do (and not to Do) with Time-Series Cross-Section Data, *American Political Science Review*, 89(3), pp 634-647.

Beck, Nathaniel and Katz, Jonathan. (2004, July).*Time-Series-Cross-Section Issues: Dynamics*, New York; NY/Pasadena; CA: New York University: California Institute of Technology.

Beck, Nathaniel. (2011). *Time Series Cross-Section Data-Dynamics-Continuous*.Annual Review Political Science. Vol. 14. pp. 331–352.

Bell, Daniel. (1973). *The Coming of Post-industrial Society*. New York: Basic Books.

Brooking, Annie.(1996). *Intellectual Capital*. Secaucus; NJ: Cengage Learning EMEA.

Busemeyer, Marius R. (April 2008). *From Myth to Reality: Globalization and Public Spending in OECD Countries Revisited*, Koeln: Max Planck Institute for the Study of Societies.

Caputo, R.K. (1998). *Management and Information System in Human Service: Implication for the Distribution of Authority and Decision Making*, New York: Haworth Press.

Castells, Manuel. (1989). *The Informational City: Information Technology, Economic Restructuring, and the Urban Regional Process.* Oxford, UK; Cambridge, MA: Blackwell

Castells, Manuel. (1996). *The Rise of the Network Society* (Vol.1). Oxford: Blackwell.

Castells, Manuel. (1997). *The Power of Identity*, Cambridge, Mass: Blackwell.

Castells, Manuel. (2001). *The Internet Galaxy*. New York: Oxford University Press.

Castells, Manuel. (2004). Informationalism, Network, and the Network Society: A Theoretical Blueprint, in Manuel Castells (ed.) *The Network Society: a Cross-cultural Perspective*, Northampton, MA: Edward Elgar. Retrieved from http://annenberg.usc.edu/Faculty/Communication/~/media/Faculty/Facpdfs/Informationalism%20pdf.ashx

Castells, Manuel., Fernandez-Ardevol, Mireia., Qiu, Jack Linchuan., and Sey, Araba. (2009). *Mobile Communication and Society: a Global Perspective : a Project of the Annenberg Research Network on International Communication*, Cambridge, Mass. : MIT Press.

Castells, Manuel and Himanen, Pekka. (2002). *The Information Society and the Welfare State: the Finnish model*, New York: Oxford University Press.

Center for International Comparisons of Production, Income and Prices at the University of Pennsylvania. (2012). *Economic Openness in Penn World Table 7.1* (PWT), 1985-2010. Philadelphia: Author. Retrieved from https://pwt.sas.upenn.edu/php_ site/pwt_index.php (accessed 24 March 2014).

Chigona, W., Beukes, D., Vally, J., & Tanner, M. (2009). Can Mobile Internet Alleviate Social Exclusion in Developing Countries?. *The Electronic Journal of Information Systems in Developing Countries* (EJISDC), 36(7), Retrieved from http://citeseerx.ist.psu.edu/viewdoc/summary?doi=10.1.1.364.1576

Colecchia, Alessandra and Schreye, Paul.(2001, July). ICT Investment and Economic Growth in the 1990s: Is the United States a Unique Case?: A Comparative Study of Nine OECD Countries. *STI Working Papers*, Paris. Author.

Coser, Lewis A. (1984). Introduction, In W. D. Halls (Trans.), *The Division of Labor in Society* (pp. ix xxiv), New York: Free Press. (Original work published in 1933).

Cook, Linda. J. (2010).Eastern Europe and Russia, In Francis G. Castles et al (Eds.), *The Oxford Handbook of the Welfare State* (pp.671-686). Oxford; New York: Oxford University Press.

Davis, Gordon B. and Olson, Margrethe H. (1985).*Management Information Systems: Conceptual Foundations, Structure, and Development* (2nd ed.), New York: McGraw-Hill.

Deininger, Klaus and Squire, Lyn. (1996). New Data Set Measuring Income Inequality. *World Bank Economic Review*, 10(3), pp. 565-591.

Division for Public Administration and Development Management (DPADM), 2014, *UN E-Government Development Database*, 2003-2012. New York: Author. Retrieved from http://unpan3.un.org/egovkb#.VBKsfZqwfIU (accessed 24 March 2014).

Ebbinghaus, Bernhard. (2010). Unions and Employers, In Francis G. Castles et al (Eds.), *The Oxford Handbook of the Welfare State* (pp. 196-210). Oxford; New York: Oxford University Press.

Esping-Andersen, Gosta. (1990). *The Three Welfare State Regime*. Cambridge: Polity Press.

Esping-Anderson, Gosta.(1999). *Social Foundations of Postindustrial Economies*. Oxford; New York: Oxford University Press.

Esping-Andersen, Gøsta.(2002). *Why We Need a New Welfare State*. New York: Oxford University Press.

European Commission (EC). (2011). *Digital Agenda for Europe: Public Service*. Brussels: Author. Retrieved from http://ec.europa.eu/digital-agenda/public-services (accessed 30 June 2014).

Foley, P. (2004). Does the Internet help to overcome social exclusion?. *Electronic Journal of e-Government*, 2(2), pp. 139-146.

Freedom House. (2014). *Freedom in the World 2014 Methodology*. Washington D.C: Author. Retrieved from http://freedomhouse.org/sites/default/files/Methodology%20FIW%202014.pdf (accessed 24 March 2014).

Freedom House. (2014). *Political Rights*, 1985-2010. Washington D.C: Author. Retrieved from http://freedomhouse.org/report-types/freedom-world#.VBKqfpqwfIU (accessed 24 March 2014).

Freedom House. (2014). *Civil Liberties*, 1985-2010. Washington D.C: Author. Retrieved from http://freedomhouse.org/report-types/freedom-world#.VBKqfpqwfIU (accessed 24 March 2014).

Galbraith, James K. and Kum, Hyunsub. (2004). Estimating the Inequality of Household Incomes: A Statistical Approach to the Creation of a Dense and Consistent Global Data Set. *UTIP Working Paper No. 22*.

Garrett, Geoffrey and Lange, Peter. (1995). Internationalization, Institutions, and Political Change, *International Organization*, 49(4), pp. 627-655.

Giddens, Anthony. (1998). *The Third Way; The Renewal of Social Democracy*. Cambridge: Polity Press.

Goos, Maarten, Manning, Alan and Salomons, Anna. (2014). Explaining Job Polarization: Routine-Biased Technological Change and Offshoring, *American Economic Review*, 104(8), pp. 2509~2526.

Gujarati, Damodar N. (2011). *Econometrics by Example*. Houndmills, Basingstoke, Hampshire; New York: Palgrave Macmillan.

Hicks, Alexander. (1994). The Social Democratic Corporatist Model of Economic Performance in the Short- and Medium-Run Perspective, In T. Janoski & A. Hicks (Eds.), *The Comparative Political Economy of the Welfare State* (pp. 189-217). New York: Cambridge University Press.

Hargittai, Eszter. (2003). The Digital Divide and What To Do About It, In Derek C.(Eds.), *The New Economy Handbook*, San Diego, CA: Academic Press. Retrieved from http://www.eszter.com/papers/c04-digitaldivide.html

Huber, Evelyne and Stephens, John.D. (2001a). *Development and Crisis of the Welfare State: Parties and Policies in Global Markets*, Chicago, IL: Chicago UP.

Huber, Evelyne and Stephens, Jonh D. (2012). *Democracy and the Left: Social Policy and Inequality in Latin America*, Chicago: University of Chicago Press.

Immergut, Ellen M. (2010). Political Institution, In Francis G. Castles et al (Eds.), *The Oxford Handbook of the Welfare State* (pp. 227-240). Oxford; New York: Oxford University Press.

International Telecommunication Union (ITU). (2010). *The World Telecommunication/ICT Indicators Database (CD)*. Geneva: Author.

Iversen, Torben& Wren, Anne. (1998). Equality, Employment, and Budgetary Restraint: The Trilemma of the Service Economy, *World Politics*, 50(4), pp. 507-546.

Iversen, Torben and Cusack, Thomas R. (2000). The Cause of Welfare State Expansion: Deindustrialization or Globalization? *World Politics*, 52(3), pp. 313-349.

Iversen, Torben. (2010). Democracy and Capitalism, In Francis G. Castles et al (Eds.), *The Oxford Handbook of the Welfare State* (pp. 183-195). Oxford; New York: Oxford University Press.

Jayashree, S. and Marthandan, G. (2010).Government to E-government to E-society. *Journal of Applied Sciences*, 10, pp. 2205-2210.

Kennard, W. E. (1999). Equality in the Information Age. *Federal Communications Law Journal*, 51(3), pp. 553-556.

Koop, Gary (2005). *Analysis of Economic Data* (2nd ed.), John Wiley & Sons Ltd: Chichester.

Korpi, Walter. (1985). Power Resources Approach vs. Action and Conflict: On Causal and Intentional Explanations in the Study of Power, *Sociological Theory*, 3(2), pp. 31-45.

Korpi, Walter. (2006). Power Resources and Employer-centered Approaches in Explanations of Welfare States and Varieties of Capitalism: Protagonists, Consenters, and Antagonists, *World Politics*, 58(2), pp. 167-206.

Labonté, R., Hadi, A., & Kauffmann, A. E. (2011). Indicators of Social Exclusion and Inclusion: A Critical and Comparative Analysis of the Literature. *Working Papers*. 2(8). Retrieved from http://www.globalhealthequity.ca/webfm_send/218.

Nahapiet, J. & Ghoshal, S. (1998). Social Capital, Intellectual Capital and the Organizational Advantage, *Academy of Management Review*, 23(2). pp. 242-266.

Leibfried, Stephan. (2010). Preface, In Francis G. Castles et al (Eds.), *The Oxford Handbook of the Welfare State* (pp. xxiii-xxv). Oxford; New York: Oxford University Press.

Lewis, Jane and Surrender, Rebecca.(2004). *Welfare State Change; Towards a Third Way?* Oxford: Oxford University Press.

Marshall, T H. (1963).*Sociology at the Crossroads and Other Essays*. London: Heinemann.

Mishra, Ramesh. (1999). *Globalisation and the Welfare State*. Cheltenham, UK; Northampton, MA: Edward Elgar Publishing Ltd.

Northrop, Alana and Kraemer, Kenneth L. (2000). The Information Age: Which Countries Will Benefit. In G. David Garson (Ed.) *Handbook of Public Information Systems* (2nd ed.), New York: Marcel Dekker Inc.

Bousrih, L. (2013). Social Capital, Human Capital and Sustainable Economic Development. *The Poznan University of Economics Review*, 13(3). pp. 42-54

Nullmeier, Frank and Kaufmann, Franz-Xaver. (2010). Post-war Welfare State Development, In Francis G. Castles et al (Eds.), *The Oxford Handbook of the Welfare State* (pp. 81-101). Oxford; New York: Oxford University Press.

Obinger, Herbert et al. (2010). *Transformations of the Welfare State; Small States, Big Lessons.* New York: Oxford University Press.

Obinger, Herbert and Wagschal, Uwe.(2010). Social Expenditure and Revenues, In Francis G. Castles et al (Eds.), *The Oxford Handbook of the Welfare State* (pp. 333-352). Oxford; New York: Oxford University Press.

O, O'Donnell, R. Boyle and V. Timonen. (2003). Transformational aspects of thee-Government in Ireland: Issues to be addressed, *Electronic Journal of e-Government,* 1(1), pp. 22-30.

Organization for Economic Cooperation and Development (OECD). (2001). Citizens as Partners: OECD Handbook on Information, Consultation and Public Participation in Policy-Making. Paris: Author.

Organization for Economic Cooperation and Development (OECD). (2001). Understanding the Digital Divide, *OECD Digital Economy Papers* 49. Paris: Author.

Organization for Economic Cooperation and Development (OECD). (2001). *The Well-Being of Nations: The Role of Human and Social Capital.* Paris: Author.

Organization for Economic Cooperation and Development (OECD). (2002). *Measuring the Information Economy.* Paris: Author.

Organization for Economic Cooperation and Development (OECD). (2007). *The Social Expenditure database: An Interpretive Guide SOCX 1980-2003.* Paris: Author.

Organization for Economic Cooperation and Development (OECD). (2009). Rethinking e-Government Services: User-centered Approaches, *OECD e-Government Studies.* Paris: Author.

Organization for Economic Cooperation and Development (OECD). (2009b). *Glossary of Statistical Terms.* Paris: Author. Retrieved from http://stats.oecd.org/glossary/ (accessed 30 June 2014).

Organization for Economic Cooperation and Development (OECD). (2012). ICT Skills and Employment: New Competences and Jobs for a Greener and Smarter Economy. *OECD Digital Economy Papers.* No.198, Paris: Author.

Organization for Economic Cooperation and Development (OECD). (2013). *OECD Skills Outlook 2013: First Results from the Survey of Adult Skills,* Paris: author.

Organization for Economic Cooperation and Development (OECD). (2013). *OECD Fact Book 2013.* Paris: Author. Retrieved from http://www.oecd.org/std/07_Labour.pdf (accessed 24 March 2014).

Organization for Economic Cooperation and Development (OECD). (2014). *Social Expenditure Database* (SOCX), 1985-2010. Paris: Author. Retrieved from http://stats.oecd.org/Index.aspx?datasetcode=SOCX_AGG (accessed 24 March 2014).

Organization for Economic Cooperation and Development (OECD). (2014). *Trade Union Density,* 1985-2010. Paris: Author. Retrieved from http://stats.oecd.org (accessed 24 March 2014).

Organization for Economic Cooperation and Development (OECD). (2014).

Unemployment Rates, 1985-2010. Paris: Author. Retrieved from http://stats.oecd.org (accessed 24 March 2014).

Parsons, Talcott. (1977). *Social System and the Evolution of Action Theory*. New York: Free Press.

Peng, Ito and Wong, Joseph. (2010). East Asia, In Francis G. Castles et al (Eds.), *The Oxford Handbook of the Welfare State* (pp. 656-670). Oxford; New York: Oxford University Press.

Pierson, Christopher. (1998). *Beyond the Welfare State* (3rd ed.). Cambridge: Polity Press.

Pierson, Paul. (1996). The New Politics of the Welfare State, *World Politics*, 48(2), pp. 143-179.

Pierson, Paul. (2001). Post-Industrial Pressures on the Mature Welfare State, In Paul Pierson (Ed.) *The New Politics of the Welfare State* (pp. 80-106). Oxford: Oxford University Press.

Pluemper, Thomas, Troeger, Vera, E. and Manow, Philip. (2005). Panel Data Analysis in Comparative: Linking Method to Theory, *European Journal of Political Research*, 44(2), pp. 327-354.

Rupasingha, Anil, Goetz, Stephan J., and Freshwater, David. (December 2000). Social Capital And Economic Growth: A County-Level Analysis, *Journal of Agricultural and Applied Economics*, 32(3), pp. 565-572.

Saunders, Peter. (2010). Inequality and Poverty, In Francis G. Castles et al (Eds.), *The Oxford Handbook of the Welfare State* (pp. 526-538). Oxford; New York: Oxford University Press.

Schiller, Herbert I. (1986). *Information and the Crisis Economy*. Norwood; NJ: Ablex Publishing Corp.

Skocpol, Theda. andAmenta Edwin. (1986). States and Social Policies, *Annual Review of Sociology*, 12, pp. 131-157.

Swank, Duane. (2010). Globalisation, In Francis G. Castles et al (Eds.), *The Oxford Handbook of the Welfare State* (pp. 318-330). Oxford; New York: Oxford University Press.

Taylor-Gooby, Peter. (2004). *New Risks, New Welfare: The Transformation of the European Welfare State*. New York: Oxford University Press.

The Economist. (2014). The Third Great Wave, *The World Economy Special Report*, 2014.10.4

Timonen, Virpi et al. (2003). E government and the Decentralisation of Service Delivery, *CPMR Discussion Paper 25*. Dublin: The Institute of Public Administration.

Toffler, Alvin. (1980). *The Third Wave*. New York: William Morrow and Company, Inc.

Transparency International (TI). (2010). *Corruption Perceptions Index 2010: Long Methodology Brief*, Berlin: TI. Retrieved from http://www.transparency.org/cpi2010/in_detail#4 (accessed 24 March 2014).

Transparency International (TI). (2011). *Corruption Perceptions Index 2011*, Berlin: TI. Retrieved from http://www.transparency.org/cpi2011/press#en (accessed 24 March 2014).

Transparency International (TI). (2014). *Corruption Perceptions Index,* 1985-2010. Berlin: TI. Retrieved from http://www.transparency.org/research/cpi/overview (accessed 24 March 2014).

United Nations Educational Scientific and Cultural Organization (UNESCO). (2002). Information and communication technology in education: a curriculum for schools and programme of teacher development. Paris: Author. Retrieved from http://unesdoc.unesco.org/images/0012/001295/129538e.pdf (accessed 24 March 2014).

United Nations Department of Economic and Social Affairs (UNDESA). (2005). *United Nations Global E-Government Readiness Report 2005: From E-government to Einclusion.* New York: UN. Retrieved from http://unpan1.un.org/intradoc/groups/public/documents/un/unpan021888.pdf (accessed 30 June 2014).

United Nations Department of Economic and Social Affairs (UNDESA). (2008). *United Nations E-government Survey 2008: From e-Government to Connected Governance.* New York: UN.

United Nations Department of Economic and Social Affairs (UNDESA). (2010). *United Nations E-government Survey 2010: Leveraging e-government at a time of financial and economic crisis.* New York: UN.

United Nations Department of Economic and Social Affairs (UNDESA). (2014). *UN E-government Survey 2014: E-government for the Future We Want.* New York: UN.

University of Texas Inequality Project (UTIP). (2014). *Estimated Household Income Inequality(EHII),* 1985-2008. Texas: Author. Retrieved from http://utip.gov.utexas.edu/data.html (accessed 24 March 2014).

Van Winden, W. (2001). The End of Social Exclusion? On Information Technology Policy as a Key to Social Inclusion in Large European Cities. *Journal of the Regional Studies Association,* 35(9), pp. 861-877.

Visser, Jelle, Martin, Sébastienand Tergeist, Peter. (2014). *Trade Union Members and Union Density in OECD Countries.* Paris: OECD. Retrieved from http://www.oecd.org/employment/emp/UnionDensity_Sourcesandmethods (accessed 24 March 2014).

Vu, Khuong M. (2009). *Measuring the Impact of ICT Investments on Economic Growth,* a paper published on Program of Technology and Economic Policy, Harvard Kennedy School of Government.

Webster, Frank. (2006). *Theories of the Information Society* (3rd ed.). London: Routledge.

Westerlund, Joakim and Edgerton, David L. (2007). A Panel Bootstrap Cointegration Test. *Economics Letters 97,* pp. 185-190.

Wilensky, Harold L.&Lebeaux, Charles N. (1975). *Industrial Society and Social Welfare: The Impact of Industrialization on the Supply and Organization of Social Welfare Services in the United States.* Berkeley; Los Angeles; California: University of California Press.

Wilensky, Herald L. (1975). *The Welfare State and Equality: Structural and Ideological Roots of Public Expenditures.* Berkeley: University of California Press.

Woolcock, Michael. (1998). Social Capital and Economic Development: Toward a Theoretical Synthesis and Policy Framework, *Theory and Society 27.* pp. 151-208.

World Bank (WB). (2014). *Urban Population (% of Total)*, 1985-2010. Washington D.C: Author. Retrieved from http://data.worldbank.org/indicator/SP.URB.TOTL.IN.ZS (accessed 24 March 2014).

World Bank (WB). (2014). *GDP Per Capita (Current US$)*, 1985-2010. Washington D.C: Author. Retrieved from http://data.worldbank.org/indicator/NY.GDP.PCAP.CD (accessed 24 March 2014).

Appendix

1. Graphs of Variables Related to ICT Industry

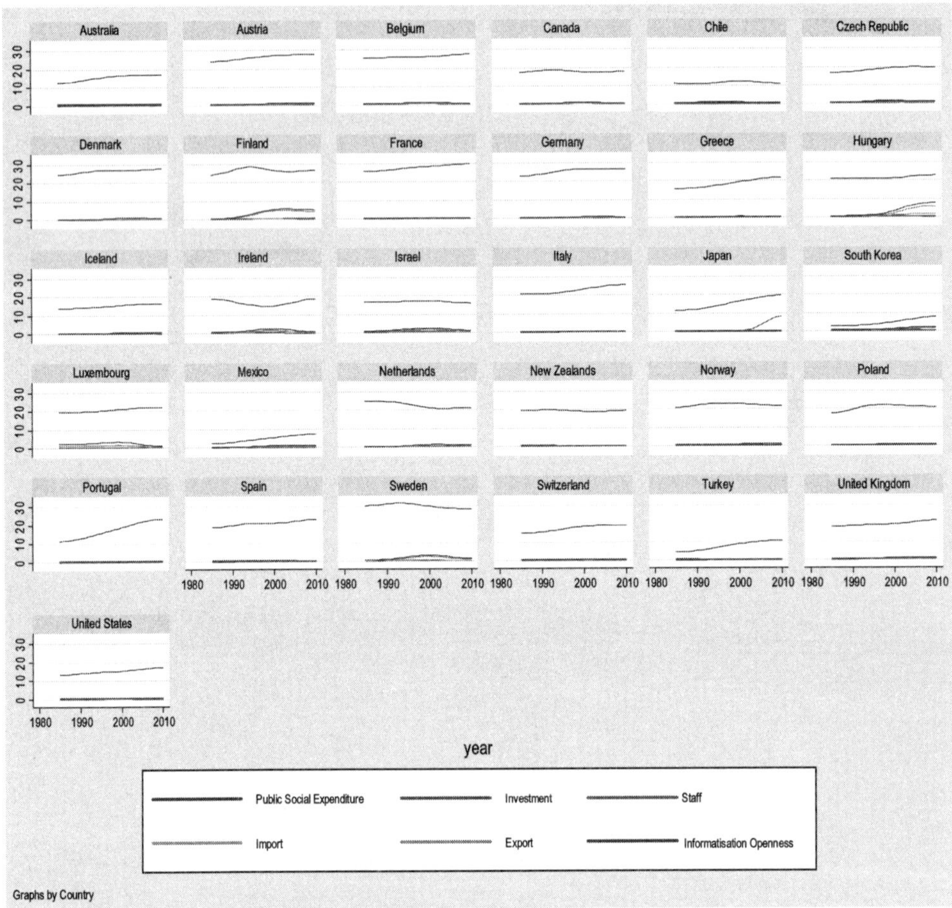

2. Graphs of Variables Related to ICT Usage

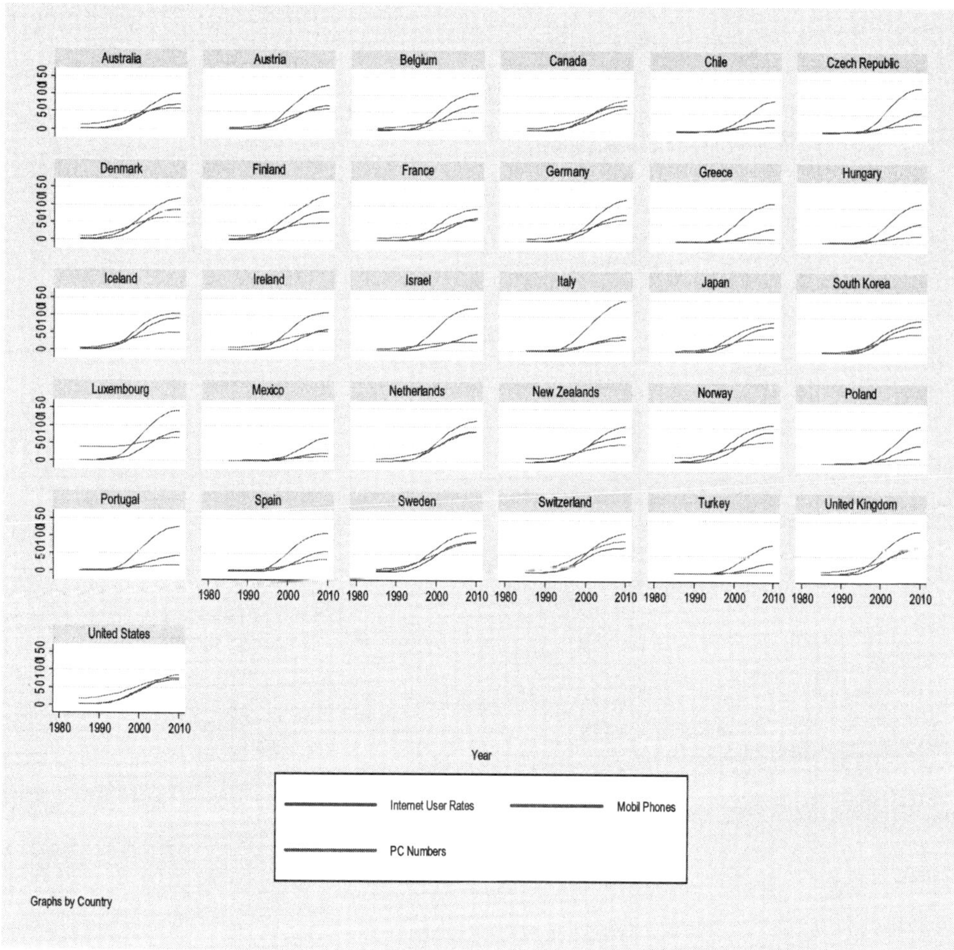

3. Results of Unit-Root Tests

	Variables	Type	Common unit-root test	Individual unit-root test
			Breitung unit-root test	Im-Pesaran-Shin unit-root test
Dependent Variable	Public Social Expenditure	Level variable	10.2237	-0.3072
		P-value	1.0000	1.0000
		Level variable with lagl	-13.3801	-33.0679
		P-value	0.0000	0.0000
		First difference	-2.2184	-0.7428
		P-value	0.0133	1.0000
		First difference with lagl	-9.9355	-9.4390
		P-value	0.0000	0.0000
		First difference with lagl & trend	1.5199	-9.0918
		P-value	0.9357	0.0000
	Estimated Household Income Inequality	Level variable	11.3403	-1.0023
		P-value	1.0000	1.0000
		Level variable with lagl	-13.7082	-41.4644
		P-value	0.0000	0.0000
		First difference	-2.2550	-0.6222
		P-value	0.0121	1.0000
		First difference with lagl	-9.9847	-8.4024
		P-value	0.0000	0.0000
		First difference with lagl & trend	1.3030	-15.5554
		P-value	0.9037	0.0000
Independent Variables	Total Investment	Level variable	6.8898	-0.5752
		P-value	1.0000	1.0000
		Level variable with lagl	-11.3025	-25.3392
		P-value	0.0000	0.0000
		First difference	-2.9274	-0.7975
		P-value	0.0017	0.0000
		First difference with lagl	-12.1713	-13.1397
		P-value	0.0000	0.0000
		First difference with lagl & trend	0.4189	-18.6642
		P-value	0.6623	0.0000
	Total Staff	Level variable	14.2904	2.9921
		P-value	1.0000	1.0000
		Level variable with lagl	-11.0740	-15.0821
		P-value	0.0000	0.0000
		First difference	-1.6644	-0.8387
		P-value	0.0480	1.0000
		First difference with lagl	-6.5141	-1.2430
		P-value	0.0000	0.1069
		First difference with lagl & trend	2.1810	-2.5098
		P-value	0.9854	0.0060
	Import	Level variable	6.9404	-0.3491
		P-value	1.0000	1.0000
		Level variable with lagl	-12.9085	-27.6691
		P-value	0.0000	0.0000
		First difference	-2.8229	-0.6321
		P-value	0.0024	1.0000
		First difference with lagl	-12.9608	-11.8743
		P-value	0.0000	0.0000
		First difference with lagl & trend	2.6579	-15.8798
		P-value	0.9961	0.0000
		Hypothesis	Ho: Panels contain unit roots	Ho: All panels contain unit roots
			Ha: Panels are stationary	Ha: Some panels are stationary

	Variables	Type	Common unit-root test	Individual unit-root test
			Breitung unit-root test	Im-Pesaran-Shin unit-root test
			(t-stat)	(W-stat)
Independent Variables	Export	Level variable	9.7391	-0.3298
		P-value	1.0000	1.0000
		Level variable with lag1	-12.9105	-27.0303
		P-value	0.0000	0.0000
		First difference	-2.6333	-0.6249
		P-value	0.0042	1.0000
		First difference with lag1	-13.5923	-16.3078
		P-value	0.0000	0.0000
		First difference with lag1 & trend	4.3745	-21.3141
		P-value	1.0000	0.0000
	Information Openness	Level variable	7.9976	-0.5708
		P-value	1.0000	1.0000
		Level variable with lag1	-12.4548	-26.5937
		P-value	0.0000	0.0000
		First difference	-2.7711	-0.5672
		P-value	0.0028	1.0000
		First difference with lag1	-13.8308	-13.3414
		P-value	0.0000	0.0000
		First difference with lag1 & trend	3.9632	-19.1423
		P-value	1.0000	0.0000
	Internet User Rates	Level variable	10.1694	0.0140
		P-value	1.0000	1.0000
		Level variable with lag1	-13.9403	-19.7893
		P-value	0.0000	0.0000
		First difference	-2.9216	-0.3663
		P-value	0.0017	1.0000
		First difference with lag1	-13.0279	-16.5121
		P-value	0.0000	0.0000
		First difference with lag1 & trend	3.4202	-18.6838
		P-value	0.9997	0.0000
	Mobile Phones	Level variable	9.3693	0.2956
		P-value	1.0000	1.0000
		Level variable with lag1	-12.6771	-20.4687
		P-value	0.0000	0.0000
		First difference	-3.1559	-0.5779
		P-value	0.0008	1.0000
		First difference with lag1	-13.4000	-16.3605
		P-value	0.0000	0.0000
		First difference with lag1 & trend	2.2054	-19.2332
		P-value	0.9863	0.0000
	PC Numbers	Level variable	15.4209	0.4980
		P-value	1.0000	1.0000
		Level variable with lag1	-16.9511	-39.4926
		P-value	0.0000	0.0000
		First difference	-2.1362	0.1530
		P-value	0.0163	1.0000
		First difference with lag1	-10.2847	-12.1205
		P-value	0.0000	0.0000
		First difference with lag1 & trend	4.6039	-10.5021
		P-value	1.0000	0.0000
		Hypothesis	Ho: Panels contain unit roots	Ho; All panels contain unit roots
			Ha: Panels are stationary	Ha: Some panels are stationary

	Variables	Type	Common unit-root test	Individual unit-root test
			Breitung unit-root test	Im-Pesaran-Shin unit-root test
			(t-stat)	(W-stat)
Control Variables	GDP Per Capita	Level variable	12.3928	-0.4750
		P-value	1.0000	1.0000
		Level variable with lag1	-11.2443	-22.0239
		P-value	0.0000	0.0000
		First difference	-2.4726	-0.8418
		P-value	0.0067	1.0000
		First difference with lag1	-10.4474	-12.3263
		P-value	0.0000	0.0000
		First difference with lag1 & trend	0.8013	-16.1254
		P-value	0.7885	0.0000
	Economic Openness	Level variable	11.0705	0.3925
		P-value	1.0000	1.0000
		Level variable with lag1	-10.4683	-15.5011
		P-value	0.0000	0.0000
		First difference	-2.9447	-0.9566
		P-value	0.0016	0.9996
		First difference with lag1	-10.5047	-10.2033
		P-value	0.0000	0.0000
		First difference with lag1 & trend	-0.5829	-10.3761
		P-value	0.2800	0.0000
	Political Rights	Level variable	1.7802	-1.9504
		P-value	0.9625	0.0021
		Level variable with lag1	0.3935	-3.5496
		P-value	0.6530	0.0002
		First difference	-17.0082	-4.6333
		P-value	0.0000	0.0000
		First difference with lag1	-10.1004	-10.2787
		P-value	0.0000	0.0000
		First difference with lag1 & trend	-11.6717	-7.7509
		P-value	0.0000	0.0000
	Civil Liberties	Level variable	3.9715	-2.7192
		P-value	1.0000	0.0000
		Level variable with lag1	1.6271	-10.6424
		P-value	0.9481	0.0000
		First difference	-16.0283	-4.1132
		P-value	0.0000	0.0000
		First difference with lag1	-5.5350	-9.0094
		P-value	0.0000	0.0000
		First difference with lag1 & trend	-9.8440	-9.6179
		P-value	0.0000	0.0000
		Hypothesis	Ho: Panels contain unit roots	Ho: All panels contain unit roots
			Ha: Panels are stationary	Ha: Some panels are stationary

4. Results of Co-integration Tests

Westerlund's ECM Panel Cointegration Test					
Variables	Statistic	Value	Z-value	P-value	Robust P-value
Dependent Variable: Public social expenditure	Gt	-4.882	-17.239	0.000	0.000
Independent Variable: Investment	Ga	-12.978	-0.791	0.214	0.000
	Pt	-14.401	-3.018	0.001	0.000
	Pa	-17.605	-7.875	0.000	0.000
Variables	Statistic	Value	Z-value	P-value	Robust P-value
Dependent Variable: Public social expenditure	Gt	-5.631	-22.371	0.000	0.000
Independent Variable: Staff	Ga	-11.347	0.544	0.707	0.000
	Pt	-13.676	-2.189	0.014	0.000
	Pa	-8.866	0.061	0.524	0.000
Variables	Statistic	Value	Z-value	P-value	Robust P-value
Dependent Variable: Public social expenditure	Gt	-6.798	-30.365	0.000	0.000
Independent Variable: Import	Ga	-11.317	0.569	0.715	0.000
	Pt	-25.518	-15.729	0.000	0.000
	Pa	-10.830	-1.723	0.043	0.005
Variables	Statistic	Value	Z-value	P-value	Robust P-value
Dependent Variable: Public social expenditure	Gt	-6.327	-27.141	0.000	0.000
Independent Variable: Export	Ga	-9.571	1.999	0.977	0.000
	Pt	-19.441	-8.781	0.000	0.000
	Pa	-7.503	1.298	0.903	0.000
Variables	Statistic	Value	Z-value	P-value	Robust P-value
Dependent Variable: Public social expenditure	Gt	-5.966	-24.664	0.000	0.000
Independent Variable: Information openness	Ga	-10.563	1.186	0.882	0.000
	Pt	-18.701	-7.935	0.000	0.005
	Pa	-9.646	-0.648	0.258	0.005
Variables	Statistic	Value	Z-value	P-value	Robust P-value
Dependent Variable: Public social expenditure	Gt	-8.912	-44.847	0.000	0.000
Independent Variable: Internet user rates	Ga	-9.599	1.975	0.976	0.000
	Pt	-24.901	-15.024	0.000	0.000
	Pa	-12.723	-3.442	0.000	0.000
Variables	Statistic	Value	Z-value	P-value	Robust P-value
Dependent Variable: Public social expenditure	Gt	-8.412	-41.422	0.000	0.000
Independent Variable: Mobile phones	Ga	-15.409	-2.782	0.003	0.000
	Pt	-29.180	-19.917	0.000	0.000
	Pa	-78.600	-63.263	0.000	0.000
Variables	Statistic	Value	Z-value	P-value	Robust P-value
Dependent Variable: Public social expenditure	Gt	-9.144	-46.442	0.000	0.000
Independent Variable: PC numbers	Ga	-4.909	5.816	1.000	0.000
	Pt	-27.892	-18.444	0.000	0.000
	Pa	-5.493	3.124	0.999	0.000
Hypothesis for Gt and Ga	H0: No cointegration for the whole panel				
(The group mean statistics)	H1: Cointegration for some countries in the panel				
Hypothesis for Pt and Pa	H0: No cointegration for the whole panel				
(The panel statistics)	H1: Cointegration for the panel as a whole.				
The robust critical values are computed using 200 bootstraps.					

Westerlund's VECM Panel Cointegration Test					
Variables	Statistic	Value	Z-value	P-value	Robust P-value
Dependent Variable: Public social expenditure	Gt	-4.104	-6.588	0.000	0.000
Independent Variable: Investment, GDP per capita,	Ga	-1.035	11.015	1.000	0.000
Economic openness, Political rights, Civil liberties	Pt	-5.689	9.862	1.000	0.000
	Pa	-0.624	9.293	1.000	0.000
Variables	Statistic	Value	Z-value	P-value	Robust P-value
Dependent Variable: Public social expenditure	Gt	-5.908	-17.500	0.000	0.000
Independent Variable: Staff, GDP per capita,	Ga	-1.580	10.686	1.000	0.000
Economic openness, Political rights, Civil liberties	Pt	-3.217	12.344	1.000	0.000
	Pa	-0.399	9.431	1.000	0.010
Variables	Statistic	Value	Z-value	P-value	Robust P-value
Dependent Variable: Public social expenditure	Gt	-6.416	-20.571	0.000	0.000
Independent Variable: Import, GDP per capita,	Ga	-1.795	10.555	1.000	0.010
Economic openness, Political rights, Civil liberties	Pt	-16.936	-1.431	0.076	0.000
	Pa	-1.810	8.56	1.000	0.000
Variables	Statistic	Value	Z-value	P-value	Robust P-value
Dependent Variable: Public social expenditure	Gt	-7.376	-26.375	0.000	0.000
Independent Variable: Export, GDP per capita,	Ga	-1.517	10.724	1.000	0.000
Economic openness, Political rights, Civil liberties	Pt	-24.078	-8.602	0.000	0.000
	Pa	-1.532	8.732	1.000	0.000
Variables	Statistic	Value	Z-value	P-value	Robust P-value
Dependent Variable: Public social expenditure	Gt	-8.326	-32.117	0.000	0.000
Independent Variable: Information openness, GDP,	Ga	-1.900	10.492	1.000	0.000
Economic Openness, Political Rights, Civil Liberties	Pt	-16.988	-1.483	0.069	0.000
	Pa	-1.705	8.625	1.000	0.000
Variables	Statistic	Value	Z-value	P-value	Robust P-value
Dependent Variable: Public social expenditure	Gt	-6.731	-22.477	0.000	0.000
Independent Variable: Internt user rates, GDP per capita,	Ga	-1.854	10.520	1.000	0.000
Economic openness, Political rights, Civil liberties	Pt	-17.308	-1.805	0.036	0.000
	Pa	-1.335	8.854	1.000	0.015
Variables	Statistic	Value	Z-value	P-value	Robust P-value
Dependent Variable: Public social expenditure	Gt	-6.246	-19.539	0.000	0.000
Independent Variable: Mobile phones, GDP per capita,	Ga	-1.482	10.745	1.000	0.000
Economic openness, Political rights, Civil liberties	Pt	-15.429	0.082	0.533	0.000
	Pa	-1.317	8.865	1.000	0.000
Variables	Statistic	Value	Z-value	P-value	Robust P-value
Dependent Variable: Public social expenditure	Gt	-4.878	-11.270	0.000	0.000
Independent Variable: PC numbers, GDP per capita,	Ga	-0.870	11.115	1.000	0.000
Economic openness, Political rights, Civil liberties	Pt	-10.510	5.021	1.000	0.000
	Pa	-0.901	9.121	1.000	0.030
Hypothesis for Gt and Ga	H0: No cointegration for the whole panel				
(The group mean statistics)	H1: Cointegration for some countries in the panel				
Hypothesis for Pt and Pa	H0: No cointegration				
(The panel statistics)	H1: Cointegration for the panel as a whole.				
The robust critical values are computed using 200 bootstraps.					

Westerlund's ECM Panel Cointegration Test					
Variables	Statistic	Value	Z-value	P-value	Robust P-value
Dependent Variable: Estimated household income inequality	Gt	-10.722	-57.249	0.000	0.000
Independent Variable: Investment	Ga	-15.515	-2.868	0.002	0.000
	Pt	-28.639	-19.298	0.000	0.000
	Pa	-10.631	-1.542	0.062	0.000
Variables	Statistic	Value	Z-value	P-value	Robust P-value
Dependent Variable: Estimated household income inequality	Gt	-6.419	-27.765	0.000	0.000
Independent Variable: Staff	Ga	-16.749	-3.879	0.000	0.000
	Pt	-32.614	-23.843	0.000	0.000
	Pa	-32.870	-21.737	0.000	0.000
Variables	Statistic	Value	Z-value	P-value	Robust P-value
Dependent Variable: Estimated household income inequality	Gt	-7.764	-36.984	0.000	0.000
Independent Variable: Import	Ga	-9.077	2.403	0.992	0.000
	Pt	-10.249	1.729	0.958	0.025
	Pa	-6.547	2.166	0.985	0.000
Variables	Statistic	Value	Z-value	P-value	Robust P-value
Dependent Variable: Estimated Household Income Inequality	Gt	-6.624	-29.174	0.000	0.000
Independent Variable: Export	Ga	-9.326	2.199	0.986	0.000
	Pt	-23.729	-13.684	0.000	0.000
	Pa	-8.546	0.351	0.637	0.015
Variables	Statistic	Value	Z-value	P-value	Robust P-value
Dependent Variable: Estimated household income inequality	Gt	-7.129	-32.634	0.000	0.000
Independent Variable: Information openness	Ga	-10.167	1.510	0.935	0.000
	Pt	-10.311	1.658	0.951	0.035
	Pa	-9.212	-0.254	0.400	0.000
Variables	Statistic	Value	Z-value	P-value	Robust P-value
Dependent Variable: Estimated household income inequality	Gt	-7.348	-34.130	0.000	0.000
Independent Variable: Internet user rates	Ga	-14.262	-1.843	0.033	0.000
	Pt	-24.261	-14.292	0.000	0.000
	Pa	-15.317	-5.797	0.000	0.000
Variables	Statistic	Value	Z-value	P-value	Robust P-value
Dependent Variable: Estimated household income inequality	Gt	-6.638	-29.268	0.000	0.000
Independent Variable: Mobile phones	Ga	-8.351	2.997	0.999	0.000
	Pt	-24.161	-14.178	0.000	0.000
	Pa	-7.694	1.125	0.870	0.000
Variables	Statistic	Value	Z-value	P-value	Robust P-value
Dependent Variable: Estimated household income inequality	Gt	-8.158	-39.685	0.000	0.000
Independent Variable: PC numbers	Ga	-5.935	4.976	1.000	0.000
	Pt	-13.103	-1.534	0.063	0.000
	Pa	5.027	2.820	0.998	0.000
Hypothesis for Gt and Ga (The group mean statistics)	H0: No cointegration for the whole panel				
	H1: Cointegration for some countries in the panel				
Hypothesis for Pt and Pa (The panel statistics)	H0: No cointegration for the whole panel				
	H1: Cointegration for the panel as a whole.				
The robust critical values are computed using 200 bootstraps.					

Westerlund's VECM Panel Cointegration Test					
Variables	Statistic	Value	Z-value	P-value	Robust P-value
Dependent Variable: Estimated household income inequality	Gt	-3.638	-3.769	0.000	0.000
Independent Variable: Investment, GDP per capita,	Ga	-1.852	10.521	1.000	0.000
Economic openness, Political rights, Civil liberties	Pt	-9.203	6.334	1.000	0.000
	Pa	-1.149	8.969	1.000	0.005
Variables	Statistic	Value	Z-value	P-value	Robust P-value
Dependent Variable: Estimated household income inequality	Gt	-3.727	-4.305	0.000	0.000
Independent Variable: Staff, GDP per capita,	Ga	-0.951	11.066	1.000	0.000
Economic openness, Political rights, Civil liberties	Pt	-1.346	14.224	1.000	0.000
	Pa	-0.201	9.554	1.000	0.000
Variables	Statistic	Value	Z-value	P-value	Robust P-value
Dependent Variable: Estimated household income inequality	Gt	-6.680	-22.163	0.000	0.000
Independent Variable: Import, GDP per capita,	Ga	-1.558	10.699	1.000	0.000
Economic openness, Political rights, Civil liberties	Pt	-21.689	-6.204	0.000	0.000
	Pa	-1.556	8.718	1.000	0.010
Variables	Statistic	Value	Z-value	P-value	Robust P-value
Dependent Variable: Estimated household income inequality	Gt	-7.003	-24.117	0.000	0.000
Independent Variable: Export, GDP per capita,	Ga	-1.695	10.616	1.000	0.000
Economic openness, Political rights, Civil liberties	Pt	-45.026	-29.637	0.000	0.000
	Pa	-2.788	7.957	1.000	0.005
Variables	Statistic	Value	Z-value	P-value	Robust P-value
Dependent Variable: Estimated household income inequality	Gt	-6.285	-19.779	0.000	0.000
Independent Variable: Information openness, GDP,	Ga	-1.557	10.700	1.000	0.000
Economic Openness, Political Rights, Civil Liberties	Pt	-18.919	-3.422	0.000	0.000
	Pa	-1.272	8.893	1.000	0.000
Variables	Statistic	Value	Z-value	P-value	Robust P-value
Dependent Variable: Estimated household income inequality	Gt	-6.554	-21.406	0.000	0.000
Independent Variable: Internt user rates, GDP per capita,	Ga	-1.701	10.613	1.000	0.000
Economic openness, Political rights, Civil liberties	Pt	-19.953	-4.461	0.000	0.000
	Pa	-1.870	8.523	1.000	0.000
Variables	Statistic	Value	Z-value	P-value	Robust P-value
Dependent Variable: Estimated household income inequality	Gt	-10.282	-43.946	0.000	0.000
Independent Variable: Mobile phones, GDP per capita,	Ga	-1.503	10.732	1.000	0.000
Economic openness, Political rights, Civil liberties	Pt	-44.525	-29.134	0.000	0.000
	Pa	-2.125	8.366	1.000	0.020
Variables	Statistic	Value	Z-value	P-value	Robust P-value
Dependent Variable: Estimated household income inequality	Gt	-6.503	-21.096	0.000	0.000
Independent Variable: PC numbers, GDP per capita,	Ga	-1.068	10.995	1.000	0.000
Economic openness, Political rights, Civil liberties	Pt	-15.904	-0.395	0.346	0.000
	Pa	-0.902	9.121	1.000	0.000
Hypothesis for Gt and Ga (The group mean statistics)	H0: No cointegration for the whole panel				
	H1: Cointegration for some countries in the panel				
Hypothesis for Pt and Pa (The panel statistics)	H0: No cointegration				
	H1: Cointegration for the panel as a whole.				
The robust critical values are computed using 200 bootstraps.					

Acronyms

DPADM Division for Public Administration and Development Management

EC European Commission

FI Freedom House

ILO International Labor Organization

IMF International Monetary Fund

ITU International Telecommunication Union

OECD Organization for Economic Cooperation and Development

TI Transparency International

UNDP United Nations Development Program

UNDESA United Nations Department of Economic and Social Affairs

UNESCO United Nations Educational Scientific and Cultural Organization

WB World Bank

저/자/소/개

■ 최 영 진

경북대학교 사회과학대학 사회복지학과를 졸업하고 독일 브레멘 대학교 사회교육학 디플롬(Diplom) 학위를 받았다. 독일 브레멘 대학교 사회정책 박사과정 수료하였다. 2010년 이후로 경북대학교, 단국대학교 등에서 청소년복지론, 아동복지론, 여성복지론, 사회보장론 등을 강의해 왔다. 복지국가, 여성복지, 청소년복지, 아동복지에 주된 관심을 두고 있다.

〈대표저서 및 논문〉
"1980년대 한국 여성노동정책의 변화"(디플롬 학위 논문)
현대사회와 여성복지(공저, 2016)
오늘의 청소년 그들은 누구인가?(공저, 2017)

정보화와 복지국가

1판 1쇄 인쇄 — 2018년 5월 1일
1판 1쇄 발행 — 2018년 5월 4일

저　　자 - 최 영 진
발 행 인 - 강 철 원
발 행 처 - 양 성 원
주　　소 - 경기도 파주시 검산로 173번길 29-20
전　　화 - 031-946-3861(代)
팩　　스 - 031-946-3864
이 메 일 - tnwpub@naver.com
홈페이지 - tnwpub.co.kr
출판등록 - 2015년 8월 31일 제 2015-000211 호

ISBN 979-11-6126-115-7

정가 17,000원